D1794962

Incorporating Diversity, Equity, and Inclusion Considerations into the 2021 Department of the Air Force Developmental Education Selection Boards

Analysis of Outcomes

RAYMOND E. CONLEY, KIMBERLY CURRY HALL, CLAUDE MESSAN SETODJI,
STEPHEN W. OLIVER, JR., SARAH W. DENTON, C. BEN GIBSON,
PAUL EMSLIE, SHAWN COCHRAN, MICHAEL SCHIEFER, MELISSA BAUMAN

Prepared for the Department of the Air Force
Approved for public release; distribution unlimited

PROJECT AIR FORCE

For more information on this publication, visit **www.rand.org/t/RRA1251-1**.

About RAND

The RAND Corporation is a research organization that develops solutions to public policy challenges to help make communities throughout the world safer and more secure, healthier and more prosperous. RAND is nonprofit, nonpartisan, and committed to the public interest. To learn more about RAND, visit www.rand.org.

Research Integrity

Our mission to help improve policy and decisionmaking through research and analysis is enabled through our core values of quality and objectivity and our unwavering commitment to the highest level of integrity and ethical behavior. To help ensure our research and analysis are rigorous, objective, and nonpartisan, we subject our research publications to a robust and exacting quality-assurance process; avoid both the appearance and reality of financial and other conflicts of interest through staff training, project screening, and a policy of mandatory disclosure; and pursue transparency in our research engagements through our commitment to the open publication of our research findings and recommendations, disclosure of the source of funding of published research, and policies to ensure intellectual independence. For more information, visit www.rand.org/about/research-integrity.

RAND's publications do not necessarily reflect the opinions of its research clients and sponsors.

Published by the RAND Corporation, Santa Monica, Calif.
© 2022 RAND Corporation
RAND® is a registered trademark.

Library of Congress Cataloging-in-Publication Data is available for this publication.
ISBN: 978-1-9774-1011-5

About This Report

The Department of the Air Force (DAF) publishes directives, memorandums of instructions, and other guidance highlighting the importance of diversity. Indeed, DAF Senior Leadership is on record stating diversity is a mission imperative. Yet, demographic data have historically been masked for most boards making decisions about career development and promotions. The 2021 Central Professional Military Education (CPME) Program Boards provided an opportunity to test the effect of changes that would make race, ethnicity, and gender data visible to board members. In addition, the DAF implemented two other diversity and inclusion–related changes for the 2021 CPME board: Board members underwent unconscious bias training, and instructions to board members concerning consideration of race, ethnicity, and gender were modified. Without careful study of the implementation, policymakers will not know whether the changes for the selection boards have had the intended effect, and whether there are unintended consequences that require mitigation efforts. The Deputy Chief of Staff for Manpower, Personnel and Services, Headquarters U.S. Air Force asked RAND Project AIR FORCE (PAF) to conduct an evaluation that measures the effectiveness of the changes and to provide insights that inform future policy refinements. This report presents the results of that evaluation.

The research reported here was commissioned by the Deputy Chief of Staff for Manpower, Personnel and Services, Headquarters U.S. Air Force, and conducted within the Workforce, Development, and Health Program of RAND Project AIR FORCE as part of a fiscal year 2021 project, "Evaluating the Effects of Incorporating Diversity, Equity, and Inclusion Considerations into Developmental Education Selection Boards."

RAND Project AIR FORCE

RAND Project AIR FORCE (PAF), a division of the RAND Corporation, is the Department of the Air Force's (DAF's) federally funded research and development center for studies and analyses, supporting both the United States Air Force and the United States Space Force. PAF provides the DAF with independent analyses of policy alternatives affecting the development, employment, combat readiness, and support of current and future air, space, and cyber forces. Research is conducted in four programs: Strategy and Doctrine; Force Modernization and Employment; Resource Management; and Workforce, Development, and Health. The research reported here was prepared under contract FA7014-16-D-1000.

Additional information about PAF is available on our website: www.rand.org/paf/

This report documents work originally shared with the DAF on October 19, 2021. The draft report, issued on October 26, 2021, was reviewed by formal peer reviewers and DAF subject-matter experts.

Acknowledgments

We are grateful for the support of our sponsors, Russell J. Frasz, Director, Force Development; and Lieutenant General Brian T. Kelly, both in the office of the Deputy Chief of Staff for Manpower, Personnel and Services, Headquarters U.S. Air Force, Arlington, Virginia.

Our primary contacts were Col Dalian Washington and Lt Col Kelli Moon. We appreciate their willingness to provide the policy background and contact information that were important for the data-gathering effort related to this research.

This research would not have been possible without the willing participation of the CPME board members and the Command Screening Board members. Their candid comments about the board guidance and use of available data were instructive and invaluable for future boards. Because we promised them anonymity, we can thank them only collectively, but we hope that we represented their individual views adequately.

We also thank representatives from Air Force Personnel Center (AFPC) and the Colonel's Group who coordinate the CPME board and Command Screening Board processes, respectively, and provided detailed information on the processes to inform our analyses.

Finally, we thank Nelson Lim, Director of RAND Project AIR FORCE's Workforce, Development, and Health Program, for his support throughout the project. We are grateful to our RAND colleagues Clara Aranibar, Perry Firoz, Anthony Lawrence, and Judith Mele for their work supporting this research. We also thank our reviewers, Miriam Matthews, Al Robbert, and Travis York.

Summary

Issue

The Department of the Air Force (DAF) promulgates directives, memorandums of instructions, and other guidance embracing the importance of diversity. Indeed, DAF Senior Leadership is on record stating that diversity is a mission imperative. Yet, demographic data have been masked for most boards making decisions about career development and promotions. The DAF wanted to assess the efficacy of making demographic data visible to board members. The 2021 Central Professional Military Education (CPME) Program Boards provided an opportunity to test the effects of unmasking the data to board members. In addition, the DAF implemented two other diversity and inclusion–related changes for the 2021 CPME board: (1) board members underwent unconscious bias training, and (2) instructions to board members concerning consideration of race, ethnicity, and gender (REG) were modified. In this report, we present the results of our analyses comparing the 2020 outcomes (before the changes in guidance) with the 2021 outcomes (after the changes).

Approach

In conducting this research, the project team used a mixed-methods approach. Specifically, the team

- analyzed board inputs and selection outcomes for the 2020 CPME board (before the changes) and 2021 CPME board (after the changes) to assess the effects on the selection likelihood for minority versus nonminority members
- conducted semistructured interviews with 2020 and 2021 board members to learn about their experiences and how they interpreted and applied the new instructions to illuminate the quantitative patterns in the data
- reviewed relevant literature to identify trends that might assist the DAF in implementing the proposed changes.

Findings

The project team derived these findings:

- Board member interviews and available data generally indicate that unmasking REG data and other changes that the DAF made for the 2021 CPME board did not have a significant effect on intermediate developmental education (IDE) and senior developmental education (SDE) board results when compared with the 2020 board.
- Most board members, for various reasons, explicitly chose not to consider REG data during the evaluation process.

- Given that this board is merely one data point, it is important to not make strong conclusions about unmasking REG data and selection board outcomes.

Recommendations

The project team offers these recommendations:

- Make adjustments to future developmental education boards:
    - Communicate diversity, equity, and inclusion goals, guidance, and intent to developmental education board members and SRs.
    - Review the IDE "definitely attend" process.

- After making the recommended changes for future CPME boards, DAF should keep the REG data unmasked for the next CPME board and analyze the results to determine whether the changes are having the desired effect.
- Leverage other aspects of human capital development and management cycle:
    - Establish REG applicant recruiting goals for the four commissioning sources.
    - Establish REG operational career-field designation goals at commissioning.
    - Update officer development/talent management guidance to squadron commanders, senior raters, and development teams.
    - Implement comprehensive rater training.

- Consider adopting strategic communications and cultural change management techniques:
    - Employ an enterprise strategic communications and change management approach.
    - Address DAF cultural norms (blind versus unblind).

Implications

As DAF implements unmasking demographic data, the research suggests that DAF will want to

- use training to educate members of the organization
- prepare for defensive responses
- implement organizational structures to address diversity, equity, and inclusion.

Also, the RAND Corporation report *Improving the Representation of Women and Racial/Ethnic Minorities Among U.S. Coast Guard Active-Duty Members* (Lim et al., 2021) developed a framework, Figure S.1, as an organizing construct that might facilitate the management and coordination of diversity, equity, and inclusion initiatives.

Figure S.1. Strategic and Tactical Enablers for Desired DEI Outcomes

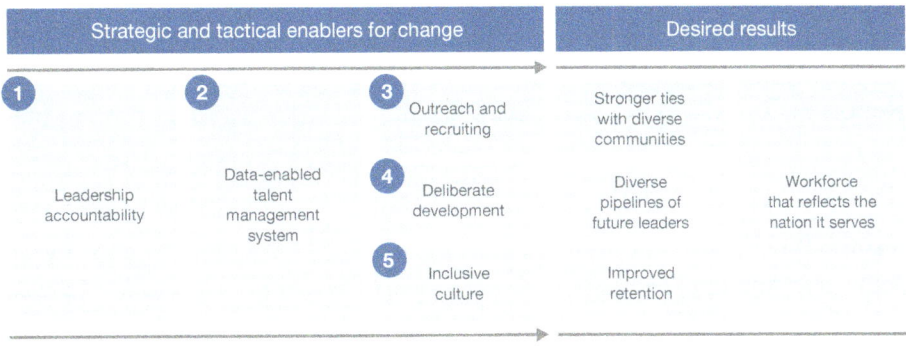

SOURCE: Lim et al., 2021, p. 136.

Contents

Figures and Tables

Figures

Tables

Chapter 1. Introduction

The Department of the Air Force (DAF) promulgates directives, memorandums of instructions, and other guidance espousing the importance of diversity.[1] Indeed, DAF Senior Leadership is on record stating diversity is a mission imperative. Yet, demographic data have been masked for most boards making decisions about career development and promotions. Moreover, recent survey findings from the DAF Inspector General revealed that many racial or ethnic minority service members lack confidence that their chain of command will treat them in an unbiased way compared with nonminority peers (Air Force Inspector General [SAF/IGS], 2020, p. 104). They also lack confidence in the system that awards opportunities for development and advancement. In response to similar challenges, the DAF and other military services are exploring ways to select more inclusive leaders and to account for equity considerations in selection boards.

The DAF wanted to assess the efficacy of making demographic data visible to board members. The 2021 Central Professional Military Education (CPME) Program boards were selected to test the effects of changes that would make demographic data visible to board members. The Air Force Officer Professional Military Education Program (PME) is essential to the continuum of learning that spans an officer's professional career. Developmental education (DE) including PME is designed to educate and professionally broaden individual officers into operational and strategic leaders who can provide innovative solutions to the future complex challenges facing the DAF (Hanser et al., 2021, p. 1). Officers selected for in-residence DE attend Air Command and Staff College, Air War College, National War College, and other such programs.

Selection to attend in-residence DE is a key gauge for DAF officers because it can be highly predictive of future promotions (Hanser et al., 2021, p. 22). For intermediate developmental education (IDE) and senior developmental education (SDE), senior raters (SRs) nominate officers, who then meet with a CPME Board that evaluates their records before other processes match the officers to specific programs and approve their designation to participate. CPME Board members consider an array of factors (e.g., leadership, depth and breadth of experience, job responsibilities), but job performance is the most important factor. The outcomes of these boards are a leading indicator of future promotion potential because the in-residence DE experience is valued by the Air Force and because the selected officers are often in the top 20 percent to 30 percent of their peers.

---

[1] As an example, see AFI 36-7001, 2019. This directive establishes guidance for diversity and inclusion implementation and management, enabling leaders to leverage diverse organizational talent and an inclusive culture to enhance mission effectiveness.

The DAF implemented seven specific changes for the 2021 CPME Board. The first three were intended to help the DAF select a diverse mix of officers for DE in-residence attendance. The seven changes are the following:

- board members underwent unconscious bias training
- board instructions were modified to permit consideration of race, ethnicity, and gender (REG)
- REG were made visible to the board
- increased emphasis was placed on recent performance (by limiting performance reports to the past five years)
- records were presented to the board by career field or developmental team category
- SRs' *definitely attends*[2] (DAs) were made visible to the board
- school slot allocations were redistributed by developmental category according to requirements.

Without careful study of the implementation, policymakers will not know whether these changes had the intended effect and whether there are unintended consequences that require mitigation efforts. The best course of action amid such uncertainty is to create and conduct a program evaluation in concert with the policy change. The Deputy Chief of Staff for Manpower, Personnel and Services, Headquarters U.S. Air Force, asked RAND Project AIR FORCE to conduct an evaluation measuring the effectiveness of the program and to provide insights that inform future policy refinements.

Study Objective and Approach

This project focused on CPME board processes before and after changes to the board information and instructions. The project team combined insights from qualitative and quantitative data, yielding a more complete and synergistic use of data than would normally be derived from separate qualitative and quantitative data collection and analysis. The team analyzed board inputs and selection outcomes for the 2020 CPME board (before the changes) and 2021 CPME board (after the changes) to assess the effects on the selection likelihood for minority versus nonminority members. The quantitative analysis included both regression models and equivalent group (*look-alike*) analyses. Further, the team conducted interviews with 2020 and 2021 board members to learn about their experiences and how they interpreted and applied the new instructions to illuminate the quantitative patterns in the data. For comparative analysis, the team also interviewed members of the 2021 Command Screening Board (CSB). Additionally, the team conducted text and sentiment analysis to gather data from performance evaluation reports and SR comments.

---

[2] SRs are allowed to designate a certain number of promotion candidates as *definitely attends* for DE, in effect guaranteeing them a spot in DE programs aimed at preparing them for future assignments.

Using this mixed-methods approach, the team identified key issues and potential actions to address them, resulting in recommendations for future boards on designing processes that select for traits that meet the future leadership needs of the DAF.

Structure of This Report

The remaining chapters in this report provide the results of our analyses and document the project's findings and recommendations. Chapter 2 discusses how the 2021 and 2020 CPME board members internalized and operationalized the guidance and data that they received. Chapter 3 compares the outcomes of the 2021 CPME board with those of the 2020 CPME board with respect to gender and racial categories. Chapter 4 compares 2021 and 2020 outcomes to explore whether similarly situated individuals from different groups have the same expected outcome. Chapter 5 summarizes the key issues and offers potential actions to address them. Chapter 6 provides our conclusions and summarizes the recommendations.

Six appendixes expand on information provided in the main report. Appendix A discusses the developmental education board process. Appendix B describes what the research indicates about masking versus unmasking gender and racial information for the boards. Appendix C reports the statistically significant officer attributes that help explain the 2020 IDE and SDE board results. Appendix D describes our approach for augmenting regression analysis with textual analysis. Appendix E provides additional information related to the equivalent group analyses. And Appendix F presents the board member interview protocols.

Chapter 2. Developmental Board Processes

To better understand CPME board members' experiences, the DE selection process, and potential impacts of 2021 changes to board guidance, the team conducted 28 interviews with 2020 and 2021 CPME board members. Additionally, to compare how CPME board members interpreted and applied board guidance, the team interviewed nine CSB members to discuss their experience with that process for the 2021 board. This chapter provides an overview of the DE selection process and changes to the 2021 CPME selection board guidance, the methodology of the qualitative data collection and analysis, and findings from interviews with both CPME and CSB panel members.

Overview of Development Education Board Processes and 2021 Changes

Each year, the DAF holds CPME boards to select officers to attend IDE and SDE in residence.[3] IDE and SDE selection boards are typically composed of nine panel members at the O-6 level and an O-7 board president. The DAF intentionally manages the makeup of board participants to ensure diversity in terms of career field, as well as REG.

Before they arrive on-site, panel members receive a memorandum of instruction (MOI) with guidance regarding the DE selection process and overall considerations for scoring candidate records. At the initial meeting, the board president recites this guidance verbatim and is available to answer questions. Once the board process starts, panel members receive candidate records in electronic form to review and score (from 6.0 to 10.0 points in half-point increments). Given the number of records and total time allotted for the board, panel members have limited time to score each record.

If two or more panel members differ by two or more points in their assessment of a given record, that record is considered a split. The panel periodically breaks from scoring to discuss and resolve any open splits. The panel members responsible for causing the splits must adjust their scores to get the gap below two points before the board process can continue. In addition, since many thousands of records are scored on a scale with just 81 possible distinct scores (60 to 100 in half-point increments), many ties occur and must also be resolved by the board to produce a complete rank ordering. Once all records are scored and the splits and ties are resolved, the board president produces a ranked list of candidates for either IDE or SDE. Further detail on board operations may be found in Appendix A.

---

[3] Air Force officers typically attend IDE in the rank of major and SDE in the rank of lieutenant colonel. Officers can attend either course via an in-residence program, which lasts approximately ten months, or an online program. Both types are technically equivalent, but attending in-residence is generally considered more prestigious, given the competitive selection process.

In 2021, the DAF made seven changes to the developmental education board process:

1. Panel members received training on unconscious bias in the form of a short video before the board began, which was not included in preceding years.[4]
2. Board instructions were modified to permit consideration of REG.
3. An officer's REG data were visible to panel members (these data were previously masked).
4. Panel members had access to only the preceding five years of an officer's record compared with the complete record used in previous selection boards; the primary aim of this change was to increase focus on an officer's recent performance.
5. Records were presented to the board grouped by career field or developmental team category as opposed to being randomly distributed, thus allowing panel members to compare candidates within a given career field more easily.
6. Panel members could see the DE recommendation from a candidate's SR; in particular, the DA designation that was masked for previous boards was made visible.
7. School slot allocations were redistributed by developmental category according to requirements.[5]

Making REG data visible to panel members is of particular interest to our study and was our primary focus when interviewing CPME board members.

Methodology

After receiving contact information from the project sponsor for 2020 and 2021 CPME board members and for 2021 CSB members, the project team reached out to each individual by email.[6] In the email, the team provided background information about the study and the interview task and asked recipients to participate in the interview process. Once we received responses from interested individuals, we coordinated with them or their staff to schedule a convenient time to conduct the interview.

We began each interview by providing background information about the study, answering participants' questions, and obtaining informed consent for participation, which emphasized that participation was voluntary and that the research team would keep any personally identifiable information confidential. Interviews with CPME board members typically ran 45 to 60 minutes, and interviews with CSB panel members typically took roughly 30 minutes. All interviews were conducted virtually via Microsoft Teams or by phone between April and July 2021. Notes taken

---

[4] The roughly three-minute video shows clips of airmen from different backgrounds interacting on the job. The narrators describe the concept of unconscious bias, explain that everyone has biases, and describe potential impacts of these biases and the importance of beginning to acknowledge and address these biases (Barth, 2020).

[5] This change was not discussed in board member interviews because it involved changes to the process after board members scored officer records.

[6] The researchers received contact information for and reached out to 17 2020 CPME board members, all 20 2021 CPME board members, and all ten 2021 CSB panel members. Contact information for the three additional 2020 CPME board members was unavailable.

during the interview by the research team were uploaded into qualitative coding software and coded to identify key themes and trends.[7] The interview protocols are available in Appendix E.

We conducted 13 interviews with 2020 CPME board members (seven IDE and six SDE), 15 interviews with 2021 CPME board members (seven IDE and eight SDE), and nine CSB panel members.[8] In addition, we held discussions with representatives from the Air Force Personnel Center (AFPC) and the Colonel's Group, who oversee the CPME board and CSB process, respectively. These discussions provided additional context regarding execution of the board processes.

Findings: CPME Board Member Interviews

Analysis of the CPME board member interview data revealed findings in four key areas:
- board member understanding and interpretation of board guidance related to diversity, equity, and inclusion (DEI)
- board member application of DEI guidance to the process of scoring officers' records
- board member opinions on unmasking REG information in officer records
- board member perceptions of other changes to the 2021 DE selection process beyond unmasking REG data.

Over the course of the interviews, board members also suggested improvements related to the role of DEI in the DE selection process. These findings are discussed in the sections that follow.[9]

Understanding and Interpretation of CPME Board Guidance Related to DEI

CPME board members from both 2020 and 2021 reported that the primary source of board guidance related to DEI came from the text of the MOIs, with little to no additional verbal context or informal discussion among board members about the topic. Table 2.1 displays the 2020 MOI language related to DEI and the changes made to the MOI language for 2021.

---

[7] Our qualitative coding methodology used a hybrid approach of deductive and inductive coding. Protocol questions guided initial coding tree development. As themes within broader codes based on protocol questions emerged, additional codes were developed and added to categorize emerging themes. One research team member completed all qualitative coding, so measures to ensure interrater reliability for multiple coders were not necessary.

[8] Interviews included discussions with board presidents. While the research team did interview all board members willing to participate, saturation for key themes was reached.

[9] Findings related to how, or whether, board members used available REG data and opinions on unmasking REG data are intentionally reported numerically. Other interview findings were not quantifiable in nature and are discussed in terms of prevalent themes.

Table 2.1. Change in MOI Guidance from 2020 to 2021

2020 MOI language	2021 MOI language
". . . acknowledging diversity is a force multiplier, I need you to recognize officers who demonstrate initiative and display an ability to lead in our increasingly diverse DAF culture. Selected officers must be the highest performers who model our core values, foster inclusiveness, and champion dignity and respect while leveraging the contribution of our Total Force." Addendum to the 2020 MOI: "To remain competitive, the Department must have members from the entire spectrum of qualified talent available. Accordingly, the [Department of Defense] needs to make every effort to encourage service from individuals of all backgrounds by providing for the equal treatment and equitable considerations of all personnel considered for development."	"To remain competitive, and acknowledging that diversity is both a force multiplier and essential within an all-volunteer force, you should look to select a diverse mix of officers who demonstrate initiative and display an ability to lead in our increasingly diverse Air Force organizations. In assessing diversity, you may consider the broad background and experiences of the candidates, including their demographics, education, experiences, source of military commission and training, prior enlistment and service experience, and any other factor. Diversity should not be interpreted as a mandate to apply weight solely based on a candidate's race, gender, or other demographic qualifier. Your assessment of each candidate must remain individualized. The Air Force needs to make every effort to encourage service from individuals of all cultural backgrounds by providing for the equal treatment and equitable consideration of all personnel considered for development."

Overall, 2021 board members found the intent of the guidance to be unclear. Board members described it as ambiguous and confusing, without adequate clarity on how to apply the guidance to the process of scoring officer records. One 2021 board member stated,

> There was an ambiguous paragraph on DEI, ambiguous to the point it was frustrating. There was no guidance on what it meant. I saw the way the paragraph was written, and it was disappointing because it was like, "We care but we don't know how to care."

Board members expressed that the guidance communicated that DEI is important to the DAF, but it also emphasized that officer performance should be the basis of scoring records. This led to confusion for many board members who found these two concepts potentially in conflict. According to one 2021 board member,

> It was kind of, "You should consider DEI, but it shouldn't change how you score a record, but you should be aware of it, but it shouldn't be a determination in how you score." So, it was kind of like doublespeak.

Some 2021 board members interpreted the guidance as directing the board not to consider REG information when scoring records, while others felt that the guidance provided no direction on how or whether to use REG data. Despite the confusion about the MOI language related to DEI, board members did not request clarification prior to the board. Of note, while REG were unmasked in 2021, board members were not notified of this change, and the availability of these data was not brought to board members' attention, perhaps contributing to their not requesting DEI guidance clarification up front.

The 2020 board members, however, largely found the MOI guidance clear and did not recall confusion about how to interpret the 2020 DEI board guidance. One 2020 board member stated,

> I think the guidance was very clear. No shades of gray there.

Notably, REG were not unmasked in officer records for the 2020 DE selection process, so 2020 board members did not have to interpret DEI board guidance in the context of unmasked demographic information.

In summary, the 2021 board members found the DEI guidance contradictory, ambiguous, and confusing, while 2020 board members, who did not consider the DEI guidance in conjunction with unmasked REG data, overall did not report confusion related to the guidance.

Application of DEI Board Guidance to DE Selection Process

When asked how, if at all, they applied the DEI guidance when scoring officers' records, 2021 board members cited different approaches, but most relayed that they did not consider REG information. Of the 15 2021 board members interviewed, ten (evenly split between the IDE and SDE boards) reported ignoring REG data when scoring officer records; nine of those did so intentionally, and one member was unaware that these data were visible at the time. Board members mentioned wanting to score based solely on job performance as the reason for this scoring approach, with some noting that the board guidance directed them to do so. Below are three examples of comments from board members who did not consider demographic data in their scoring.

> Since there was no formal guidance, I did not take race or gender into my calculus when scoring records and based my scoring on performance only.

> To be honest I did not apply [REG data] at all. I tried to make a conscious effort to not look at that block. It was tough because I looked at the commissioning source and that's one line down from race and ethnicity. It was challenging to not look at it, but I really tried not to. I didn't want to make any judgment as it relates to race and ethnicity because [the guidance] said not to let it impact my scoring and I didn't want it to.

> My scan pattern [of officer records] didn't really include going to the upper left corner or wherever [REG] is in the [record]. I would not go there as part of my scan. I did not factor it into my scoring.

Two of the 15 CPME board members, both serving on the SDE board, reported that they used REG information as a kind of "tiebreaker" when they were waffling between two scores for an officer's record. In those cases, if an officer was a racial or ethnic minority and/or female, these board members would round up to the higher score. In cases where these two board members were able to make a firm decision about the score, however, they did not factor demographic data into their scores. For example, one board member stated,

> If you're reviewing an airman and were torn between an 8 and 8.5 and they're an airman of color, that might help tip the scale. If the person is a white guy, it tells me he's probably had some advantaged opportunities, so it's easier for me to go on the low side.

The other board member who applied demographics as a tiebreaker commented,

> Keep it in mind, they never specifically said "give a boost to diversity" because that would go against the equal opportunity act. But it was mentioned that CSAF [Chief of Staff of the Air Force] said diversity is a mission imperative and that we could see race, gender, ethnicity. What I took from that is if you're really on the bubble, that [REG] could be used as a tiebreaker, but that was never explicitly stated anywhere. . . . If I wasn't quite sure of where to go with an individual and was on the fence with my scoring, then I'd look at the race/ethnicity/gender and maybe use that as the decider.

Three of the 15 board members intentionally sought out and observed the REG data for each officer record but relayed that they did not directly consider this information as a scoring factor. One board member used this demographic information to identify any trends by REG in officers' pre-board DAF career opportunities. Another board member reported reviewing racial or ethnic minority or female officers' records with more of an eye for positive factors. That board member commented,

> I would say it didn't impact my scoring because I never thought "hey, this is a female so I'm going to bump her half a point." But there's probably a chance that if I saw a minority female that I looked at the record in a more positive note and looked harder for good things versus just scoring it. But I didn't overtly try and bump up those records at all. Almost like an unconscious bias in a positive manner.

The third board member in this category described being unsure of how awareness of REG affected scoring. While not intentionally considering demographics as a factor, this board member recognized that intentionally observing this data point for each record could have had some influence on scores, even if unintentional.

For the 2020 DE selection process, REG data were masked in officer records. When asked if these demographics could be inferred from records in 2020, some board members reported that limited demographics could be inferred for some candidates. However, all 2020 board members stated that inferred demographics did not factor into their scoring decisions. One board member commented,

> I didn't have a lot of time in my grading regimen. I didn't look at sex, nationality, gender, race, any of that. If I saw the person's name then great, but generally the only way to pick up on that was the pronouns in the senior rater comments. But nowhere did anyone call out race or ethnicity and I didn't go looking for it. I went looking for the best officers and the folks that had excelled throughout their career up to that point.

We asked these board members how, if at all, they would have used this information if it had been visible when they were scoring officer records, in light of the guidance that they received. While a few 2020 board members were unsure, most board members shared that they would not have considered REG when scoring records. One 2020 board member stated,

> No, it wouldn't have made a difference. Not in a tiebreak, split or anything. . . . There's no time to [consider demographics] either. Unless I'm told to do that as a board member, I don't think it's necessary because in my opinion, I think it's all about performance.

Some 2020 board members added that they would not consider REG unless board guidance explicitly required them to use it as a scoring factor. One commented,

> Based on that guidance that you read to me, I still don't know if I would look at anything other than performance because the guidance doesn't explicitly say "treat race/gender as a part of your scoring calculus." I wouldn't take it into account unless there was explicit guidance that said give preference to minorities.

A small number of 2020 board members, primarily SDE board members, did think they would consider REG if they were intentionally unmasked. One member said,

> Assuming the verbiage was the same from last year to this year, and given that you could now see the gender and the race, I would say you have to consider that when you think of . . . two records being equal, understanding that minorities of all types are underrepresented, I think you would have to give consideration to the minority member because of the importance of diversity in the force.

A small number of 2020 board members also noted that their views on the role of DEI in the DE selection process might have shifted, given the changing racial justice environment in the country since the 2020 process. One board member noted,

> If you were to ask me how you would have considered [REG] a year ago and how I would tackle it now? I have learned a lot of things I had no clue about before. I have no doubt it would have influenced how I score . . . especially with how charged the environment has been the last year. Some commanders chose to have a conversation and others did not, so I don't think you'd have an equal playing field. That's an evaluation on my part.

In summary, most 2021 board members intentionally did not use REG data in scoring— preferring to score solely on performance. Most board members who served in 2020 before REG data were unmasked said that they would not have considered the data when scoring records unless explicitly told to do so.

Stance on Unmasking Race, Ethnicity, and Gender Data

Regardless of how they used or would have used the demographic data, the project team asked all board members from both years whether they believed that REG information *should* be visible in the DE selection process.[10] We start with the 2021 CPME board members. Most of these board members (11 out of 15) relayed that they did not believe that this information should be unmasked. Some felt that, if job performance is intended as the sole basis for scoring, then REG data is unnecessary—and even distracting, since board members already have a great deal of information to process in a short time for each record. Some board members who felt REG data should not be visible believed that the scoring process should be as blind as possible to avoid the potential for bias to seep into scoring. One board member commented,

> I don't think [REG] should [be unmasked] because it's not a factor. If you unmask it, then the opportunity is there for someone to use it based on how they want to. If race/ethnicity and gender are not supposed to be considered, then it shouldn't be unmasked.

Others pointed out that unmasking REG can introduce the perception that the DE selection process is not fair and that those selected may have been chosen for their demographics rather than their performance. One board member stated,

> If they mask the data, I think it provides confidence back to the force that it's a fair system.

Two of the 15 2021 board members believed that REG data *should* be visible to board members when scoring records. They felt that unmasking these data promoted transparency in the process because often demographics may be inferred from the records by names or pronouns regardless of visibility. They also felt that unmasking this information allowed board members to consider the "whole person" when making scoring decisions. One board member commented,

> I do [think REG should be unmasked] because I think that you're taking a holistic view of the officer and that's part of who they are. The board process means we are all independently grading, and we resolve splits and ties, and having [REG] there allows it to come into arbitrating tiebreakers and splits.

Two additional 2021 board members reported that they did not object to unmasking race/ethnicity and gender information but believed that more guidance is needed for how to use these data in the scoring process. One of these board members stated,

> Unless the Air Force tells me to do something with [the demographic data], it's probably more hurtful than helpful [to include].

---

[10] Prior to asking this question, the project team informed 2020 board members that REG data had been unmasked in the 2021 DE selection process.

Turning to the 2020 board, five of the 13 members whom we interviewed believed that REG data should be masked, four felt that it should be unmasked, and the remaining four were unsure or agnostic.

In summary, a majority of both 2020 and 2021 board members favored masking the data to avoid the perception that the process is biased or unfair.

Perceptions of Other Changes to the 2021 DE Selection Process

After discussing the role of REG data, board members were asked to weigh in on additional changes to the 2021 DE selection process.

Addition of Unconscious Bias Training

Most 2021 board members felt that the unconscious bias training video at the start of the board was a positive addition.[11] Some had seen this video before but thought it was a good reminder for board members to be aware of their unconscious bias prior to scoring records. One board member said,

> It's always good to reflect on those kinds of things and be aware of the unconscious biases that everyone has. So, to see the video again, it forces you, even if only for a moment, to take a moment of reflection and spike awareness. Seeing the video before going into the board process, it's a good reminder of the importance of the job we do scoring. Reflective, yes, but more of a rededication of my duty as an officer to perform my duties on the board.

Although most felt that the training video was a positive addition, board members generally did not feel that it affected their scoring. One board member stated,

> I thought it was a well-done video, but I didn't think it changed anyone's mind. . . . I thought the video made it clear that the Air Force values diversity but didn't make it clear what we should do.

A small number of board members felt that unmasking REG conflicted with the unconscious bias training—that making demographic data visible allowed unconscious bias to seep into the scoring process. One board member commented,

> I thought the video was a great lead-in, especially considering the current environment and focus on this topic. But again, I go back to, it's almost in direct conflict with, "hey, you might have unconscious bias, and we are going to unmask this information so you can see it, but don't use it in scoring," those things all conflict. You're giving people the tools to apply unconscious bias by giving us the race, gender, and ethnicity information.

---

[11] The team did not ask 2020 board members for their opinions on this change, because they did not view the video that was part of the CPME board process.

Focus on Recent Performance

Limiting officer records to a five-year window to focus on recent performance received mixed reviews from 2021 board members. Some liked the change and noted that they would focus on recent performance even if the entire record had been available. They saw it as a time saver to not have this additional information present when reviewing records. One 2021 board member commented,

> If we had been asked to score the entire records, we would've been there a month. . . . I think you can get a pretty good sense of performance based on looking at the last five years.

However, other 2021 board members reported that they would prefer to see officers' entire record, and some viewed the additional information as necessary for candidates who fell toward the middle of the scoring range or were "on the bubble." In particular, board members mentioned a desire for all training reports (TRs) for each officer's record. They noted that performance in Squadron Officer School (SOS) and Air Command and Staff College (ACSC) were visible in some officers' records but not others because this training fell within the five-year window only for some officers. Board members were interested in seeing whether officers had received a distinguished graduate (DG) award from these programs, and for those whose SOS and ACSC fell outside the five-year window, the only way that board members had visibility on DGs was if SR comments happened to mention it. One board member said,

> Loved [the change to the five-year window]. But they need to give us all the training reports. That's the only measure we have to see how they do against their peers in other career fields.

Among 2020 board members, most saw limiting officer records to a five-year window as a positive change, with one noting that this was recommended by their board in the 2020 DE selection process out-brief session. This board member stated,

> That's what we recommended at the out-brief of our board. I think it's positive for SDE because young people do a lot of stupid stuff and some grow into their commitment.

Board members also reported that they tended to focus on recent performance and that having just the five-year window available would speed up the scoring process. However, a few 2020 members noted that having visibility into an officer's entire record is valuable in some instances.

Officer Records Grouped by Developmental Team

The grouping of records by development teams (DTs) received universally positive feedback from board members. The 2021 board members reported that it was much easier and faster to review records from the same Air Force Specialty Code (AFSC) together because they can compare "apples to apples." Grouping records also allowed them to become familiar with the specifics of a particular AFSC, including AFSC-specific awards, and not have to retain that information sporadically throughout the review process. One 2021 board member stated,

> I thought it was a positive [change]. It is hard to jump between career fields every other report. If you can focus your mind on one career field and work your way through it and then move to another, it allows you to see how folks are doing against others in their own career field. That was a big improvement from other boards I've been on in the past.

Board members from 2020 agreed that batching records in this manner would have made their scoring process more streamlined and easier. One 2020 board member said,

> I think that would be very useful because in 2020 it was random and would go from operators to civil engineers to aviators. So, lumping them together so you scored all operators, all logisticians, all civil engineers, I think that would be a very good change. It would make it easier.

Unmasking Senior Raters' "Definitely Attend" Designations

Making SRs' DA designations visible to IDE board members in 2021 received mixed reviews.[12] Some board members used DA as a quality indicator when scoring records, while others tried to ignore this information completely. One 2021 board member stated,

> I used [the DA designation] pretty strongly. [The board] had a conversation about the fact that the DA process exists to allow commanders and senior raters to push a member and get them a school slot. . . . On a number of occasions for a record that I thought was average, but a commander put a DA, I found myself scoring higher than I would've if I had not seen that.

Overall, there was consensus among IDE board members that SRs used DAs in an inconsistent manner. Some board members raised concerns about SRs using DAs to "game the system," meaning that SRs did not give their top-ranked candidates a DA because they thought those high achievers would be selected for DE anyway, and they saved their DAs for lower-ranked candidates. As one board member speculated,

> I think the intent was to give the DA to one of your top two or three officers, and some senior raters were giving their DA to #12 or something, which I don't think was the intent of the DA. That sends a message to the board that senior raters are gaming the system to get more of their officers to school. . . . There were a number of [board members] that said that after they saw the disparities among senior raters, everyone started ignoring it.

Board members from 2020 also had mixed views on the usefulness of unmasking DAs and similarly raised concerns about the inconsistency in how SRs awarded these designations. One 2020 board member noted that SRs' comments can sometimes include the DA information, so it was available for some officers' records but not others in 2020.

---

[12] DA designations are not given to SDE candidates, so this question was asked only of IDE board members.

In summary, the 2021 board members largely found other changes to the DE selection process to be positive (e.g., unconscious bias training, focusing on recent performance, grouping officer records by developmental team). However, unmasking SRs' DAs got mixed reviews, and some raised concerns about SRs using DAs to "game the system." The 2020 board members agreed with 2021 board members' assessments of these changes to the DE selection process.

Suggested Improvements to the Role of DEI in the DE Selection Process

Board members suggested several improvements related to the role of DEI in the DE selection process. These suggestions included changes to DEI guidance, how DEI is integrated into the process, and other considerations for the DAF.

Board Member Diversity

Board members recommended that the boards themselves be more demographically diverse. The 2021 members, in particular, noted that their boards were lacking in REG diversity. Board members perceived a demographically diverse board as critical for providing different perspectives to the scoring process. One board member commented,

> The makeup of the board itself along the same lines as diversity. I was on the IDE panel, and we had one female and she was Hispanic I think, and we had one male African American, and everyone else was a white male. So we talked about the lack of diversity on the panel itself and the potential impacts that could have on the panel itself considering the [demographic] information was unmasked on the records. . . . It seems like we screwed up the makeup of the board.

Board members did recognize and appreciate the diversity of AFSCs present in board membership and acknowledged the difficulty in achieving both demographic and career field diversity in the board's composition. Some board members noted that the lack of demographic diversity might have occurred because of last-minute replacements for board members who had been tapped to participate but had to drop out. Board members suggested the DAF consider having a demographically diverse bench of board member candidates to accommodate last-minute changes while maintaining demographic diversity of the board.

Board members also noted that more notice of board participation would be beneficial for planning purposes. In particular, officers with family obligations may need additional lead time to participate on a CPME board, given the time commitment away from home.[13]

Clear DEI Board Guidance

Many board members said that the DAF should provide clearer board guidance on DEI and that the ambiguity of the guidance was frustrating. One 2020 board member commented,

> It's a garbage statement. It's impossible to apply unless you have some sort of quota system. A) It doesn't explain why it's a force multiplier, so you don't know

---

[13] The IDE and SDE boards typically run for two weeks.

what attributes to measure in a performance report—they need to be able to articulate the attributes of DEI that make it a force multiplier; B) it's impossible to look at a record and discern whether the person, based on their performance report, if they are fostering an environment of dignity and respect. . . . We don't have an inclusivity measure in the Air Force so that doesn't appear in the performance reports. [The DEI guidance] is a wink from the SecAF [Secretary of the Air Force] that if you see someone that's not a white male and their record isn't quite as strong that we should pick them. . . . It's frustrating. SecAF, just tell us what you want us to do.

A 2021 board member also expressed a desire for more clarity,

I think [the guidance] ought to be a more tangible way of defining how panelists should value [REG] information: a tiebreaker, a discriminator among equals, or it gives an extra half-point. And also, I think they need to explain the why. I think most people get it, but because we value a diverse workforce, we need to take deliberate steps to act on that. . . . And the Air Force needs to articulate the why to us and our service.

However, while in the minority, a few board members did find the guidance clear and did not believe it required additional specificity. For example, one 2021 board member said,

I think like anything we all have our backgrounds and experiences which impact how we look at records. I think it's fine to say consider DEI just like you consider career progression and other things in the records. It's just another thing folks can consider, but I'm hesitant to say [the guidance] should dictate how we should consider it.

Some racial or ethnic minority and female board members raised a particular concern about the lack of clarity:[14] Ambiguity places the burden on the board member to interpret the guidance, which can be awkward for the few minority or female members on the board. For example, if demographic data is used as a scoring factor and a racial or ethnic minority or female candidate's record ends up as a split, a minority or female board member might feel uncomfortable having to defend their scoring differences if related to demographics.

Board members also sought clearer DEI board guidance because they felt the lack of clarity could introduce the perception that the selection process is biased or unfair. One 2021 board member commented,

There needs to be clarification that this isn't necessarily a point to put your thumb on the scale, but to consider that sometimes that through the process that unintended or blatant bias may drive those records not to the look the same as others. . . . There needed to be clarification that this wasn't an attempt to put a thumb on the scale to get people to advance who should not or were not qualified.

Racial or ethnic minority and female board members had a unique perspective on this concern that was raised by the broader group. They felt that if perceptions of unfairness emerged,

---

[14] The REG of board members was not collected as part of the interview; however, many board members volunteered their REG during the discussion.

racial or ethnic minority and female officers would not believe that they had been selected based on merit and could lose the confidence that they need as leaders. Additionally, others might believe they are undeserving of their positions or opportunities and did not earn them through their performance, which could have negative implications for diverse leaders.

Timing of DEI Interventions

Many board members stated that CPME boards are not the right time for DEI interventions. They thought that the boards come too late in an officer's career for this type of intervention, particularly for SDE, and that DEI should come into play in the years prior to DE selection to better develop diverse officers and increase the diversity of the pool of officers who are competitive for DE. Board members emphasized that the focus should be on building and strengthening the pipeline of diverse candidates that the CPME board will review. One board member commented,

> You can't start when they are halfway through their career. You have to start before they walk through the door, but that's a 15-year commitment. There's not a quick way to get a quick win, and more senior leaders would rather the quick wins happen on their watch.

Another board member said,

> If you want to increase representation in developmental education, the board is not the place to do that. It's in the units and how we develop a person's record over time with opportunity and a level playing field to compete so the record itself is what wins the day. So it's more systemic.

Other board members saw the timing of DEI considerations in the DE selection process as less than ideal. One board member suggested that if REG are considered in the process, that should happen at the end, after the records are scored.

> Some ways I feel it'd be better if it's masked, and then show the demographic breakdown of how you and your board members scored and where the minorities flush out. I think that may provide more of a learning point, or not. Maybe it will show we were unbiased and fair in this snapshot assessment. . . . I think keeping it objective at the beginning, and then showing objectively how the board scored and how the preponderance of minorities played out, and then talk about if this is the intent. I think giving them an example based on their own inputs and scoring, and then giving them a chance to make this "more right," maybe that would be a better way to do it.

In summary, board members recommended that the boards themselves be made more demographically diverse and that the DAF provide clearer board guidance on DEI to eliminate ambiguity. Minority and female board members were concerned about the burden of having to defend DEI-based scoring differences, and about perceptions that racial or ethnic minority and female members did not earn their nominations. In addition, board members questioned the timing of DEI interventions in both the career lifecycle and the DE selection process.

Findings: Command Screening Board Member Interviews

Given the reported confusion around the intent of DEI guidance in the DE selection process and the desire of many board members for more clarity about the use of REG data, the project sponsor recommended that the research team speak with recent CSB panel members about their experiences. The recent CSB also had REG unmasked in officer records, as well as a statement about DEI in the board guidance. We compare the findings from these interviews to those of CPME board members to explore whether DAF officers who are more senior had a different perspective or interpretation of the guidance and the role of DEI in selection processes.[15] It is important to note that unlike CPME boards, REG data were visible to CSB members in officers' records in past years and were not new for the CSB in 2021. Although use of REG data was not prohibited in past years, the board language was expanded in 2021 to align with CPME board guidance and more explicitly allow consideration of demographics.

Interpretation and Application of CSB Board Guidance Related to DEI

CSB members received an MOI as well as a CSAF intent memo focused on DEI. DEI language in the CSB's MOI stated,

> To remain competitive, and acknowledging that diversity is both a force multiplier and essential within an all-volunteer force, you should look to select a diverse mix of officers who demonstrate initiative and display an ability to command in our increasingly diverse Air Force organizations. In assessing diversity, you may consider the broad background and experiences of the candidates, including their demographics, education, experiences, source or military commission and training, prior enlistment and service experience, and any other factor. Diversity should not be interpreted as a mandate to apply weight solely based on a candidate's race, gender, or other demographic qualifier. Your assessment of each candidate must remain individualized. The Air Force needs to make every effort to encourage service from individuals of all cultural backgrounds by providing for the equal treatment and equitable consideration of all personnel considered for command opportunities.

CSB panel members reported that the intent of this guidance was clear to them and that they did not seek further clarification.[16] They noted that, with such a senior-level group, panel members had served on numerous boards in the past and were familiar with this type of DEI guidance language. One panel member commented,

> I was amongst other deputy commanders, so we are all experienced in this piece of our responsibilities, so it was not new for us. Communication has been pretty

---

[15] CSB members were at the O-9 level with an O-10 board president. Findings related to how, or whether, board members used available REG data, and opinions on unmasking REG data are intentionally reported numerically. Other interview findings were not quantifiable in nature and are discussed in terms of prevalent themes.

[16] Of note, the CSB is not a statutory board like promotion selection boards, allowing more informal discussion about the board guidance beyond the official MOI and written guidance.

crystal clear the last four years so there's not room for doubt on what their intent and guidance is. Frankly communication has been excellent.

Still, even though CSB panel members generally perceived the board guidance as clear, they interpreted and applied this guidance in fundamentally different ways.[17] One board member described the clarity and interpretation of board guidance as follows:

> I think [the interpretation] varied by person, but definitely . . . [the guidance] was crystal clear, and each person had to interpret how to balance the guidance and their scoring.

Five of the nine panel members interviewed reported using REG information when scoring records. Like some CPME board members, some of these panel members said that they used these data as a "tiebreaker," meaning that if the panel members were undecided between two scores (using half-point increments) for a given candidate, they would default to the higher score for a diverse candidate and not necessarily do the same for other candidates. Some of the panel members who said that they used the demographic information when scoring records noted that they did so only in certain cases. For example, they bumped up scores of diverse candidates who demonstrated strong performance in nondiverse career fields. One panel member stated,

> If two records are the same and one of them is a diverse candidate, then I'd choose the diverse candidate. . . . What you're doing is saying you have two individuals that are absolutely equal, but I know that I haven't scored many females in this AFSC, so if two are the same, then I am inclined to give the female in that case a half-point bump up.

According to another panel member,

> My personal process was giving a half-point increase off the average based on a diverse demographic and continuing to evaluate the rest of the individual's reports for performance. . . . If I don't see continued performance, I would take that half-point for diversity away. Strong records of diverse candidates got a half-point bump, but if the record wasn't strong then I would not give that half-point bump.

Four of the nine panel members interviewed reported that they did not use REG information when scoring officer records. One described this approach as,

> Frankly, for me, [REG] didn't weigh into my scoring rubric. . . What I looked for was leadership qualities against their peers. . . . I understand where the Air Force wants to go to ensure we have the most diverse workforce possible, but it didn't factor into my ratings. I looked at all records fairly.

Some of these panel members noted that demographics were—and should be—taken into consideration *after* the scoring process. They described increasing the number of candidates that they send forward to increase the diversity of the selected pool. Specifically, the board can look

---

[17] Perspectives of the board president are included in CSB interview findings. While the board president does not officially score officer records as part of the CSB process, we asked the board president how, if at all, he would have used REG data as a scoring panel member.

at the demographic outcomes of the ranked candidate list resulting from the scoring process, and if the candidate pool that is "above the line" lacks adequate diversity, the board president can decide to add diverse officers who scored above a certain threshold (but did not make the original cut) to the pool sent forward for command selection. One CSB panel member commented,

> We had a small amount of people with quality scores below the line, and we'd go back and look to see if we should bring them above the line because we weren't adding enough diversity. . . . We were totally blind and agnostic of the race/ethnicity and gender in scoring, but then we considered it in the qualified pool to see if we had enough diversity, and we'd have conversations about each person [whom we considered moving up above the line].

It is important to note that the CSAF intent memo provided to CSB members explicitly mentioned considering REG in this manner, after the scoring process. The CSAF intent memo stated that the CSB should

> Make every effort to place qualified, eligible diverse applicants who meet the standard board score on the command candidate list for their respective CSB category, regardless of pre-established ratios.

While the general consensus seemed to favor the approach of increasing the pool of candidates sent forward for command selection to achieve diversity objectives as described above, one panel member did not agree, stating,

> My gut is that I'm against that. I've seen it be OK when it's literally a tenth of a point of margin. The good news is that it's a discussion that always takes place, but it generally doesn't happen. I am more comfortable with the methodology of bumping [the scores of] strong diverse candidates up.

Stance on Unmasking Race/Ethnicity and Gender Data

Despite the board being split on the use of REG data in scoring records, most panel members (seven of the nine interviewed) thought that this information should be visible during the scoring process. One board member stated,

> Yes [REG should be visible] . . . especially if your target is having a more diverse force. . . . It's hard to do without having precise data. The awareness is the biggest piece of it, with the training and education on why it's a mission imperative that we have a diverse force and ability to understand that if you are looking at a diverse candidate, then there might be things in the record that indicate disparity in opportunity.

Two of these seven noted that it is better to use this information after scoring, when deciding whether to expand the candidate pool, but still thought that it should be visible during scoring.

Two of the nine panel members interviewed did not believe that REG should be visible while scoring. One believed that the entire process should be blind, stating,

> I personally think it shouldn't be visible because then you can remove all unconscious bias. It's difficult because we use personal pronouns as you're

reading performance reports, so we would have to change how we write. But if there was a way to not have personal pronouns, no names . . . that would be great because I don't think it matters given we are trying to promote the most qualified individuals.

The other board member felt that this information should not be visible during scoring but should be observed after the scoring process to take into account when deciding whether to expand the ranked list of candidates for command.

In summary, CSB panel members reported that the guidance on how to use DEI guidance in their decisionmaking was clear, yet they interpreted and applied this guidance in different ways (e.g., as a tiebreaker when scoring records, to bump up diverse candidates' scores in nondiverse career fields, not using DEI considerations when scoring officer records, and increasing the number of candidates that they send forward to increase the diversity of the selected pool). A majority believed that REG data should be visible but had mixed views on whether REG data should be introduced before or after the scoring process.

Role of DEI in the DE Selection Process

Given that DEI was the focus of the study, we also asked CSB panel members to weigh in on the role of DEI in the DE selection process. Panel members advocated for IDE and SDE boards using the same approach as the CSB (although individual CSB board members took different approaches, as indicated by their comments above). One panel member described the reasoning for all boards to have REG visible as follows:

> [DE boards] should be similar to the CSB because it's again to the awareness piece. We select our [IDE and SDE] board members generally from command ranks because they are brought into the Air Force as an enterprise leader, so they understand the guidance and what we are trying to accomplish.

However, an important difference exists between CPME boards and CSB boards regarding how REG come into play after the scoring process. The CSB does not pick officers for specific command billets but instead merely provides hiring authorities with a list of potential commanders, and there is no statutory limit on the length of this list. Accordingly, the ranked list of candidates produced by the CSB readily allows for the cutoff line to be moved to increase the number of candidates sent forward, potentially increasing the diversity of the pool of candidates for command. However, only a set number of DE opportunities are available, so the CPME boards do not have an opportunity to increase the number of selected candidates to increase the diversity of the candidate pool. For CPME boards, pulling someone above the cutline bumps another candidate out of that spot for a school slot.[18] CSB panel members who discussed this issue had varied approaches and were often unclear or undecided about the best course of action.

---

[18] Of note, while the CSB process does allow for increasing the number of candidates sent forward for command selection, increasing this pool reduces each individual's chance of being selected for command.

For example, a panel member described the need for factoring REG into scoring for CPME boards because of this issue:

> There's a fixed number of seats [for DE], and movement of the line only adds people to the alternates, which means that this one piece of the CSB doesn't translate well. . . . That's why it's important to have race/ethnicity and gender data as a consideration in scoring.

Another panel member preferred that REG be masked during IDE and SDE board scoring and taken into account once a ranked list was created but was unsure how to address the issue of limited school slots.

> I think [REG] should be masked and used at the end. . . . You have to try and figure out . . . this is a really thorny issue . . . some would use the word quota . . . but we need to figure out what right looks like for DEI in the DE environment and then work back from the target and figure out how to, through a fair and equitable process, create a fair and equitable environment. Fundamentally we know we value it, but we can't make it a concession, and we have to figure out how to generate the right outcome for what we need. You're asking questions I don't have the answers to.

Another panel member described permitting a diverse candidate to bump another candidate off the IDE or SDE list as follows:

> CSB is a little bit easier in that way because in IDE/SDE you can't bring all four above the line because that means others get bumped off. . . . I am fundamentally OK with that situation . . . because we fundamentally scored the records based on performance and there's little difference between the ones near the cut line, and if it means that one person gets bumped off to bring a diverse candidate up, then I am absolutely OK with that because they could've all gone to school but we need to value diversity.

A different panel member did not agree with bumping candidates from above the cut line and replacing them with diverse candidates farther down the list but suggested adding school slots to accommodate those diverse candidates just below the cut line.

> I'm not for bumping, so the question is if the Air Force is willing to add a handful of school slots if it meant getting a few more diverse candidates.

In summary, many panelists advocated for all boards to have REG data visible, but they lacked consensus on how to address the limited number of school slots and the fact that, unlike the CSB board, CPME boards cannot increase the diversity of the candidate pool by increasing the number of selected candidates.

Suggested Improvements to DEI's Role in the CSB Process and Other Considerations

CSB panel members were asked for their thoughts on any improvements to DEI board guidance and related communication, the role of REG in the CSB process, and other considerations related to DEI in the CSB process and in current officer management and selection processes more generally.

When asked about current board guidance related to DEI, panel members generally reported that they did not think the guidance itself needed any improvement. However, some panel members discussed a desire for additional DEI context, including broader DAF demographic data to identify potential representation gaps and to help inform their scoring approach. Panel members suggested that these data could include demographics of the overall DAF, comparisons to the relevant population benchmarks, demographics by career field, and demographics of the pool of candidates who opted in for CSB board review compared with those who opted out of command consideration. One panel member commented,

> One thing that would be helpful is showing the current as-is state of DEI before the board gets into scoring so the race/ethnicity and gender data is contextualized and everyone has the baseline of where we are at and gets a sense of the trend line.

Another panel member agreed and said,

> It would be helpful just to know . . . what our [demographic] breakdown is before we score. I want to make sure I am being equitable across the board and score the same way but . . . this is our challenge right now—individuals build up these track records and if the system didn't allow for some to be provided the same opportunities, then you're going to be scoring a record and not be able to put it in that context. So having upfront, statistics . . . makeup of the USAF, makeup of society, challenges we've had over the years . . . if we think there is a particular area where [demographic diversity] is lacking and, if all things are equal in the records, then we should push those diverse candidates.

Another panel member discussed the additional context and DEI understanding that is needed beyond the written guidance:

> We probably do need a little more at the beginning of the board—talk about the benefits of racial diversity and ethnic and gender diversity. Have a discussion and make sure all board members are on the same page regarding what the Air Force means by diversity. There is an assumption that we are all educated and fully understand this. We've got to change the culture—that's not a bad thing—we have to help ourselves work into this. We can't do it overnight. There needs to be a little more education and dialogue upfront.

Beyond suggesting that additional DEI context be provided to the CSB, panel members also commented on the timing of DEI interventions when asked about potential improvements regarding the role of DEI. Like CPME board members, CSB panel members emphasized that DEI interventions needed to come earlier and more consistently in officers' careers to have an impact on the diversity of DAF leadership. One panel member commented,

> If you are only including it in the CSB process, for a lot of people it's too late. I think you need to bring it into the DT process so there's opportunity when they are still captains and majors. . . . Identify folks that need mentoring to give the opportunity to receive feedback and implement it before they get to DE and CSB.

Similarly, a panel member stated,

Conclusion

Interviews with CPME and CSB members revealed several key takeaways about the DE selection process and the role of DEI (Table 2.2). The DAF should consider these takeaways when determining the best way forward for future selection processes.

In general, CPME board members found board guidance related to DEI ambiguous and were unclear on its intent. Some CPME board members interpreted the guidance as instructing them not to consider REG in scoring, which we do not believe was the DAF's intent in unmasking these demographics, while others felt that they were not given any clear direction on whether or how to use these data. CPME board members expressed a desire for more clarity in the board guidance and more explicit direction on how to use REG in the scoring process. In responding to this finding, the DAF will need to consider the best way to strike a balance between providing clear guidance and being overly directive. Notably, CSB members generally found board guidance related to DEI to be clear and did not seek additional clarification. This may demonstrate that more-seasoned senior officers better understand the DAF's intent and overarching goals with respect to DEI and how unmasking REG supports those goals. Additionally, CSB members received the CSAF intent memo focused on DEI in addition to the MOI, which provided additional context and guidance. Still, CSB panel members did note a desire for additional context about DAF demographic trends at the start of the board. Providing this type of information would likely also provide CPME board members context that would help clarify the DAF's intent related to DEI and integration of REG into selection processes.

Most 2021 CPME board members chose to ignore REG information and did not consider it when scoring officers' records, even after receiving the board guidance related to DEI. These board members expressed the viewpoint that selection processes should be based solely on performance factors and thought that they needed explicit guidance from the DAF to use REG data in scoring before they would do so.[19] In general, 2020 CPME board members agreed, and most stated that they would not have used REG data as a scoring factor if it had been available during their board. Again, the CSB panel largely differed from CPME board members, with just over half of CSB members considering REG in the scoring process. This is likely a result of more-seasoned senior officers having perhaps a more nuanced interpretation of the board guidance that included an understanding of the DAF's overall intent with respect to DEI. In addition, past CSBs had included REG in officer records, perhaps normalizing the inclusion of this information, and the CSAF intent memo offered explicit guidance related to increasing the pool of diverse applicants sent forward for command selection.

Most CPME board members thought that REG should be masked and that the DE selection process should be blind to demographics, which is not surprising given their lack of consideration of demographics data in scoring. These board members thought that the

---

[19] A small number of 2021 board members did consider demographics when scoring, with some increasing scores for records of racial or ethnic minorities and women in some instances.

introduction of demographics could allow for bias and introduce the perception that the process is not fair. Again, at the general officer level on the CSB, we see differences in opinion from CPME board members. CSB panel members overwhelmingly thought that REG should remain visible for not just the CSB, but for all selection processes. These panel members expressed that these data are necessary to implement the DAF's intent to improve the diversity of the force.

Board members from CPME and CSB did agree that selection boards for developmental education and command are too late in an officer's career to make a significant impact on the diversity of DAF senior leaders. They felt that earlier interventions throughout officers' careers are necessary to build a diverse pipeline for senior leadership.

Table 2.2. Summary of Findings

	DE Boards		CSB
	2021 (REG unmasked)	**2020** (REG masked)	(REG unmasked)
How clear was board guidance related to DEI?	Ambiguous and confusing	Relatively clear	Clear
Did you use/would you have used REG data in scoring records?	Most did not (10/15)[a]	Most would not unless specifically directed	Mixed: used–5/9, did not use–4/9
Should REG data be unmasked?	No (11/15)	Mixed: no–5/13, yes–4/13, not sure–4/13	Yes (7/9)
Were additional measures positive or negative?			
Unconscious bias training	Positive	N/A	N/A
Focus on recent performance	Mixed	Positive	N/A
Officer records grouped by DT	Positive	Positive	N/A
Unmasking SRs' DAs	Mixed (concerns about inconsistency)	Mixed (concerns about inconsistency)	N/A

[a] Of the remaining five board members, two used REG data as a tie-breaker, and three were unsure of REG influence—although they did not intentionally use the REG data in scoring.

Chapter 3. Developmental Education Board Outcomes

In the previous chapter, we discussed how CPME board members perceived the role of DEI guidance in the selection process. In this chapter, we compare the outcomes of the 2021 and 2020 CPME boards to explore whether the DAF's changes improved the diversity mix of officers for in-residence DE. We focused on factors that seemed important to board members as they rank-ordered nominees from the top to the bottom percentiles while making use of the innovative method of textual analysis where SRs' specific sentiments and words used in their comments are considered.

To provide context for this analysis, we show the population at three distinct points in the process with an emphasis on racial groups and gender: the eligible pool of officers, the officers nominated by their SRs, and the officers sent to a DE assignment as a result of the CPME board ranking and the DE seats allocated to each DT. Table 3.1 shows this information for Black, Hispanic, Asian, and female service members at each of those points for years 2019, 2020, and 2021. As an example, for IDE in 2021, women represented 13.2 percent of the eligible officer pool, obtained 16.4 percent of the nominations from their SRs, and received 21.5 percent of the IDE seats. For SDE in 2021, female officers were 12.2 percent of the eligibles, obtained 14.0 percent of the nominations, and received 17.5 percent of the SDE seats. While there is potentially an intersection between race and gender that would be good to assess, as was done in the DAF Inspector General (IG) Disparity Review Addendum (Inspector General Department of the Air Force, 2021), the sample sizes within minority groups and gender were too small to conduct any meaningful analysis at that intersection for this evaluation.

Table 3.1. Minority Representation Within the Named Pool of Officers

DE_Level	Group	Pool	2019 Share (%)	2020 Share (%)	2021 Share (%)	2019 Count	2020 Count	2021 Count
IDE	Asian/Pacific Islander (non-Hispanic)	Eligible	6.4	6.7	6.5	337	371	343
		Nominated	6.7	6.5	6.8	110	117	112
		Designated	*4.6	8.4	6.6	25	46	33
	Black (non-Hispanic)	Eligible	4.6	5.3	5.5	240	295	286
		Nominated	4.9	5.5	6.3	80	98	104
		Designated	4.7	7.1	7.0	26	39	35
	Hispanic	Eligible	6.4	6.9	7.0	338	384	369
		Nominated	6.5	7.0	6.9	106	126	114
		Designated	*4.6	5.3	6.8	25	29	34
	Other (non-Hispanic)	Eligible	1.2	1.3	1.2	62	74	61
		Nominated	1.3	1.0	0.9	22	17	14
		Designated	1.3	1.3	0.8	7	7	4
	White (non-Hispanic)	Eligible	78.8	77.0	77.1	4137	4271	4039
		Nominated	78.3	77.0	76.6	1278	1377	1260
		Designated	82.7	75.0	76.9	454	412	387
	Female	Eligible	11.7	13.0	13.2	614	721	690
		Nominated	14.9	16.9	16.4	244	302	269
		Designated	15.1	21.7	21.5	83	119	108
SDE	Asian/Pacific Islander (non-Hispanic)	Eligible	4.5	5.0	5.2	212	244	241
		Nominated	4.6	4.8	4.9	65	67	66
		Designated	2.8	5.1	4.4	7	13	10
	Black (non-Hispanic)	Eligible	4.9	5.1	4.7	235	248	221
		Nominated	6.1	6.1	6.9	87	86	93
		Designated	*2.0	3.1	4.4	5	8	10
	Hispanic	Eligible	5.6	5.7	5.8	265	280	269
		Nominated	5.3	5.0	5.8	75	71	79

DE_Level	Group	Pool	2019 Share (%)	2020 Share (%)	2021 Share (%)	2019 Count	2020 Count	2021 Count
	Other (non-Hispanic)	Designated	4.9	3.5	3.9	12	9	9
		Eligible	1.7	1.5	1.5	80	76	70
		Nominated	1.6	1.4	1.3	23	20	18
		Designated	1.2	2.0	1.3	3	5	3
	White (non-Hispanic)	Eligible	79.7	78.8	78.6	3793	3866	3664
		Nominated	79.3	78.9	76.6	1128	1112	1038
		Designated	87.0	83.9	82.5	214	214	189
	Female	Eligible	11.4	12.0	12.2	541	591	567
		Nominated	11.9	12.9	14.0	169	182	190
		Designated	13.8	10.6	17.5	34	27	40

NOTE: This table and the rest of the report follow a prioritization of race and ethnicity so as to create one mutually exclusive dimension from the two columns and 33 combinations of race from which military members may select. Members are assigned to the first racial category that they claim in the following sequence, regardless of how it is combined with other categories, as long as they have not already been assigned to a previous category: Hispanic, Black, American Indian/Alaskan, Asian/Pacific Islander, Other, and White.
* = the group's share of the designated pool is statistically significantly lower than its share of eligibles.

Our detailed analyses start with officers nominated by their SRs. We did not perform additional analyses of the eligible population. For our analysis, we used the inputs available to board members plus additional administrative data to model the rank order of the nominated officers as derived from scores assigned by CPME panel members. This included textual analysis of performance reports. The 2020 data model estimates were used to predict the rank order in 2021 and compare the prediction to the actual observed rank order. The analysis combined traditional statistical methods with machine learning and artificial intelligence methodologies (see Appendix D for more discussion). Several key findings were gleaned from our comparisons of the 2020 and 2021 boards:

- Our models found no evidence of positive or negative changes from 2020 to 2021.
- IDE outcomes for female nominees were better than our models predicted, especially among women working for male SRs.
- Average orders-of-merit (OOMs) for women exceeded the IDE and SDE board averages.
- Black and Hispanic members fared at predicted rates, which were at or below board averages.
- Poor retention is one reason that women are underrepresented in the higher grades.
- We did find two groups that appear to be disadvantaged by the current IDE selection system, although not due to REG: (1) officers who became SOS distinguished graduates prior to the five-year performance window that was visible to the board, and (2) unit level flyers (ULFs).

The bottom line is that the new MOI diversity language and unmasking REG to the CPME board do not appear to have significantly changed diversity nominee outcomes (gender may have often been apparent prior to unmasking).

Two Approaches for Comparing the 2020 and 2021 Board Results

We took two approaches that independently led to the overall finding that DAF's changes do not significantly change diversity nominee outcomes. First, we developed IDE and SDE predictive linear regression models to explain 2020 OOM percentiles, and the results of that analysis were used to predict the OOM in 2021 to assess whether the dependencies in 2020 remained in 2021. The OOM was scaled so that the higher the OOM percentile, the better-ranked an officer is. For simplicity, we use percentile or percentage interchangeably in this chapter when referring to the OOM, as a percentile can be defined as the percentage below a specific OOM value of interest. For our second approach, we developed prescriptive linear regression models to explain 2021 IDE and SDE rank-order percentiles. The findings from both methods were similar, as we demonstrate below.

For the first approach, the linear regression models were based on administrative data, some of which were not visible to CPME board members. For example, REG were not visible in 2020, but being female was a positive predictor of 2020 IDE OOM. Race and ethnicity were not predictive in either 2020 model. The models also included variables derived from textual analysis using natural language processing (NLP), a class of techniques for developing software for automatic or semiautomatic understanding and manipulation of human language.

For the first approach, we used 2020 models to score 2021 records. The model had a good variability explained by the covariates with a model R-square of 0.56 on a sample of 1,587 officers who were IDE eligible. The 2020 model predicted that women competing for IDE in 2021 would have an average OOM percentile of 53 (Figure 3.1, panel A). Their actual OOM was the 55th percentile, which exceeded the 50th percentile average for all nominees, and that is statistically significant (p-value=0.003). Figure 3.1, panel B shows that in 2021, the average OOM ranking for Black nominees competing for IDE was below average, just as predicted by our 2020 model, which reflects findings from boards whose members did not know that the nominees were Black. Figure 3.1, panel C indicates that in 2021, Hispanics competing for IDE received OOM rankings that were much better than their 2020 average, as our 2020 model predicted would be the case. Because the predicted 2021 IDE OOMs based on the 2020 rules closely resembled the actual 2021 results, it appears that the 2021 rule changes did not significantly affect the IDE board outcomes.

Figure 3.1, panel D shows that women competing for SDE received similar average OOM rankings in both years, as our 2020 model predicted. Figure 3.1, panel E demonstrates that Black officers competing for SDE in 2021 received below-average OOM rankings, as predicted. Figure 3.1, panel F indicates that Hispanics competing for SDE in 2021 predictably received below-average OOM rankings. Because their predicted 2021 SDE OOMs according to the 2020 rules closely resembled the actual 2021 results, we also conclude that the 2021 rule changes do not appear to have significantly affected SDE board outcomes for female, Black, and Hispanic members.

Our first approach to this analysis, the predictive model, was constrained by a very compressed timeline because our DAF partners had an immediate need for our best estimates. Our second approach, the prescriptive model, has a stronger statistical foundation in assessing directly the correlations between officer attributes and outcomes in 2021. As was the case with the first approach, being female was a positive predictor of the 2021 IDE rank-order. Race and ethnicity were not predictive in either 2021 model. Hence, there is additional evidence that the 2021 rule changes do not appear to have significantly affected the CPME board outcomes.

Figure 3.1. Average IDE and SDE OOM for Female and Minority Members

A. Female Service Members (IDE)

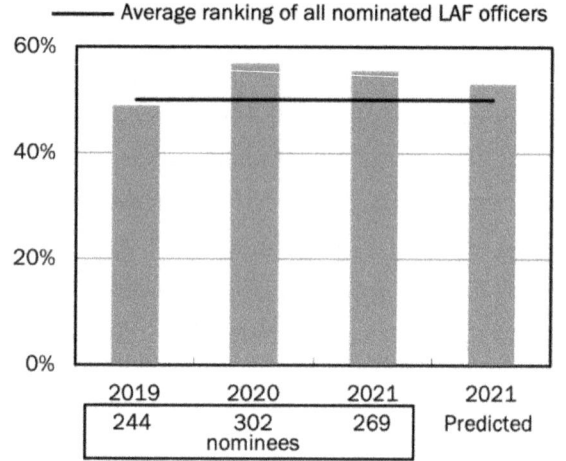

B. Black Service Members (IDE)

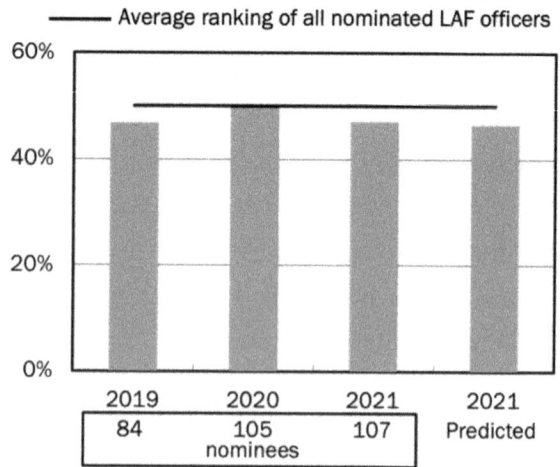

C. Hispanic Service Members (IDE)

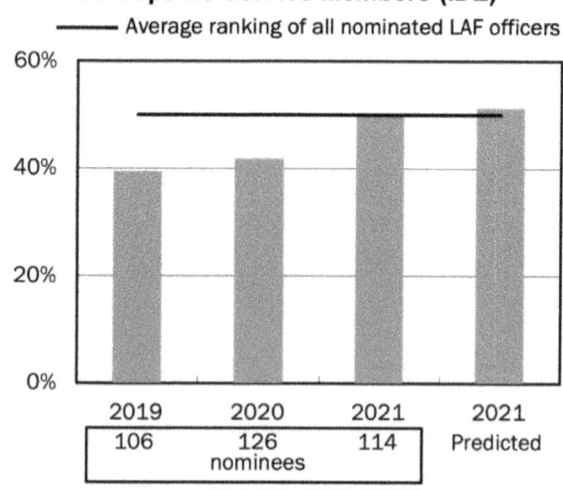

D. Female Service Members (SDE)

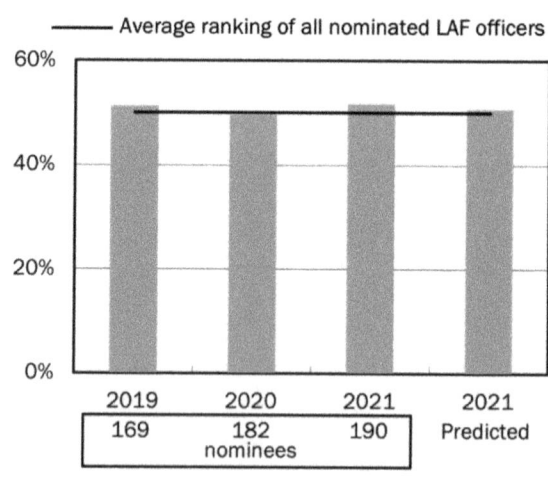

E. Black Service Members (SDE)

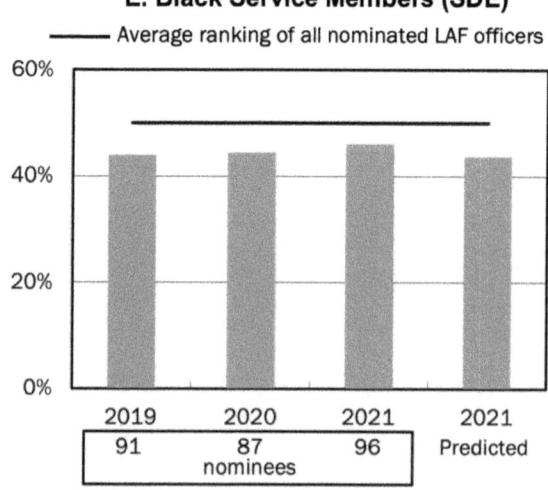

F. Hispanic Service Members (SDE)

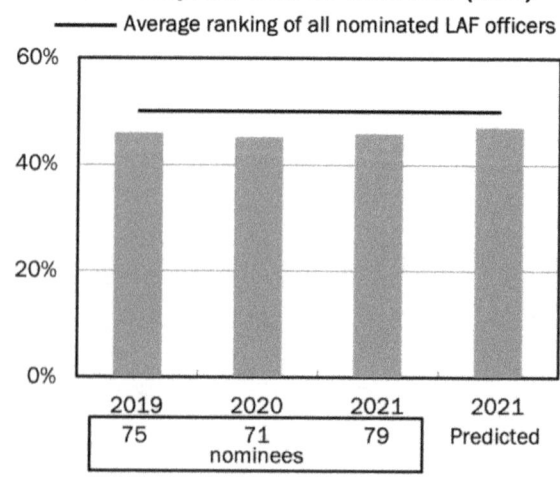

2021 IDE Model

Appendix C discusses the statistically significant attributes that help explain the 2021 IDE board results. In our modeling, we found 41 attributes to be statistically significant (Table C.1 in Appendix C lists those attributes with information on their distribution on different groups). Even though the average unadjusted IDE OOM is expected to be at 50 percent, from our IDE OOM model, a baseline officer with none of the 41 attributes is expected to have an OOM at the 43rd percentile point (model intercept), and then from there any additional attribute a nominee possesses will lead to a decrease or an increase of their OOM ranking. For example, a nominee who was stratified #1 by an SR with six to nine nominees had an average IDE OOM percentile of 79 percent (where 100 percent was the top-ranked competitor) after the boards score all the nominees' records, producing the OOM. Three percent of all nominees fell into this stratification grouping (#1 of six to nine), and their average OOM increased by 286 percentile points (the IDE model coefficient) from the 43-point start, all other things being equal.

Stratification is the most important attribute for explaining IDE board results. The model shows that being stratified in at least the top 40 percent of at least six nominees had a positive effect, while being stratified in the bottom 30 percent of at least six nominees had a negative effect. There was a wide range of average OOM percentiles—from 88 percent to 29 percent—as a function of stratification. The corresponding model coefficients ranged from plus 31 points to minus 13 points, and every nominee was stratified. The following factors were important in the analysis:

- *SR grade.* The higher the grade, the greater the positive impact. The 2 percent of nominees with O-10 SRs gained 15 percentile points.

- *Gender differences between SR and nominee.* Male nominees working for female SRs lost 5 percentile points on average. Female nominees with male SRs gained 3 points. Officers with SRs in Air Education and Training Command lost 9 points, and Hispanic nominees were overrepresented in that group.

- *Nominee milestones prior to the IDE board.* Those who were above the promotion zone (APZ) to O-4 lost 20 points, and Hispanics were APZ at higher rates. Source of commission (SOC) DGs gained 4 points, and Black and Hispanic members were SOC DGs at lower rates. While *SOC DG* was visible on the selection brief, *SOS DG* was not visible to the 2021 CPME board unless the SOS TR was rendered within the past five years or SRs mentioned it in their remarks. SOS DGs who had visible TRs gained 19 percentile points. But SOS DGs whose TRs were not visible gained only 7 points, even though their SRs were free to mention being an SOS DG (at the opportunity cost of absorbing some of the character-constrained space available for comments). Hence, masking SOS TRs seems to have penalized some. Overall, 11 percent of nominees were SOS DGs, and 10 percent were women; 13 percent were White, 5 percent were Asian, 6 percent were Hispanic, and 5 percent were Black.

- *DA.* In addition to usually being well-stratified, IDE nominees with DA assurances gained 6 additional points (DA was unmasked for the 2021 board). About 22 percent of nominees had SRs who could not give a DA, and they lost 8 OOM percentile points, a 14-point difference relative to the DAs. Female, Black, Asian, and Hispanic members were overrepresented in the group that had no DA opportunity.
- *Duty history.* The 10 percent of nominees who were Weapons School grads gained 13 percentile points. More than half of nominees had some sort of executive officer experience, which had a positive impact on OOM. Women were overrepresented in the executive group. Fifty-two percent of nominees had no meritorious service medal (MSM), which resulted in a loss of 7 percentile points on average. Seventy-four percent of ULF pilots had no MSM, and, because of the current pilot shortage, 80 percent of pilots were ULFs.
- *Textual sentiments in the Officer Performance Reports.* Very few sentiment words were observed in the Officer Performance Reports (OPRs), and most of them did not affect the ranking. When sentiments of fear were observed in 2 percent or more of the words used in an officer's OPR, the result was, on average, a 4-point drop in ranking, while OPRs with comments on stratification led to a potential 8-point increase. Examples of *fear* seen in OPRs include words such as *arson, assault, case, confession, conspirator, death, escape, fatal, fire, force, homicide, lines, loom, lose, offender, penal, penalty, prison, sentence, stab, suspect, terror,* and *threat.*[20]

Additional IDE Observations

Female, Black, and Hispanic nominations do not appear to present current disparities compared with male and White nominations. Figure 3.2, panel A shows that eligible female members have been nominated for IDE above overall average rates. Figure 3.2, panels B and C demonstrate that eligible Black and Hispanic members have been nominated at the average rates.

---

[20] Here is an example of an OPR statement that includes *arson*: "Developed lead for fatal stabbing of AD member—suspect behind bars—death penalty trial looms. Vigorously solved crime; analysis **arson** cover-up homicide—full suspect confession." One that includes *assault* is as follows: "Led joint US/UK child sexual assault case—secured vital testimony/evidence—offender sentenced to 12 yrs in prison."

Things need to happen—accessions, coaching, mentoring—to see the value of DEI and meet our goals. All of that will increase opportunity and create an equal playing field, which will increase the diversity of folks that make it to the board to be screened, which will help us have more diverse selections.

On this topic, another panel member said,

> We have to start with the right accessions, and then as we go along we have to value diversity when we are doing PME, training, when leaders and commanders get up and chat about diversity, they have to speak with authority. There's a whole range of DEI things that we have to get after in the Air Force, but it really starts with accessions.

Several CSB panel members raised another concern for DAF senior leadership to consider. When discussing the use of REG data in the CSB and other selection processes, panel members expressed concerns about the accuracy and completeness of the demographic information available. Specifically, panel members discussed the trend of airmen declining to disclose their race or ethnicity and the implications for selection processes that were taking demographics into account. Two panel members commented,

> We need to better understand diversity. . . . We allow the member to tell us what their [race or ethnicity] is and . . . we see growing numbers in the lower ranks that "decline to comment" on their racial/ethnic information or put "other," which get lumped in with diverse candidates. If we are going to use the racial/ethnic and gender data, then we need to have stricter guidance or more detailed guidance on how to promote and score records. Then we also need to understand and know the validity of the racial/ethnic data on those records are accurate and correct.

> Declining to respond puts them into the pool of diverse candidates and puts the board in an awkward position in that it's not clear. . . . The board found themselves in the position of inferring demographics by name or someone knows them. . . . But the reality is that we don't know [race or ethnicity] when they decline to respond. . . . I believe that this generation that's entering, the decline to respond is becoming more regular, and then when you try to start figuring out if you're treating folks equitably, it's hard to figure that out when more and more people are declining to respond.

While panel members did not have solutions to their concerns about racial and ethnic data accuracy, they felt that it was important to consider in the context of potentially basing selection decisions on these data.

In summary, CSB panel members saw no need for changes to the DEI guidance itself but wanted more information about DAF demographics and benchmarks as context for decisionmaking, and early discussions about DEI so that board members are on the same page about how to use it. They also emphasized that the CSB board comes too late in officers' careers to have an impact on the diversity of DAF leadership.

Figure 3.2. Average IDE Nomination and Designation Rates for Female and Minority Service Members

A. Female Service Members (Nomination)

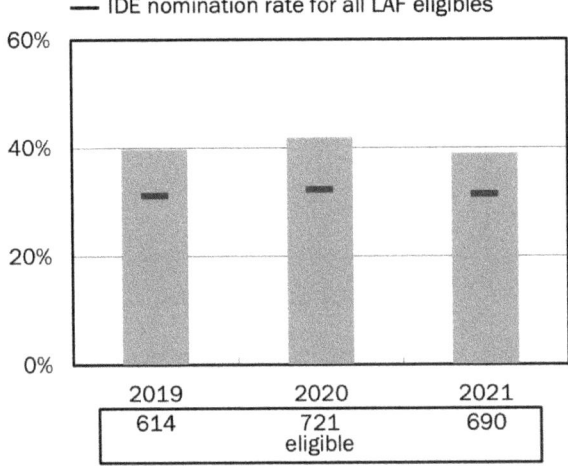

B. Black Service Members (Nomination)

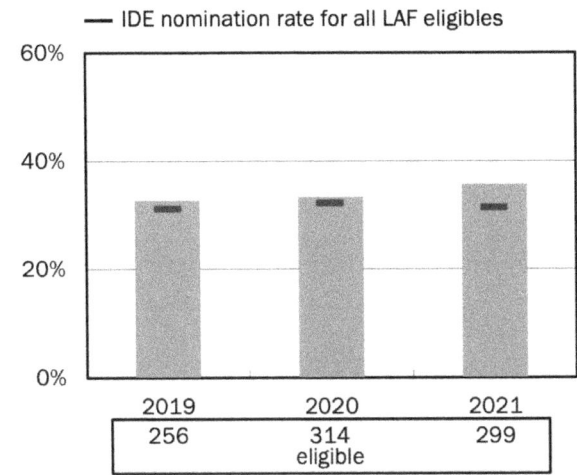

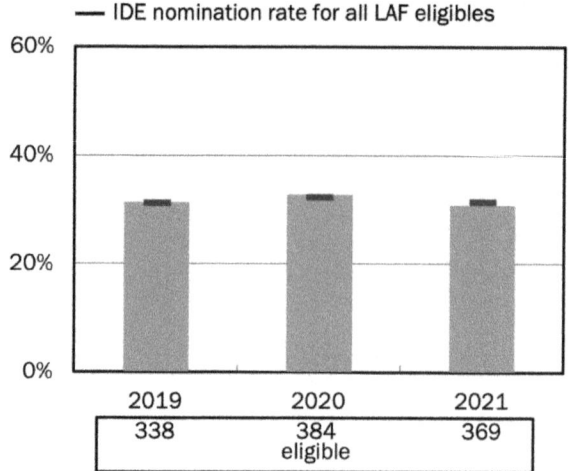

C. Hispanic Service Members (Nomination)

— IDE nomination rate for all LAF eligibles

2019	2020	2021
338	384	369
	eligible	

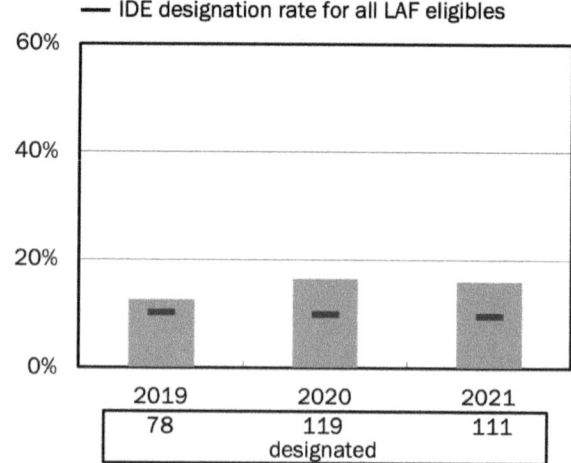

D. Female Service Members (Designation)

— IDE designation rate for all LAF eligibles

2019	2020	2021
78	119	111
	designated	

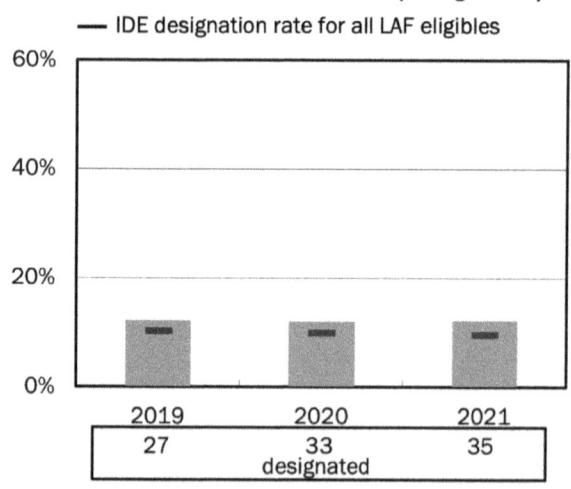

E. Black Service Members (Designation)

— IDE designation rate for all LAF eligibles

2019	2020	2021
27	33	35
	designated	

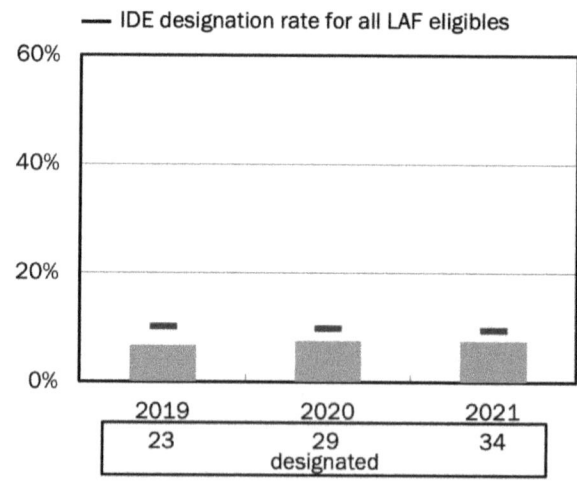

F. Hispanic Service Members (Designation)

— IDE designation rate for all LAF eligibles

2019	2020	2021
23	29	34
	designated	

Female and Black IDE designation rates[21] also do not appear to show disparity compared with male and White IDE designation rates. Figure 3.2, panels D and E show that female and Black eligibles have ultimately been designated for IDE above overall average rates. Figure 3.2, panel F points out that Hispanic eligibles have been designated slightly below overall average rates. The 2021 estimates account for DT IDE quotas, individual OOMs within DTs, DAs, and officers whose attendance was deferred for operational reasons (*Ops Deferred*) by DT from the 2020 cycle. At this time, we do not know which nominees who met the 2021 IDE board will eventually be Ops Deferred and replaced by alternates.

---

[21] Among officers eligible for DE, some are nominated by SRs for DE, but only a subset of those is designated or selected for DE.

Four Aspects of the IDE System That Need Attention

In addition to concluding that the new MOI diversity language and unmasking race/ethnicity and gender to the CPME board do not appear to have significantly changed diversity candidate outcomes, we found that four aspects of the IDE system require attention or review: the DA program; the redistribution of IDE quotas by the DT; masking SOS TRs; and a potential disconnect between IDE board timing and rated management, all of which we discuss below.

Definitely Attend

SRs were allowed to issue a certain number of DAs according to the number of officers who were eligible for IDE and the type of SR (Table 3.3). The officers with this DA designation get scored along with other records but are designated regardless of their OOM.

One concern with the DA program is that 22 percent of nominees had no opportunity to earn a DA, and women and minorities were overrepresented in that 22 percent. Not having a DA had a negative influence, in part because DA was unmasked in 2021. A second concern with the DA program is that too many officers with weaker records take the place of very strong officers. Even though the CPME board knew who the DAs were, it ranked 17 percent of them (n=46) in the bottom half. Also, just ten of the 46 were female, Hispanic, or Black, which suggests that SRs did not use DAs as an on-ramp for target groups.

Starting in 2020, SRs awarded increased numbers of DAs—from 194 in 2019 to 275 in 2020 and 269 in 2021. The increase in the number of DAs raises three issues. First, DAs reduce the influence of the IDE board. In 2021, 54 percent of the IDE quota was absorbed by DAs who were guaranteed to attend IDE. Within the DTs, 100 percent of Mobility Air Forces' (MAF's) IDE quota was filled by DAs, and the CPME board had zero influence over which MAF officers would attend IDE. Within the rated DTs, some nominees with strong OOMs were displaced by DAs.

A second issue is that DAs diminished the impact of limiting the CPME board to a five-year look. SRs who issued DAs and who determined more than half of the IDE selects could consider the entire record.

A third issue is that DAs limited the impact of changes to the MOI. The SRs who determined more than half of the IDE selects were not bound by the MOI.

Table 3.2 reflects our estimate of the impact on women and minorities in 2021 if the IDE nominees had been the same but there had been no DAs.

Table 3.2. Percentage of Nominees Who Would Attend IDE Under Different Policies

	Current Policy (%)	"No DA" Policy (%)	Difference (%)
Women	41	43	2
Black	31	36	5
Hispanic	25	31	6
Air Force average	30	30	0

IDE Quota by Development Team

The data also showed that the SRs nominated ULF pilots at lower rates, and those ULFs were concentrated in MAF and Combat Air Forces (CAF) DTs. In addition, about 60 percent of the IDE quota was filled by nominees who had guaranteed IDE slots, which meant that the IDE board played a limited role in identifying the officers who would attend IDE. Finally, many SRs had one too many or one too few relative to their maximum quota. Six percent were off by two or more. One SR nominated seven too many, and another SR with a maximum of 40 nominated just 22. Using a smaller denominator probably did not hurt the #1 stratified nominee in that management level. But, in another management level that nominated three under quota, being #1 of six would have been better than #1 of three. All these IDE quota observations can be correlated with REG (in addition to the fact that women and minorities were small numbers in the nominated sample), and thus they have the potential to influence the IDE DEI.

2021 SDE Model

Appendix C discusses the statistically significant attributes that help explain the 2021 SDE board results. In our modeling, we found that 38 attributes were statistically significant (Table C.2 in Appendix C lists those attributes with information on their distribution on different groups). The model had good variability explained by the covariates with a model R-square of 0.65 on a sample of 1,323 officers SDE eligible. In our SDE OOM model, each nominee starts with 70 percentile points. That starting point is then increased or decreased according to the 38 factors in the model. The following factors played a role in SDE board results:

- *Stratification.* This is the most important attribute that explains SDE board results. There was a wide range of average OOM percentiles—from 88 percent to 24 percent—as a function of stratification. The corresponding model coefficients range from plus 34 points to minus 17 points, and every nominee was stratified. Nominees who were stratified #3 of three, #4 of four, #4 of five, or #5 of five lost 11 points on average, and Black, Asian, and Hispanic members were overrepresented in that group.

- *SR grade.* The 1 percent of nominees with O-10 SRs gained 18 percentile points. The small percentage of nominees who worked for one of the six SRs above the management level (President, Vice President, Chairman of the Joint Chiefs of Staff, Secretary of Defense, SecAF, CSAF) gained 29 percentile points.

- *Nominee milestones prior to the SDE board.* The 9 percent who were below the promotion zone (BPZ) to O-5 gained 19 points, but just 2 percent of Black, 5 percent of Hispanic, and 8 percent of Asian nominees were in that group compared with 10 percent of White members. The 44 percent who attended traditional IDE in-residence gained 9 points, but just 36 percent of Black and 24 percent of Asian nominees had that box checked. The 15 percent who were SOC DGs gained 5 points, but just 8 percent of Hispanic and 6 percent of Asian nominees were SOC DGs. While SOC DG was visible on the selection brief, SOS DG and ACSC DG were not.

- *First and last looks.* Nominees receiving their first and last SDE looks lost 4 and 5 percentile points, respectively. The 1 percent who graduated from historically black colleges and universities (HBCUs) lost 11 points. Based on their OOMs within their DTs, we are projecting that none of the 15 HBCU nominees will be designated.

- *Duty history.* The 21 percent who had no experience as a commander lost 18 percentile points on average, and Hispanics and Asians were overrepresented in this group. The 11 percent of nominees who were Weapons School grads gained 6 percentile points, but female, Black, Asian, and Hispanic members were underrepresented. Special Warfare nominees gained 16 points, but only 1 percent of the nominees have that attribute. Current instructors lost 7 points. Female, Black, Asian, and Hispanic members were overrepresented in the group with Headquarters Air Force experience, a group that gained 3 points on average.

- *Textual sentiments in the OPR.* Women nominees were more likely than men to have received positive words relative to trust and less likely to have negative words related to fear or anger in OPR comments. However, the appearance of those words did not seem to affect nominees' board ranking. Similarly, there were some slight race and ethnicity differences observed; for example, Asian members tended to have fewer sentiment words—positive or negative—compared with White members. As another example, Black service members were more likely than White members to receive comments related to fear or sadness, but ultimately those sentiment words were not associated with board ranking. Given that African Americans, particularly males, have been stereotyped as not intelligent, violent, and dangerous in some cases,[22] it is reassuring that negative comments did not influence their ranking.

Additional SDE Observations

Female, Black, and Hispanic nomination rates do not appear to present disparities compared with male and White nomination rates. Figure 3.3, panels A and B show that women and Black eligibles have been nominated for SDE at rates higher than the overall average. Figure 3.3, panel

---

[22] Oliver, 2003.

C demonstrates that Hispanics have been nominated slightly below overall average rates. Figure 3.3, panel D indicates that female eligibles have ultimately been designated for SDE at near or above average rates. Figure 3.3, panels E and F show that Black and Hispanic eligibles have been designated at below overall average rates. The 2021 estimates account for DT SDE quotas, individual OOMs within DTs, and Ops Deferred by DT from the 2020 cycle. At this time, we do not know which nominees who met the 2021 SDE board will eventually be Ops Deferred and replaced by alternates.

Figure 3.3. SDE Nomination and Designation Rates for Female and Minority Service Members

A. Female Service Members (Nomination)

— SDE nomination rate for all LAF eligibles

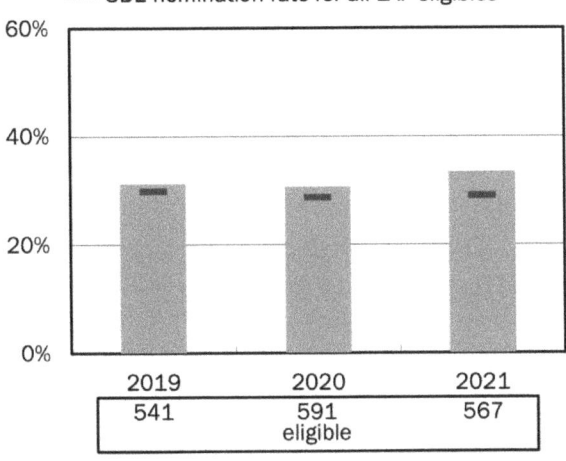

2019	2020	2021
541	591	567
	eligible	

B. Black Service Members (Nomination)

— SDE nomination rate for all LAF eligibles

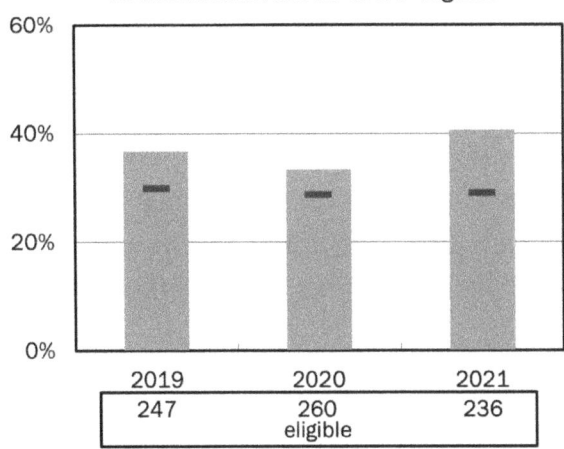

2019	2020	2021
247	260	236
	eligible	

C. Hispanic Service Members (Nomination)

— SDE nomination rate for all LAF eligibles

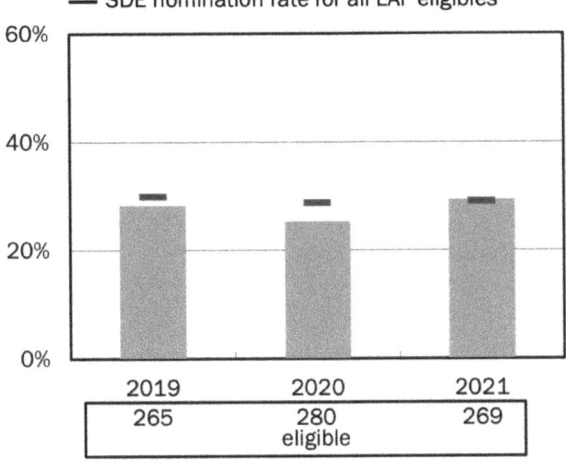

2019	2020	2021
265	280	269
	eligible	

D. Female Service Members (Designation)

— SDE designation rate for all LAF eligibles

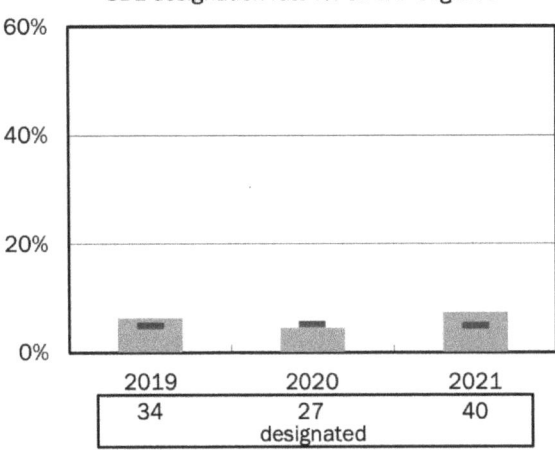

2019	2020	2021
34	27	40
	designated	

E. Black Service Members (Designation)

— SDE designation rate for all LAF eligibles

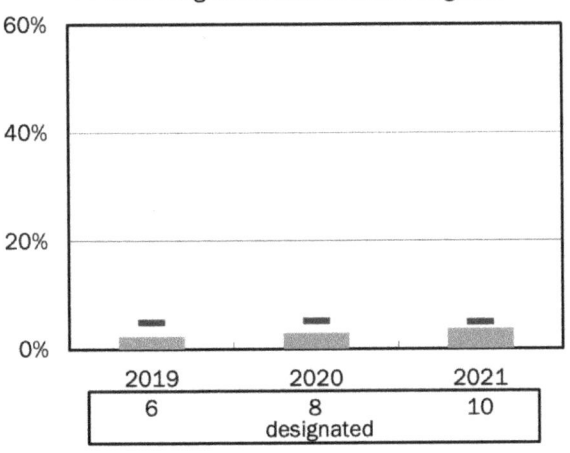

2019	2020	2021
6	8	10
	designated	

F. Hispanic Service Members (Designation)

— SDE designation rate for all LAF eligibles

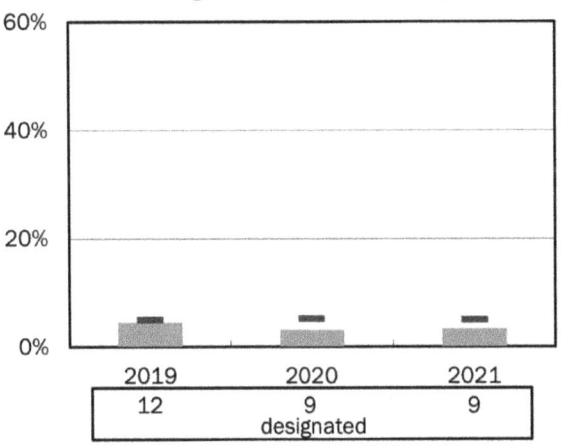

2019	2020	2021
12	9	9
	designated	

In the data, SDE nomination rates by DT ranged from 20 percent to 54 percent, which meant that SDE board members had a greater range of choices in some DTs. SRs were able to nominate up to 30 percent of their eligible SDE candidates, and all SRs were able to nominate at least one candidate. As for the reasons for the lower CAF and MAF SDE nomination rates, SRs tended to nominate ULF pilots at much, much lower rates, and those ULFs were concentrated in the MAF and CAF DTs.

Also, only about 10 percent of the SDE quota was filled by nominees with guaranteed SDE slots—that is, officers who were Ops Deferred or last-look nominees who were selected for DE at their promotion board. This was in stark contrast to the IDE board that saw more than 60 percent of the quota filled by officers with guaranteed IDE seats.

Pre-Commissioning Opportunities to Increase Diversity in DE Selections

Based on our findings, the DAF has several opportunities to increase diversity in DE selections prior to a candidate accepting a commission.

More operational specialties. Given that the DAF is trying to increase diversity in the higher grades, modifying DE selection procedures may be late-to-need. An approach that incorporates efforts to achieve diversity both in recruitment for long-term goals and in the higher grades for the near future is essential. Since the early 1990s, many in the DAF have believed that one key to modifying the demographic composition of senior leadership was to recruit and commission additional competitive females and minorities who wanted to become pilots. Table 3.3 shows that for officers who were eligible for IDE in 2021, women and minorities were still underrepresented among pilots.

Table 3.3. Pilot Proportions of 2021 IDE Eligibles

	Total (% pilots)	Female (% pilots)	Black (% pilots)	Hispanic (% pilots)
All eligibles	41	17	16	28
U.S. Air Force Academy (USAFA) graduates	62	30	33	54

Classification. Classifying graduating cadets into AFSCs offers another pre-commissioning opportunity. If the DAF continues to promote to O-5 and O-6 authorizations by AFSC and grade, disproportionally classifying women and minorities into AFSCs with rich authorization structures would be helpful. To some extent, this is already happening. Whether or not a classification strategy would yield additional female and minority general officers is unclear.

Retention. Figure 3.4 indicates that female retention rates are very low. For example, by the tenth year of service, just 42 percent of women entering the cohort remain in the service compared with 60 percent overall. Reasons for this difference are beyond the scope of this study,[23] but because females become pilots at lower rates, fewer incur the ten-year active-duty service commitment for attending pilot training. Women may also be making family choices as a function of frequent deployments and permanent changes of station. To the extent that the commissioning programs could produce more female pilots, the actual number of female pilots retained will increase.

Figure 3.4. Estimated Line of the Air Force Cohort Continuation

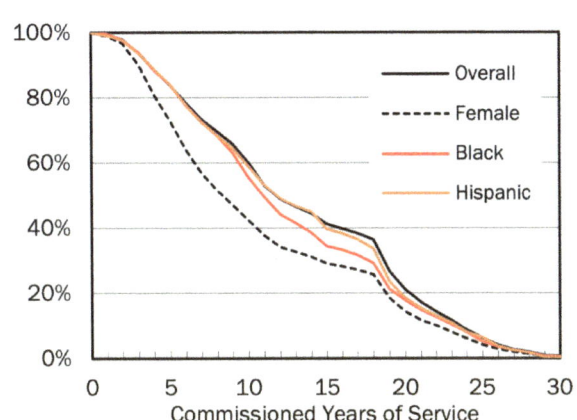

Advanced academic degrees. If there is a relationship between academic preparation and future success in the DAF, promotion and DE designation differences might be narrowed through relevant advanced academic degrees (AADs). Although the DAF masks AADs to CPME boards and to O-4 and O-5 promotion boards, half of junior officers obtain them anyway. Table 3.4 displays AAD completion rates for some groups of 2021 IDE eligibles. Female, Hispanic, and Black members all had PhDs, Air Force Institute of Technology (AFIT) master's degrees, or off-duty master's degrees near or above the averages for all eligibles. Note that the top 25 percent from USAFA had much higher AAD rates. Hispanic members and the bottom 75 percent from USAFA had lower AAD rates. While the DAF wants lower-grade officers to focus on performance first, it is possible that having a relevant AAD would enhance job performance. While we do not recommend changing AAD masking policy, supervisors might wish to encourage junior minority officers to pursue AADs that would strengthen their writing, speaking, and analytical thinking skills and take steps to encourage female, Black, and Hispanic members who express interest in pursuing AAD. Table 3.5 shows that female, Black, and Hispanic members with AADs were nominated for IDE at much higher rates in 2021.

---

[23] For a discussion of barriers to retaining female officers in the U.S. Air Force, see Keller et al., 2018.

Table 3.4. 2021 AAD Completion Rates for IDE Eligibles

	Ph.D. (%)	AFIT Master's (%)	Off-Duty Master's (%)
All eligibles	0.9	9	49
USAFA DG	4.3	44	29
Top 25%, not DG	1.6	16	49
2nd quartile	0.5	10	46
3rd quartile	0.3	7	46
Bottom 25%	0.0	5	42
Female	1.0	11	62
Black	1.0	7	61
Hispanic	0.5	10	50

Table 3.5. 2021 IDE Nomination Rates

	Had an AAD (%)	No AAD (%)
All eligibles	38	22
USAFA DG	44	19
Top 25%, not DG	42	24
2nd quartile	41	27
3rd quartile	37	16
Bottom 25%	42	27
Female	42	31
Black	44	16
Hispanic	36	23

Assignments. Another post-commissioning opportunity would be to give preferential assignments to target groups. That already appears to be happening for women. Table 3.1 indicates that women become executive officers at much higher rates. And Figure 3.5 shows that female pilots in the promotion zone (IPZ) to O-5 have been ULFs at lower rates. Figure 3.5 also suggests that the assignment system is already providing Black and Hispanic pilots who have been ULFs at about the average rate with some large variations from year to year for Black pilots. Figure 3.6 shows that female, Black, and Hispanic pilots who are IPZ to O-6 are already ULFs at lower rates.

Figure 3.5. Pilots IPZ to O-5 by Gender and Minority Group

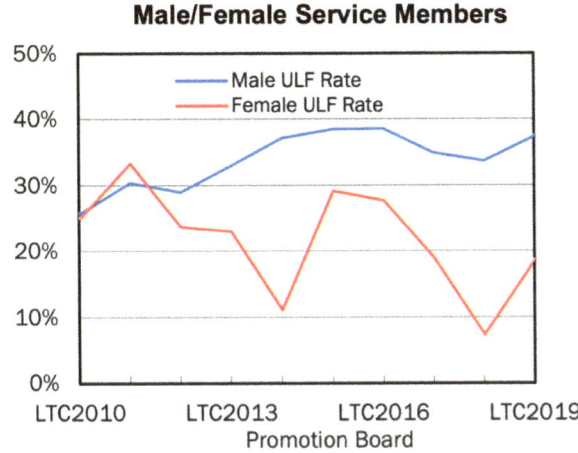

Male/Female Service Members

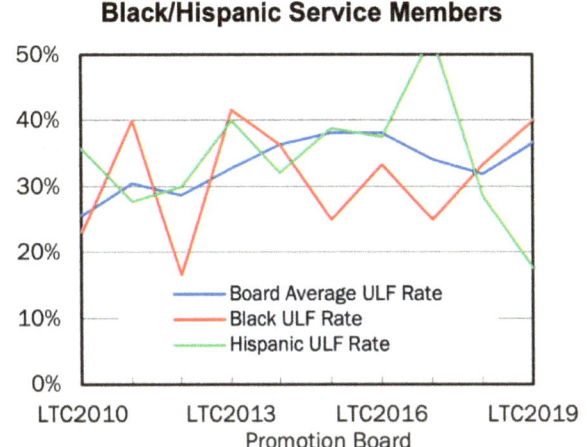

Black/Hispanic Service Members

Figure 3.6. Pilots IPZ to O-6 by Gender and Minority Group

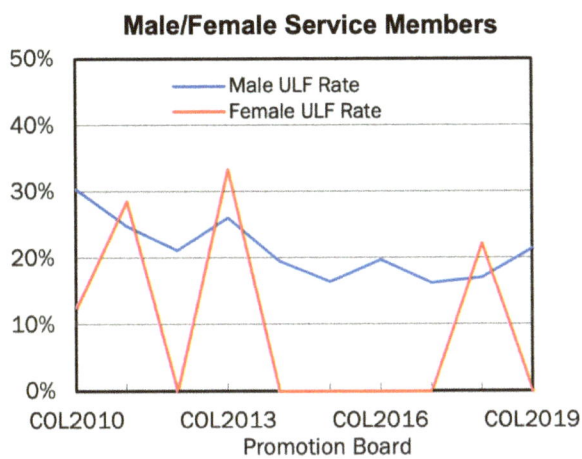

Male/Female Service Members

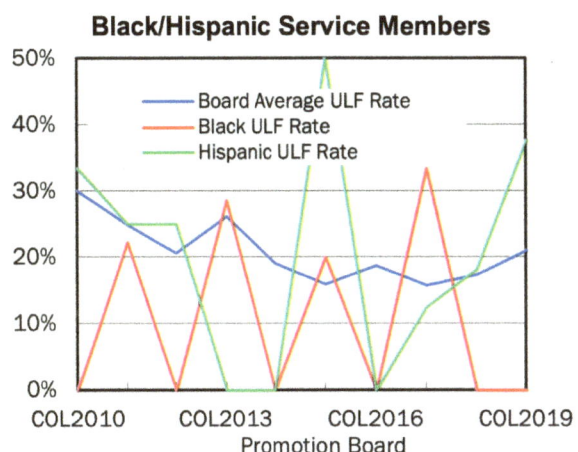

Black/Hispanic Service Members

Ramifications of Redistributing IDE and SDE Quotas

In the data in 2021, IDE and SDE quotas were substantially shifted from the CAF, MAF, and Special Operations Forces DTs to nonrated DTs.[24] These redistributions have at least two ramifications. First, more than 100 additional pilots annually will receive a strong message that they are not on track to make O-6. This could influence their retirement timing plans and levels of effort. Second, these redistributions will yield more nonrated generals and/or lead to reduced selectivity for key rated general officer requirements.

---

[24] The DAF realigned in-residence IDE and SDE school slots according to a review of the requirements by development category.

45

Conclusion

The changes that DAF implemented in the 2021 DE selection process, making some pertinent information available to the CPME board members, at least for now have not affected the board ranking. For IDE, the 2020 trends predicted that, in 2021 women would have better OOM compared to men, and that trend was like the actual pattern observed in the 2021 data. Similarly, for minority groups, the trends in 2020 predicted well the observed ranking in 2021, suggesting that the changes have not had the intended effect. For SDE, the same results were observed for 2021, in which the rankings in the different groups were like those predicted by the 2020 trends. These results corroborate the results of the interviews that also found CPME board members usually did not understand how to implement the new changes.

Chapter 4. Equivalent Group (Look-Alike) Analysis

In the previous chapter, we compared the outcomes of the 2021 and 2020 CPME boards to explore whether the DAF's changes improved the diversity mix of officers for in-residence DE and what factors seemed important to board members as they arrayed nominees from the top to the bottom percentiles. In this chapter, we compare men and women as well as different racial and ethnicity groups to explore whether the changes for the 2021 boards resulted in different outcomes than the 2020 boards. More specifically, this equivalent group analysis—also known as *look-alike* analysis—examines whether observed differences are explained by nonequivalence or by differences that already exist in the groups being compared.

Purpose of Look-Alike Analyses: Exploring Cause and Effect

The evaluation of the impact of the rule changes in the CPME board process is designed to assess cause and effect: whether the new rules really lead to changes in board ranking and that the changes are not explained by the characteristics of the different groups being compared. In this analysis, we explore the causal effect on CPME board rankings—that is, what the CPME board ranking of Black service members would have been if they had been White and what the board ranking would have been for those service members in 2021 had the changes in the CPME board process not been implemented (i.e., the same process as in 2020). The methodology used for the analysis is described in detail in Appendix E.

Two Possible Causes of Observed Disparities: True Disparity (Indicating Potential Bias) or Imbalance Between Group Characteristics

Directly observed differences between, for example, Black and White groups may not necessarily reveal cause and effect, especially if the differences can be explained by differences in qualifications between Black and White members. If the qualifications do not explain the differences, this situation suggests that a *true disparity* may exist. As a definition, a *true disparity* is what cannot be explained by differences in characteristics or qualifications that influence the outcome. Nevertheless, one needs to recognize that, in practice, analysts are subject to data limitations in which essential characteristics might be unmeasured.

There are two main potential sources of observed differences between groups: (1) the true disparity and (2) the imbalance between groups. The *imbalance between groups* refers to any difference (observed or unobserved) between the characteristics of the groups, except race, that affects the CPME board ranking. For example, if White members are more likely to have a greater number of MSMs, a characteristic that is visible to the CPME board, and the board members consider the number of MSMs as a tiebreaker in their rankings, then an observed difference between White and Black groups can be explained by the imbalance in MSMs. Thus, when comparing only White and Black members with exactly the same number of MSMs, no difference in ranking would be expected. This is the basis for the notion of equivalent or look-alike groups; if there is a way to make White and Black service members look alike on all characteristics (e.g., MSMs) that differ between the two race groups and that influence the ranking outcome, then we would expect no meaningful difference between the look-alike White and Black rankings. Although traditional linear or logistic regression will take correlated predictors into account, if the propensity of Black and White populations to have those predictors is not equal, then the larger group's propensity or distribution into those predictors drives the calculation of coefficients. The process of propensity balancing actually reshapes the majority group to resemble the minority group's distribution, and then reduces the total weighted frequency of the larger group to match the smaller group. This allows the coefficients to be driven equally by both groups when evaluating the predictive value of the independent variables.

If a difference still exists in the ranking between White and Black members after making the groups equivalent, the difference is attributed to true disparity, since the group differences cannot be explained by imbalances in observed characteristics or qualifications that affect the outcome. *True disparity* can be thought of as the variability (i.e., heterogeneity) of the outcome relative to the different group characteristics. Decomposing observed differences into these components— *true disparity* (unexplained differences) versus an *imbalance of characteristics* (explained differences)—can be useful for decisionmaking, as we explain below. (See Appendix E for more details on the methodology.)

Policies Can More Easily Mitigate Explained Differences Than Unexplained Disparities

The look-alike analysis and the potential decomposition of the observed difference into an *explained portion* (that is, the part that is due to the imbalance between the groups) and an *unexplained portion* (that is, the true disparity) are well suited to inform decisionmaking intended to improve equity and inclusion in the DAF.

The explained difference can always be remediated by decisions to train, incentivize, or push service members of the different groups to have enough of the characteristics that lead to a better board ranking (e.g., MSMs). Note that this assumes that all qualifications and characteristics that go into the CPME board ranking are well-known and well-studied for their impact on the CPME board decisions and that they are not mediated by a true disparity in and of themselves (for example, where the MSM itself is more difficult for women or persons of color to achieve because of true disparity).

On the other hand, mitigating *true disparity*—the unexplained causal impact of race or gender on the board ranking—requires deeper policy decisions, because there might be conscious or unconscious bias on the part of the CPME board. For example, providing clear rules and guidance on how a board member is supposed to rank a candidate and having them follow such rules to the letter might be a solution. Nevertheless, one will recognize that no matter the rules and guidance, human predispositions will still influence decisionmaking—but minimizing personal feelings can be effective. Studies have reported that more elaborate training methods and tools that intensively educate and train people on how to mitigate personal biases can eliminate such predispositions.[25]

Evaluation of IDE Board Outcomes

This equivalence group analysis will address two research questions for the IDE evaluation:

- Which characteristics differ along REG lines and are also important for CPME board ranking?
- Is an officer who is a member of a racial or ethnic minority or a woman any less or more likely to be ranked high than an equally situated officer who is White or male?

We consider two different outcomes in these analyses. The first is the ranking that the IDE board settled on, which will allow us to assess *whether the ranking of one group is, in general, higher* than those of the other groups. Like the definition in Chapter 3, the board ranking was operationalized into percentiles, with the best-ranked officer at the 100th percentile and the lowest-ranked officer at 0. The second outcome that we considered is the *likelihood of a woman or minority being in the top 25th percentile* of the ranking, or the top-ranked group.

We answered the first question by examining which characteristics present significant differences between the groups being compared. To assess the effectiveness of the propensity score method being used to estimate the true disparity, if there is any, we also reported whether such differences in characteristics were eliminated after the propensity score weighting to produce groups that look alike for comparison (full results reported in Appendix E). We then examined the second question by statistically adjusting the characteristics of Whites and men so that they are comparable to minorities and women (as described in the methodology section), and then comparing their ranking and likelihood of being ranked in the top tier. If large, statistically significant REG gaps exist in the board ranking after this rigorous controlling for relevant differences in observable characteristics and experiences, then it would appear that something unobserved about the system (presumably relating to race or gender) presents a true disparity and, thus, a barrier to equal opportunity. Finally, we compared the 2020 estimates with the 2021 estimates to assess the impact of the rule changes that occurred in 2021.

IDE Board Rankings: Significant Differences Between Races but Not Genders

To examine whether large gaps exist in IDE outcomes, we looked at the percentile rankings and examined where the demographics group fell within them after controlling for relevant differences. Given that the CPME board gives the best ranking to the top qualified candidates and the lowest ranking to the candidate ranked last, the higher the ranking, the better—and,

---

[25] Poos, van den Bosch, and Janssen, 2017.

consequently, the higher the percentile, the better. With the percentile ranking used as the main outcome, the average across the population ranked will be at the 50th percentile, since the top candidate will be at the 100th percentile, and the bottom candidate will be at 0. Consequently, in an equity and inclusion setting, the average ranking for men or for women is also expected to be at the 50th percentile. For the top-tier outcome, members ranked in the top 25th percentile will be assumed to be in the top-tier group. In that setting, across the population, the average likelihood of being in the top tier will be at 25 percent, and, if everything is equal, the average in groups to be compared will also be 25 percent. Note that, as in the case of the ranking percentile, for the top-tier outcome, the higher the proportion, the better, because it will indicate that individuals in that group have a higher likelihood of being in the top tier.

Figure 4.1 provides the distribution of the IDE board ranking between men and women from 2020 to 2021. For the average ranking, women were more likely to be ranked higher in 2020, with an average ranking at the 57th percentile compared with the 49th percentile for men. Similarly, in 2021, the average ranking for women was at the 55th percentile compared with the 49th percentile for men. These represent 8– and 6–percentage point differences, which are both statistically significant. The spread is also similar among the top ranked groups. In 2020, women had a 32-percent chance of being in the top group of the ranking compared with a 24-percent chance among men, which is an 8–percentage point difference. In 2021, the difference was 10 points, where women had a 33-percent chance of being in the top group compared with a 23-percent chance for the men. All these differences are also statistically significant.

Figure 4.1. Observed IDE Board Ranking for Men and Women

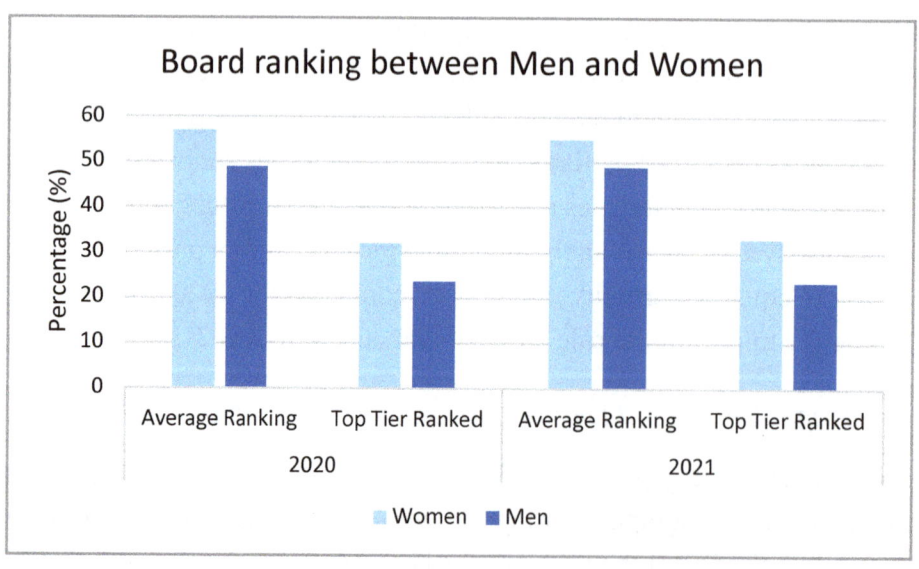

For the race comparisons (shown in Figure 4.2), White officers tended to be ranked higher than their minority peers. For 2020, the average ranking among White members was at the 51st percentile compared with the 49th percentile for Black, 45th for Asian, and 41st for Hispanic members. These differences are statistically significant. For the top tier, White members had a 26.5-percent chance of being in the top tier compared with 22.9 percent for Black, 24 percent for Asian, and 10 percent for Hispanic members. These differences are marginally significant. Here, it is necessary to note that the minority group is small: The 10 percent among Hispanic members is just five out of 50 officers. The 2021 results are similar but nonsignificant. The average ranking for White members was, again, at the 51st percentile compared with the 47th percentile for Black, 42nd for Asian, and 54th for Hispanic members (again, the sample is small, with just 42 Hispanic members in 2021). For the top tier, White members have a 25.7-percent chance of being in the top group compared with 21.1 percent for Black, 16.7 percent for Asian, and 31 percent for Hispanic members, all of which differences are nonsignificant.

Figure 4.2. Observed IDE Board Ranking Between Race Groups

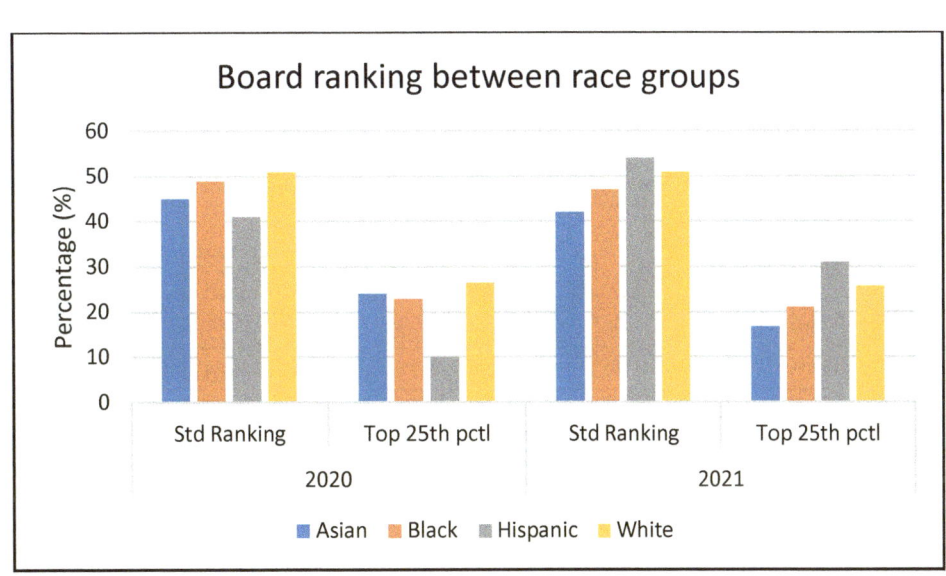

Overall, there were significant differences between men and women, and women were more likely to have a better IDE board ranking. However, mostly nonsignificant differences are observed between the minority and White groups. All the observed differences seemed to remain the same from 2020 to 2021 before any proper selection bias adjustment.

Rankings by Gender: Unchanged Before and After New Rules

We considered factors that potentially influenced the IDE board ranking (listed in Appendix E) to explain the observed differences between men and women. First, we assessed the observed differences between men and women and then conducted a comparison to assure that, after propensity score adjustment, such differences disappeared on the look-alike samples. The differences in characteristics between men and women are reported in Appendix E (Table E.1a and Table E.1b), which also provides estimates of how the propensity score adjustment of those characteristics was balanced. In general, in terms of the baseline attributes, women were more

51

likely (23.7 percent) than men (14.6 percent) in 2020 to receive a DA. After making the men look like the women using the propensity score weight, the equivalent group of men had a 23.1-percent chance of receiving DA—similar to a 23.7-percent chance for women. A similar pattern between men and women is observed in 2021, when a marginal difference in DA existed between women (20.9 percent) and men (16.2 percent), but after propensity score weighting, the probability of DA in the equivalent group of men increased to 21.0 percent. Propensity score weighting also erased differences between men and women for other characteristics, such as being a DG from squadron school, being a weapon school graduate, the number of MSM received, the SR's rank, and being aide-de-camp or executive assistant for a high-ranking officer.

With all these characteristics balanced between men and women, we incorporated the balancing method with a modeling tool to assess the covariate and propensity score–adjusted estimates of the difference between men and women on the board ranking. Table 4.1 reports the results of the estimation from the look-alike sample of men and women.

Table 4.1. Propensity Score–Adjusted Estimates of IDE Board Ranking in 2020 and 2021

	2020 Board ranking estimates				2021 Board ranking estimates				2020 to 2021 changes	
	Women	Adjusted estimate		p-value	Women	Adjusted estimate		p-value	Estimate	p-value
		Men	Diff			Men	Diff			
Ranking average percentile	56.6%	49.5%	7.1%	0.000	55.5%	49.7%	5.8%	0.001	–1.3%	0.308
Top tier proportion	32.1%	24.0%	8.1%	0.003	33.1%	24.5%	8.6%	0.001	0.5%	0.808

NOTE: The percentile ranking is discussed with the term percentage of OOM above the specific ranking of the last officer ranked in the OOM for simplicity.

After controlling for the different characteristics—making the men equivalent to the women—in 2020, the women still had an average ranking that was 7.1 percentage points higher than the men. For the likelihood of being in the top tier, the chance for women was 8.1 percentage points higher than for men in that year. A similar result is observed in 2021: Women had a better average ranking (5.8 points more than men) and more likelihood of being in the top tier (8.6 points more than men). Put together, the ranking did not change much between 2020, when the old rules were in effect for the IDE board, and 2021, when the new rules began. The overall ranking changed by only 1.3 points, and the top-tier ranking changed by only 0.5 points after the rule changes—and both are nonsignificant (as seen by the p-values in the rightmost column of Table 4.1). Consequently, the rule changes do not appear to have closed the existing gap between men and women on the IDE board ranking.

Rankings by Racial and Ethnic Groups: Rule Changes Had Little Effect

For the racial and ethnic group comparisons, we compared White members to Black, Asian, and Hispanic members separately. The same characteristics used in the gender comparisons are also used for assessing equivalence of the different race groups. The equivalence tables for racial and ethnic group comparisons are reported in Appendix E (Tables E.2a to E.2d). In general, in 2020, White members were less likely to be female and less likely to have SRs who were not allowed to award DAs. On the other hand, White members were more likely to be DGs from squadron officer school and to have colonels as SRs. For the other characteristics, White members seem to have had a higher distribution compared with some minority groups and a lower distribution compared with others. After the propensity score weighting made the groups look alike, the distributions for all these observed differences between the racial/ethnic groups were balanced in comparison with the White group.

After balancing all these characteristics between the White group and each of the minority groups, we calculated the covariate-adjusted estimates of the difference between the White and minority groups on the board ranking. (See Appendix D for more details on the estimation method.) Table 4.2 reports the results of the equivalence group estimation. After we controlled for the different characteristics, in 2020, only small, statistically nonsignificant differences are observed between the White and minority groups. For the average ranking, the White group had a ranking 5 points better than the Asian group and 4.5 points better than the Hispanic group, while the Black group had a ranking that is 0.5 points better than the White group. None of these differences are significant. Similarly, the White group was slightly more likely to be in the top tier than the Asian group (1.28 points), considerably more likely than the Hispanic group (7.4 points), and slightly less likely than the Black group (0.2 points). The nonsignificant difference in the White-Hispanic comparison is most likely caused by the very small sample size in Hispanics, making the estimates between White and Hispanic groups more unstable. Similar nonsignificant results were observed in 2021, except for the small group of Hispanics. It is worth pointing out that the other minority groups also had very small sample sizes in 2021.

Taken together, no significant difference was observed in 2020 between the White and minority groups (Asian, Black, and Hispanic), and the same nonmeaningful differences were observed in 2021. There were not much ranking differences by race groups before the rule changes, and the status quo was maintained after the rule changes.

IDE Board Summary

In summary, there were some characteristics, experiences, and qualification gaps between gender groups and between racial and ethnic groups that were observed, and the propensity score method was able to make the groups look alike. In addition, whether it was gender or race or ethnicity, the IDE board ranking rule changes did not seem to affect the way that the board members ranked the officers. In the case of gender, some notable differences before the rule changes persisted in 2021 after the changes. In the minority group comparisons, no meaningful difference was observed in 2020, and those minor differences were similar in 2021, after the rule changes.

Table 4.2. Propensity Score Adjusted Estimates of IDE Board Ranking in 2020 and 2021

Outcome	Target group Being Compared	2020 Board Ranking Estimates					2021 Board Ranking Estimates					2020 to 2021 Changes	
		Sample Size	Target Estimate	Adjusted Estimate		p-value	Sample Size	Target Estimate	Adjusted Estimate		p-value	Estimate	p-value
				White	Difference				White	Difference			
Ranking average percentile	Asian	75	44.7%	49.7%	−5.0%	0.107	66	41.7%	45.5%	−3.8%	0.201	1.2%	0.462
Top tier proportion			24.00%	25.28%	−1.28%	0.765		16.67%	18.03%	−1.36%	0.716	−0.09%	0.975
Ranking average percentile	Black	83	49.4%	48.9%	0.5%	0.868	95	46.6%	49.0%	−2.3%	0.323	−2.8%	0.087
Top tier proportion			22.89%	22.69%	0.2%	0.965		21.05%	21.79%	−0.74%	0.822	−0.94%	0.725
Ranking average percentile	Hispanic	50	41.2%	45.7%	−4.5%	0.136	42	53.6%	44.9%	8.7%	0.004	13.3%	0.000
Top tier proportion			10.00%	17.37%	−7.37%	0.118		30.95%	23.20%	7.75%	0.138	15.12%	0.000

NOTE: The percentile ranking is discussed with the term percentage of OOM above the specific ranking of the last officer ranked in the OOM for simplicity.

Evaluation of SDE Board Outcomes

For the SDE evaluation, the research questions were like those for the IDE evaluation:

- Which characteristics differ along racial and ethnic or gender lines and are also important for SDE board ranking?
- Is an officer who is a member of a racial or ethnic minority or a woman any less or more likely to receive a high ranking than an equally situated officer who is White or male?

For this part of the evaluation, we again looked at two outcomes, the board ranking and the likelihood of being in the top tier. If large, statistically significant REG gaps exist in the rankings after rigorous controls for relevant differences in observable characteristics and experiences, then it would appear that something unobserved (presumably relating to REG) led to a true disparity. We again compared the 2020 estimates to the 2021 estimates to assess the impact of the rule changes that occurred in 2021.

SDE Board Rankings: Men and Women Are Similar, and Significant Differences Between Minority Groups in 2020 Disappear After the 2021 Rule Changes

Figure 4.3 provides the distribution of the SDE board ranking for men and women from 2020 to 2021. The average rankings for both years were similar, and none was statistically significant. In 2020, the average woman was ranked around the 49th percentile, while the average man was at the 50th percentile. In 2021, the average woman was ranked at the 52nd percentile, while the average man was again at the 50th percentile. The pattern was the same for the top-tier ranking. In 2020, the likelihood of a woman being top ranked was 23.5 percent compared with 25.2 percent for men. In 2021, women had a 28.3-percent chance of being in that group compared with 24.6 percent for men.

Figure 4.3. Observed SDE Board Ranking for Men and Women

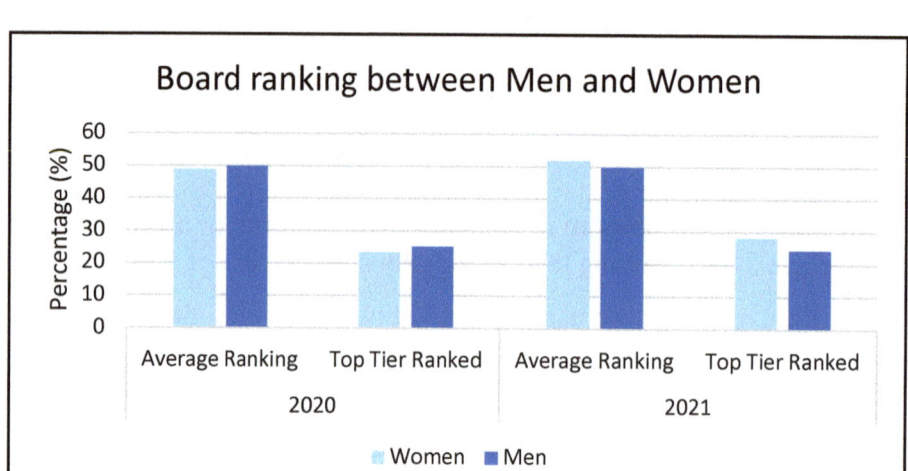

In the racial and ethnic comparisons, some differences observed in 2020 tend to disappear in 2021 (see Figure 4.4). Before the rule changes, the average White candidate was at the 51st percentile versus 57th for Asian, 43rd for Black, and 45th for Hispanic candidates. These differences were statistically significant. For the likelihood of being in the top tier, the White group has a 26.1-percent chance compared with 29.4 percent for Asian, 14.3 percent for Black, and 15.7 percent for Hispanic groups, and these differences were marginally significant. However, after the implementation of the rule changes in 2021, the averages for the groups— White (51 percent), Asian (54 percent), Black (47 percent), and Hispanic (43 percent)—were not statistically different. Similarly, the likelihood of being in the top tier in 2021 for the White (26.2 percent), Asian (25 percent), Black (18.5 percent) and Hispanic (23.1 percent) groups were not statistically different.

Figure 4.4. Observed SDE Board Ranking Between Racial and Ethnic Groups

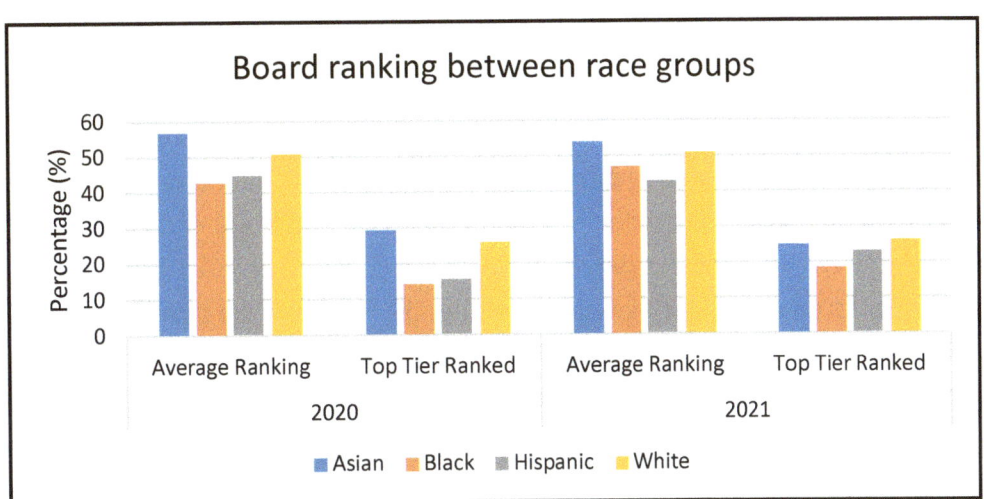

Overall, there were some significant observed differences between the minority groups in 2020, but none remained significant after the rule changes were implemented. Like the observation in the IDE evaluation, the sample sizes were very small for Hispanic (fewer than 36) and Asian (fewer than 52) groups, which could make the observed differences with the White group unstable.

Rankings by Minority Groups: Look-Alike Comparisons Are Similar for 2020 and 2021, with Mixed Results on Confounding Factors

The equivalence tables for race and ethnicity comparisons for SDE are reported in Appendix E (Tables E.4a to E.4d). After balancing and adjusting for propensity score, the results in 2021 are similar among the groups. In general, White members (14.5 percent) were more likely than Black (2.6 percent) and Hispanic (9.8 percent) members to be selected for SDE by the CPME board. They were also more likely to be weapon school graduates and to be married. For many of the confounders, the relationships are mixed, with the White group having more favorable qualifications than some minority groups but not others. For example, the White group (26.7 percent) was more likely than the Hispanic group (15.7 percent) to be assigned to Headquarters Air Force and less likely than Asian (32.4 percent) and Black (41.6 percent) groups. As in all our analyses, the propensity score adjustment did make the different groups look alike on all characteristics where differences were found before. The comparison results and look-alike adjustment were similar in 2021 as well.

Table 4.3 reports the results of the look-alike analysis. In 2020, the Asian group had a ranking 4.5 percentage points better than the White group in 2020, and a 5.3-point advantage in 2021.

For the likelihood of being in the top tier, no difference was observed between the White and Asian groups in 2020 or 2021. Accordingly, from 2020 to the rule changes in 2021, only a very small difference was seen in the advantage that the Asian group had in the average ranking. We note that the Asian group had a very small sample size (34 in 2020 and 36 in 2021), so these changes can be volatile. For the comparison of Black and Hispanic to White groups, no significant difference was observed in either outcome in 2020 or 2021. It is worth noting that significant *changes* were observed in the top-tier comparisons of Black and Hispanic to White groups, even though no significant *difference* was observed in either year. This is due to a reverse of nonsignificant effect; for example, in 2020, the White group was more likely to be in the top tier by 3 percent (too small to be significant), but then in 2021, the Black group was slightly more likely to be in the top tier by 3.51 percent (again too small to be significant). The difference between them was 6.5 percent and significant. While this can be a true difference, it can also be an artifact of randomness.

Taken together, no meaningful difference was observed in 2020 between the White and the minority groups except for the Asian group, and the same nonmeaningful difference was observed in 2021. There was not much change in the SDE board rankings from 2020 to 2021 between the different minority groups and the White group. The rule changes do not appear to have had an effect on closing the existing gap between rankings.

Rankings by Gender: Experiences Make a Difference

Many experience and background characteristics that can potentially affect the SDE board ranking showed differences between men and women. The equivalence tables for gender comparisons are reported in Appendix E (Tables E.3a and E.3b). In general, women were less likely to be DGs of SOS, to be weapon school graduates, to be in major command headquarters, or to be married. At the same time, women were more likely to be assigned to Air Force headquarters, to be aide-de-camp to a high-ranking officer, or to have graduated from historically black colleges or Hispanic-serving institutions. The sample in 2021 had very similar distributions and differences (between men and women). After propensity score adjustment, the sample of men was made like the women on all these characteristics, providing equivalent groups of men and women to be compared.

Table 4.3. Propensity Score-Adjusted Estimates of SDE Board Ranking in 2020 and 2021

Outcome	Target Group Being Compared	2020 Board Ranking Estimates					2021 Board Ranking Estimates					2020 to 2021 Changes	
		Sample Size	Target Estimate	Adjusted Estimate White	Adjusted Estimate Difference	p-value	Sample Size	Target Estimate	Adjusted Estimate White	Adjusted Estimate Difference	p-value	Estimate	p-value
Ranking average percentile	Asian	75	56.6%	52.1%	4.5%	0.018	66	53.9%	48.6%	5.3%	0.026	0.8%	0.656
Top tier proportion			29.41%	27.91%	1.5%	0.530		25.00%	25.01%	−0.01%	0.998	−1.51%	0.599
Ranking average percentile	Black	83	42.9%	42.8%	0.1%	0.936	95	46.8%	44.6%	2.2%	0.404	2.0%	0.363
Top tier proportion			14.29%	17.29%	−3.01%	0.258		18.52%	15.01%	3.51%	0.217	6.51%	0.004
Ranking average percentile	Hispanic	50	45.2%	43.8%	1.4%	0.500	42	42.6%	42.5%	0.1%	0.956	−1.2%	0.566
Top tier proportion			15.69%	20.15%	−4.46%	0.182		23.08%	18.83%	4.25%	0.170	8.71%	0.002

NOTE: The percentile ranking is discussed with the term percentage of OOM above the specific ranking of the last officer ranked in the OOM for simplicity.

For the men and women look-alike sample, we used the doubly robust method to evaluate the covariate-adjusted estimates of the difference between men and women on the SDE board ranking. Table 4.4 shows the results of the double robust estimation.

Table 4.4. Propensity Score Adjusted Estimates of SDE Board Ranking in 2020 and 2021

| | 2020 Board Ranking Estimates | | | | 2021 Board Ranking Estimates | | | | 2020 to 2021 Changes | |
| | Women | Adjusted Estimate | | p-value | Women | Adjusted Estimate | | p-value | | |
		Men	Difference			Men	Difference		Estimate	p-value
Ranking average percentile	48.7%	47.4%	1.3%	0.424	51.6%	52.2%	−0.6%	0.727	−1.9%	0.138
Top tier proportion	23.5%	23.0%	0.5%	0.852	28.3%	27.3%	1.0%	0.719	0.5%	0.813

NOTE: The percentile ranking is discussed with the term percentage of OOM above the specific ranking of the last officer ranked in the OOM for simplicity.

After we controlled for the different officer attributes, making the men equivalent to the women on those characteristics, in both 2020 and 2021, there was no meaningful difference in the men and women rankings. In 2020, women had a 1.3-percent higher ranking, and in 2021, men had a 0.6-percent higher ranking. As for being in the top tier, in 2020, women had a 0.5-percent higher likelihood compared with men, and in 2021, women were 1.0-percent more likely to be in the top tier. Overall, there seemed to be no meaningful difference in the ranking of men and women in 2020 or 2021, when the rule changes in the SDE board ranking process took effect.

SDE Board Summary

In summary, whether it was gender or race or ethnicity, the SDE board ranking rule changes did not seem to influence the way that the board members ranked the officers. In the case of gender, there were no meaningful differences before the rule changes, and the status quo continued in 2021 after the changes. For racial and ethnic groups, the results in 2021 were very similar to the results before the rule changes in 2020. These results are like the IDE board ranking evaluation.

Conclusion

The goal of the process changes for CPME boards was to provide more information and instructions on what to consider and what not to consider when evaluating service members in the hope that such changes would close any existing gaps in how officers are ranked by the SDE and the IDE boards. First, most differences in board ranking were explained by differences in the characteristics and the experiences of the officers in the different groups being compared. Even in the few cases where unexplained disparities were observed in 2020, most differences remained after the rule changes in 2021, suggesting that the implemented changes were not effective.

The finding that the rule changes were not effective is not surprising in light of the qualitative results from this study, in which many board members reported not being able to effectively adopt the changes because they had no clear guidance on exactly how to implement them. For these changes to be effective, the DAF will have to assess this need, since so few true disparities exist, and to assess in cases where disparities do exist whether to provide further guidance to the board members for implementation. For the explained differences between groups, long-term changes will be required to instill the experience and qualifications that the minority groups need to prevent disparities in promotion outcomes. As is often the case, systemic inequality is so embedded within the overall structures and systems of our society that it can produce subtle (sometimes even imperceptible) nudges that are mutually reinforced to produce an overall opportunity and outcomes gap.

Chapter 5. Summary of Issues and Potential Actions to Address

Our quantitative and qualitative analyses reveal that the multiple changes that the DAF made for the 2021 CPME board processes did not have their intended effect: Despite updated DEI guidance to the board and unmasking REG data, there were no significant changes to in-residence DE selection outcomes for REG officer diversity groups when comparing 2021 results to those of previous boards. In addition, the team found no evidence of unfair or nonobjective consideration for or against minority and female officers in the DE selection process.

Given the 2021 CPME board results, the team concludes that passive measures, such as emphasizing the importance of DEI or showing unconscious bias videos, will not significantly alter outcomes.[26] Changing the quantity or ratio of REG officers selected for DE will require the DAF to increase representation in the candidate pool—a long-term solution—while taking deliberate, active measures to improve opportunities for REG officer candidates in the short term.

Drawing on the combined insights from qualitative and quantitative data, we will explore in this chapter adjustments for future CPME boards and propose "left of board" actions[27] that the DAF should consider to achieve greater minority and female officer representation at in-residence DE and senior ranks. The team will also offer observations about the benefits of more comprehensive, regular, and transparent communication to the officer corps to dispel uncertainty, confusion, and myths related to the DAF's desire to field a more representative senior officer population. Finally, we will discuss the project team's conclusion that a deliberate, DAF-wide change management approach is needed to modify DAF cultural norms concerning "blind" development, performance evaluation, and promotion selection; to synchronize actions to reduce real and perceived disparities across the force; and to accelerate changes designed to account for equity considerations in the selection process.

Adjustments for Future Developmental Education Boards

CPME board member feedback and the project team's statistical data analyses suggest that further changes to future CPME board information and instructions are needed if the DAF wants to significantly improve racial and ethnic minority officer selection outcomes.

---

[26] The authors acknowledge that the 2021 board results are a single data point, and project team conclusions must be validated by data from future boards.

[27] *Left of board* refers to personnel management actions and initiatives that affect the opportunities and strength of an officer's record that happen well before (i.e., *left of*) their eligibility for the CPME board.

Communicate DEI Goals, Guidance, and Intent to CPME Board Members and Senior Raters

Multiple CPME board members said that the DEI guidance in the 2021 board MOI was ambiguous and confusing. Others stated that it was difficult to determine how or whether to use the unmasked REG data in their evaluation of nominated officers' potential, and most did not use these data at all. Many board members requested more clarity. Both CPME and CSB board members also expressed desire for additional DEI context—the "why" behind diversity efforts— prior to scoring records, such as current officer diversity demographics and trends, relevant population benchmarks, and diversity demographics by officer career fields.

In light of this feedback, the project team believes that the DAF should provide clearer guidance and intent for future CPME boards. This should start with logical stretch goals for REG officer representation at in-residence DE, using an approach like the USAFA applicant pool recruiting goals established in 2014 to reflect America's eligible population.[28] Setting stretch goals[29] offers multiple benefits. Published goals communicate the DAF's commitment to inclusion, opportunity, and institutional growth. DAF-wide goals also provide the impetus for data collection, focus the efforts of a wide array of responsible stakeholders toward a common purpose, and enable periodic executive leader reviews. Goal data collected can be further used to inform barrier analyses and derive potential left-of-board actions that the DAF could implement to make desired CPME board outcomes[30]—progress toward the goal—more likely. Potential DE stretch goals that the DAF should consider include the following:

- rate of CPME board designation/selection of eligible REG officers (by category) equals the DAF-wide average rate of eligible officer CPME board designation/selection.
- percentage of REG officers (by category) designated or selected for in-residence DE equals the percentage of eligible REG officers (by category) meeting the CPME board.

In addition to published REG goal(s), the project team recommends that the DAF enhance DEI guidance in the CPME board MOI to eliminate board member confusion and enable the guidance to be more consistently applied to meet the DAF's intent. According to CPME board member feedback, recommended questions to answer in the MOI are the following:

---

[28] See Nelson Lim, Louis T. Mariano, Amy G. Cox, David Schulker, Lawrence M. Hanser, "Improving Demographic Diversity in the U.S. Air Force Officer Corps," Santa Monica, Calif.: RAND Corporation, RR-495-AF, 2014, Chapter 2.

[29] Stretch goals, as recommended in this report, are not quotas. *Stretch goals* are defined by the authors as desired outcomes that are published to align and drive coherent policies and actions across a large, dispersed group of institutional stakeholders and to enable the organization to measure progress over time. In comparison, *quotas* compel selection decisions to meet mandated targets. This report does not advocate quotas.

[30] Quotas are strictly forbidden. Affirmative action regulations permit goals that serve as "targets reasonably attainable by means of applying every good faith effort to make all aspects of the entire affirmative action program work" and that the goals "may not be rigid and inflexible quotas, which must be met." See Department of Labor, "Affirmative Action Frequently Asked Question," fact sheet, Washington, D.C., January 7, 2021, for more discussion.

- How does the DAF recommend board members incorporate unmasked REG data in their evaluation of officers' record of performance and future potential?
- Should board members use REG data as a tiebreaker between those with otherwise equivalent job and leadership performance when scoring a record?
- Does current equal opportunity law permit the use of REG data in evaluating personnel and/or making selection decisions?[31]
- What known, data-supported REG disparities could have negatively impacted eligible officers' opportunities and records of performance?
- What is the purpose of the unconscious bias training video, and how does it relate to unmasking REG?

Additionally, we recommend that enhanced board guidance include legal precedent related to equal opportunity law and the consideration of demographics to address concerns raised by some board members. Enhanced board guidance should link consideration of REG data to DAF DEI goals within the context of current legal interpretation of equal opportunity law. Revised and enhanced guidance language should undergo rigorous legal review to ensure that it is not in conflict with existing equal opportunity law and legal precedent of its interpretation. The team also recommends that the CPME board president lead a discussion with board members on the DAF's DEI goals and MOI DEI guidance prior to live record scoring.

Finally, the project team believes that the DAF should include its published REG stretch goal(s) and DEI guidance matching the CPME board MOI in its annual IDE/SDE Designation Board Personnel Services Delivery Memorandum (PSDM) that provides procedural guidance used by DAF SRs nominating officers to the CPME board. Though SR nomination of eligible officers is the first step in the annual DE selection process, the PSDM currently contains *no* language or guidance to SRs on DEI considerations or data on DAF-documented REG disparities. The project team believes that this inconsistency is a gap that should be closed if the DAF is to increase minority officer representation at in-residence DE.

Review the IDE Definitely Attend Process

Important secondary findings of the project team's qualitative and quantitative analyses of the 2021 CPME board involve the dynamics surrounding the DA process for IDE.[32]

Except for Asian officers, racial and ethnic minority officers saw a slight increase in IDE designation under the DA program. Female officers experienced a significant increase—nearly 10 percent—in IDE designation under the DA program. The data results detailed in Chapter 3

---

[31] See U.S. Equal Employment Opportunity Commission, "CM-604—Theories of Discrimination," guidance document, August 1, 1988, for discussion of legal theories of employment discrimination and adverse impact. Also see Appendix B in this report for historical and current use and interpretation of equal opportunity law and race-conscious policies in section processes.

[32] On January 5, 2022—as this report was in RAND review for publication—the DAF announced an in-residence IDE nomination process change, effective for the 2022 annual developmental education designation cycle, which discontinued the DA program for IDE ("Air Force Announces IDE in-Residence Nomination Process Change," 2022).

also reveal the unintended consequence of a nearly 40-percent increase in the number of DAs allocated to SRs to award since the process was introduced in 2019. Finally, the data show that 22 percent of 2021 IDE eligible officers were aligned to a SR who lacked a DA recommendation to allocate and that IDE-eligible REG officers appear to be overrepresented in that 22 percent.

DE board members gave mixed reviews on the utility of unmasking DA recommendations to make them visible to the board during record scoring. However, there was broad consensus that SRs used the DA inconsistently, and many board members raised concerns about SRs "gaming the system." In 2021, fully 54 percent of the IDE designation quota went to officers with a DA recommendation, significantly reducing the influence and independence of the IDE board. For some career-field DTs, the IDE board had little or no input on which officers were selected for IDE. For example, 100 percent of the 2021 MAF rated officer IDE quota was filled by officers designated as DA. As noted in Chapter 3, this resulted in a notable reduction in designated officer quality for several of the rated officer DTs: Officers with significantly higher OOM board scores were displaced by officers with lower board scores who received SR DA recommendations. Looking across all career-field DTs, 17 percent of officers with DA recommendations ranked in the bottom half of the board's OOM.

The DAF should assess how to balance the benefits of the DA process for future IDE boards while mitigating the second-order effects of the large number of DAs on IDE designee quality, reduced REG officer DA opportunities, and potential negative downstream impacts for officers with stronger records *not* selected to attend in-residence DE. The project team recommends several changes to minimize these effects:

1. significantly reduce the total number of DAs awarded to rebalance influence toward the CPME board
2. employ a Management Level Review (MLR)–like process to aggregate awarding of DAs (similar to officer promotion MLRs for Definitely Promote (DP) recommendations) to ensure that every IDE-eligible officer has an opportunity to compete for a DA
3. narrow guidance to SRs in the PSDM, clarifying that the DAF's intent for DA recommendations is to ensure consistency of purpose and opportunity for all IDE-eligible officers meeting the CPME board
4. clarify MOI guidance to the CPME board; is the DA a guaranteed attendance chit for late bloomer and/or REG officers, or is it the strongest in-residence recommendation (but not a guarantee) that an SR can give, similar to a DP recommendation to a promotion board?

Higher-Leverage Approaches to Diverse Officer Development

A key finding of the equivalent group (look-alike) analysis detailed in Chapter 4 is that when identifiable feature differences in officer records of performance are eliminated, majority and REG officer DE selection outcomes are statistically equivalent. Therefore, the team concludes that the DAF must leverage other aspects of human capital development and management—well prior to the selection boards—to increase minority and female officer representation in critical leadership positions and senior leader ranks.

Establish REG Applicant Recruiting Goals for All Four Commissioning Sources

A previous RAND study concluded that increasing diversity in the officer corps starts with recruiting and accessions.[33] DAF officers are commissioned from four sources: Air Force Reserve Officer Training Corps (AFROTC); Officer Training School (OTS); USAFA; and "direct accession" for specialized professions, such as doctors, lawyers, and chaplains. AFROTC produces the largest percentage of officers serving in the DAF at approximately 40 percent, followed by USAFA at 23 percent and OTS at 20 percent. Currently, only USAFA has established REG applicant goals used by recruiters.[34]

As discussed earlier in this chapter, published goals provide multiple benefits. This has been the case with the USAFA applicant pool goals set by the SecAF in 2014. The Academy's percentage of Black applicants for the classes of 2020 to 2024 ranged from 12.9 percent to 15.3 percent, exceeding the DAF goal of 10 percent (see Table 5.1). In fact, the percentage of all minority students entering USAFA closely matches the Academy's applicant pool goals.[35]

The project team believes the DAF should establish REG applicant goals for AFROTC and OTS to match those at USAFA. These goals would serve to standardize data collection, align the efforts of multiple agents in the DAF recruiting enterprise, enable development of tailored REG applicant recruiting strategies, and drive periodic progress reviews. Each of these areas should be regularly coordinated and collectively reviewed by Air Education and Training Command, USAFA, the Headquarters Air Force Deputy Chief of Staff for Manpower, Personnel and Services (HAF/A1), and the Assistant Secretary of the Air Force for Manpower and Reserve Affairs (SAF/MR).

---

[33] Lim et al., 2014.

[34] See IG DAF, *Independent Racial Disparity Review (Report of Inquiry S8918P)*, Arlington, Va., December 2020, pp. 36–38.

[35] See Appendix E for comparative discussion of the U.S. Supreme Court's "strict scrutiny" framework as applied to race conscious admissions policies in colleges and universities.

Table 5.1. USAFA Applicant Pool (Class of 2020–2024)

Race or Ethnicity	USAFA Goal	Applicant Pool Class of:				
		2020	2021	2022	2023	2024
American Indian/Native Alaskan (%)	1	1.30	1.30	1.30	1.20	1.20
Asian American (%)	8	8.50	9.10	9.60	9.80	10.40
Black (%)	10	15.00	15.30	13.50	13.30	12.90
Native Hawaiian/Other Pacific Islander (%)	1	1.80	1.30	1.60	1.80	2.10
Hispanic/Latino (%)	10	12.70	12.90	13.10	13.40	13.90

SOURCE: USAFA; see also IG DAF, 2020, p. 37.
NOTE: Excludes international students.

Establish REG Operational Career-Field Designation Goals at Commissioning

Similarly, the team recommends that the DAF set operational career-field designation stretch goals for REG category officers at commissioning. Data continue to show that minority and female officers are overrepresented in the support career fields and underrepresented in the operations career fields. The operations career fields make up the largest percentage of the DAF officer corps at every rank, including senior leaders and general officers. To increase REG officer presence downstream in the key, visible DAF and Joint leadership positions that officers from the operational specialties fill, it is necessary to increase the flow of REG officers in these career fields into the talent pipeline. Further, career-field designation goals must link to REG recruiting efforts, applicant counseling, academic major selection, AFROTC scholarship awards, etc. As it works to increase the diversity of operational career fields, the DAF should also make coordinated efforts on development and organizational climate to maximize retention of REG officers in its operational career fields.

Update Officer Development/Talent Management Guidance to Squadron Commanders, Senior Raters, and Development Teams

A 2014 RAND study, *Improving Demographic Diversity in the U.S. Air Force Officer Corps*, concluded that "many of the predictors of promotion to the more senior levels actually begin with characteristics that are determined early in an officer's career, including career field. Furthermore, promotion prospects are not reset at each level, but rather these important characteristics accumulate over time."[36] Our data analysis detailed in Chapter 3 validated that this 2014 study conclusion is still true in 2021.[37]

Given this conclusion, the team believes that any DAF strategy to increase REG officer representation at in-residence PME, in key leadership and command positions, and in senior

---

[36] Lim et al., 2014, p. 48.

[37] As the DAF has recently implemented alternative authorities provided in NDAA 2019 and other new talent management policies (see list on p. 71), further analysis is needed to determine if this conclusion remains valid.

leader ranks must include earlier, consistent force development opportunities and experiences for REG officers. Representative examples of these selective opportunities and experiences include the USAF weapons school, wing-level and above executive officer positions, general officer aides-de-camp, and MAJCOM and/or career-field developmental "spotlight" programs. Squadron commanders, SRs, and career-field DTs play critical roles in recommending, stratifying, and selecting officers for these opportunities.

Therefore, the project team recommends that the DAF update development and talent management guidance to commanders, SRs, and DTs to emphasize DEI in both individual approaches and centralized processes to address disparities—real and perceived—in counseling, mentoring, and providing development opportunities for all officers. This guidance should also be promulgated to MAJCOMs and functionals who have developed in-house officer "executive development" programs.

Implement Comprehensive Rater Training

A large body of leadership and management literature documents common human psychological tendencies and the potential negative impacts of performance evaluation bias.[38] Given the critical roles that raters, commanders, and SRs perform in the DAF Officer Evaluation System as discussed above, the team recommends that the DAF develop and implement comprehensive training on various unconscious biases that can affect officer performance evaluation and identification for opportunities. This training would aim to improve the accuracy of performance ratings. The team believes that a new rater training program should include academics and guided discussion on identifying and mitigating racial and cultural bias, halo effects, confirmation bias, and recency bias. Studies have shown that single unconscious bias training sessions do not result in significant behavioral changes, and multiple sessions over time are more likely to result in reduced impact of biases.[39] In its course design, the DAF should heed recent evidence that training raters on "what not to do" is insufficient.[40] Employing a frame of reference approach will balance bias mitigation content with discussion of "what right looks like" to include behavioral anchors, performance dimension definitions, competencies, and levels of performance.[41] Rater training should also include a focus on the potential impact of biases on stratification, as our data analysis reveals that stratification is the most significant predictor of CPME board OOM.

---

[38] For a representative example, see John C. Polanco-Santana, Alessandra Storino, Sidhu P.Gangadharan, and Tara S. Kent, "Ethnic/Racial Bias in Medical School Performance Evaluation of General Surgery Residency Applicants," *Journal of Surgical Education*, Vol. 78, No. 5, September–October 2021.

[39] For a summary of the literature on pitfalls of unconscious and implicit bias training and examples of strategies to ensure that such training effectively reduces unconscious and implicit bias, see Hanover Research, *The Impact of Implicit Bias Training*, Arlington, Va., March 2019, pp. 7–10.

[40] Angelo S. DeNisi and Kevin R. Murphy, "Performance Appraisal and Performance Management: 100 Years of Progress?" *Journal of Applied Psychology*, Vol. 102, No. 3, 2017.

[41] DeNisi and Murphy, 2017, p. 425.

To widen reach and accelerate near-term impact, the team recommends that the DAF consider parallel rollouts of new rater training at multiple officer education and training venues to include the commissioning programs, SOS, the Leader Development Course, MAJCOM and functional Squadron Commander courses, and Group and Wing Pre-Command Training. For the initial DAF-wide launch, it may also be desirable to conduct just-in-time comprehensive bias training at the start of DT meetings, promotion boards, and developmental selection boards such as AFIT master's and Ph.D. programs, USAF Weapons School, and PME.

Strategic Communications and Cultural Change Considerations

The project team believes that accelerating change requires significantly more emphasis on communication and change management informed by clarity and awareness of current DAF cultural norms. The remainder of this chapter offers recommendations to address collateral issues identified in the team's analysis.

Employ an Enterprise Strategic Communications and Change Management Approach

Over the last three or four years, the DAF implemented multiple, rapid, and significant reforms to its officer talent and performance management processes, with most reforms rolled out individually. These interdependent reforms were designed to enable more flexible, suitable, and sustainable developmental pathways within career fields and throughout an officer's career.

Recent changes include the following:

1. introducing a new Talent Marketplace to improve assignment visibility and matching
2. implementing a new annual Officer Instructor and Recruiting Special Duty selection process
3. creating a new two-line, potential-focused promotion recommendation form
4. adopting merit-based promotion sequencing and eliminating below-the-zone promotions
5. splitting the Line of the Air Force (LAF) into officer developmental categories for promotion
6. introducing officer career field briefs at promotion boards
7. establishing an Air Force Ph.D. office
8. adjusting resident DE selection processes and distance learning eligibility criteria
9. unmasking REG data and promulgating new DEI guidance to CPME selection boards.

Other changes will soon be implemented, including a new Officer Evaluation System. This volume of change, implemented this quickly, has enormous potential to fuel uncertainty and confusion among the rank-and-file officer corps, as well as the commanders and SRs who counsel, evaluate, and recommend officers for development and promotion opportunities.

Therefore, the team recommends that the DAF implement a strategic communications campaign, employing a change management approach, which engages all ranks of the current officer corps, to clarify the DAF's intent; place cumulative officer talent management reforms in relative context; and dispel uncertainty, confusion, and myths related to the DAF's desire to field a more representative, diverse senior officer population. The team believes that there is a significant need to communicate clearly and consistently on these issues to all DAF officers, not just to racial or ethnic minority and female officers.

A proven method for initiating a DAF-wide communications campaign is the traditional HAF/A1, MAJCOM/A1, and AFPC road show "spread the word" briefs. For example, senior officer briefers, accompanied by subject-matter experts, could

1. discuss the intent and linkages between the officer talent management and DEI reforms
2. provide increased data transparency to confirm the need for significant changes (these data should also be centrally accessible to all officers and updated regularly)
3. address perceptions and realities for REG officers informed by the DAF/IG disparities feedback and analysis
4. preview adjustments, next steps, and additional planned officer talent and performance management changes.

Augmenting spread the word road shows with consistent content on DAF public affairs and social media platforms during SecAF and CSAF base visits, Facebook Live officer engagements, and discussions at pre–command training courses offer additional avenues for aligned change messaging.

The key goals—and benefits—of the recommended strategic communications campaign are to *increase the awareness* and understanding of all officers using common data and analysis; *build consensus* on areas of concern that the DAF is addressing; *gain feedback and buy-in* from officers, commanders, and SRs on office talent management and DEI reforms; and *improve the alignment* of DAF-wide implementation efforts.

Address DAF Cultural Norms (Blind Versus Unblind)

Finally, the project team concluded that the DAF's senior leaders must recognize and address current DAF cultural norms concerning "blind" development, performance evaluation, and promotion selection to reduce real and perceived disparities across the force and accelerate changes designed to account for equity considerations in the selection process.

Team interviews with 2020 and 2021 CPME board members and 2021 CSB members—all serving colonels and general officers—portray a spectrum of viewpoints on the appropriate use of unmasked REG data and DEI considerations by central selection boards. CPME board member interviews revealed a dominant cultural norm of "REG blind"—that is, most board members scored an officer's record of performance and demonstrated potential without regard to REG. Through these interviews, the team found that many CPME board members lacked significant understanding of the perceptions, challenges, and barriers faced by minority and female officers. In contrast, CSB board members displayed more understanding of the "big picture" behind the DAF's diversity efforts but were split on their willingness to use REG data in their evaluation of officers' records.

Appendix B discusses in detail the blinding versus unblinding (masking versus unmasking) dynamics in DE selection processes. There is robust literature requiring thoughtful consideration of both the perceived benefits and unintended consequences of blinding, as well as the potential benefits of unblind (i.e., *awareness*) approaches. However, the full range of these perspectives is not currently informing the mainstream DAF debate on DEI. Importantly, there was no strategic communication to the officer corps explaining the rationale or purpose or intent of unmasking REG data for the 2021 CPME board. Any significant alterations to the DAF blind norm will require a careful, deliberate DAF-wide change management approach incorporating significant senior leader commitment and messaging.

Comprehensive Implementation

The project team believes that the recommendations outlined in this chapter are realistic and implementable by the DAF in the near term. The team asserts that taking these actions will improve REG outcomes across the officer corps management lifecycle, moving toward proportional representation in the senior officer ranks and in key DAF and Joint leadership positions. Further analysis—including detailed REG barrier analyses—may derive additional actions that the DAF should consider to pursue its REG goals.

This effort, as with any significant institutional change effort, has certain essentials for successful execution: well-defined, published goals; visible, enduring senior leader commitment; a coordinated plan of actions and milestones for implementation; clear, aligned communications at all organizations levels; and an actively managed culture change effort supported by a coherent strategic narrative.

Chapter 6. Conclusion and Recommendations

This report aimed to answer a central question for the DAF: Should DE boards be blind or unblind with respect to REG? The DAF's culture has emphasized performance and endeavored to be blind to demographic data (discussed in Chapter 5 and Appendix B). However, research indicates that masking REG information does not necessarily reduce the impact of bias on selection processes, has little impact on objective assessment of quality, and may even perpetuate prejudice over time (discussed in Appendix B). It may seem intuitive that masking identifying information can reduce bias, but research has shown that masked and unmasked peer reviews are equivalent and have marginal impact on the influence of unconscious bias.[42]

The 2021 CPME boards, the focus of this report, provided the DAF with an opportunity to make demographic data visible to board members and, subsequently, assess whether these additional data made a difference. In our analysis of outcomes, we found that unmasking REG data did not have a significant effect on the 2021 IDE and SDE board results in the sense that not much change was observed from 2020 to 2021 after the unmasking. Our interviews with board members revealed that most explicitly chose to not consider REG data during the process for various reasons. Also, given that this board is merely one data point, it is important to avoid making strong conclusions about unmasking REG data and selection board outcomes.

Despite the lack of difference in outcomes, the 2020 and 2021 CPME boards did elicit revealing feedback from board members about how they applied DEI guidance, how they used REG data, and their opinions about unmasking REG data. This feedback informed the recommendations in Chapter 5 for future boards, especially those occurring later this year and during the next calendar year. If the DAF hopes to alter the culture around unmasking REG, the effort will require leadership, communications, and time for people to change their habits and shift the culture in the desired direction.

Insights from Other Research for Implementing Change

In the report "Moving Beyond Implicit Bias Training,"[43] the authors posit three policy insights that we believe would be helpful for the DAF as it implements change.

Use trainings to educate members of the organization. Guidelines for organizations that want to produce effective, evidence-based diversity trainings suggest not only reframing the trainings

---

[42] Nora S. Newcombe and Mark E. Bouton, "Masked Reviews Are Not Fairer Reviews," *Perspectives on Psychological Science*, Vol. 4, No. 1, 2009, pp. 62–63.

[43] Ivuoma N. Onyeador, Sa-kiera T. J. Hudson, and Neil A. Lewis, Jr., "Moving Beyond Implicit Bias Training: Policy Insights for Increasing Organizational Diversity," *Policy Insights from the Behavioral and Brain Sciences*, Vol. 8, No. 1, 2021.

to focus on raising awareness of bias, as a first step, but also equipping trainees with strategies for behavioral change (p. 21). Unpublished RAND research notes that organizations are trending toward online, voluntary learning tools and resources. This allows leaders and employees to learn about potential bias at their own pace.[44]

Prepare for, rather than accommodate, defensive responses. As organizations launch diversity initiatives, Onyeador, Hudson, and Lewis, 2021, recommend that they

> "be prepared for potential resistance and expect some defensive responses. Organizations can plan to document how defensiveness manifests and to respond to defensiveness by correcting misperceptions; linking diversity efforts to the organization's mission, values, and goals; and providing incentives for reaching diversity targets" (p. 21).

Implement organizational structures to address DEI. Citing research by Bailey et al., 2017,[45] and Hatzenbuehler et al., 2010,[46] Onyeador, Hudson, and Lewis note that the challenge is not just the people; inequalities may be embedded in the structures of the organization and society at large (p. 22).

Borrowing a Framework to Address Diversity, Equity, and Inclusion

Although it was beyond the scope of this project, Lim et al., 2021, p. 136 developed a framework for the U.S. Coast Guard that integrates several strategic and tactical enablers needed to achieve desired DEI outcomes—the third policy insight from Onyeador, Hudson, and Lewis. The framework could help the DAF link its myriad initiatives to desired results. This framework, depicted in Figure 6.1, provided Lim et al. with an organizing construct for 40 recommendations to the Coast Guard related to five areas, which we discuss below.

---

[44] 2021 RAND research by Devon Hill, Kirsten M. Keller, Monica Rico, Melissa Shostak, and Miriam Matthews.

[45] Zinzi D. Bailey, Nancy Krieger, Madina Agénor, Jasmine Graves, Natalia Linos, and Mary T. Bassett, "Structural Racism and Health Inequities in the USA: Evidence and Interventions," *The Lancet*, Vol. 389, No. 10077, 2017.

[46] Mark L. Hatzenbuehler, Kate A. McLaughlin, Katherine M. Keyes, and Deborah S. Hasin, "The Impact of Institutional Discrimination on Psychiatric Disorders in Lesbian, Gay, and Bisexual Populations: A Prospective Study," *American Journal of Public Health*, Vol. 100, No. 3, 2010.

Figure 6.1. Strategic and Tactical Enablers for Desired DEI Outcomes

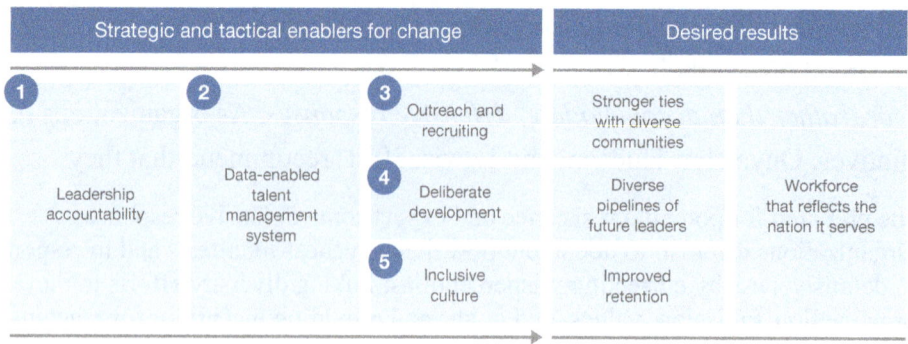

SOURCE: Lim et al., 2021, p. 136.

Leadership Accountability. Accountability involves establishing behavioral standards and ensuring that leaders personify them. A RAND report on culture change states, "when a behavior change is sought, in some cases undesired behaviors should be expected and seen as learning opportunities for honest feedback."[47] The most important part of accountability is the "actual execution of existing policy"[48] because failure to effectively execute DEI policies fuels cynicism and diminishes a sense of belonging among personnel. Accountability also involves developing metrics and benchmarks to measure and track organizational and cultural change. For example, the National Defense Authorization Act (NDAA) of 2021 requires the military services to develop rigorous and extensive metrics to track their diversity and inclusion efforts and report annually to Congress and the public.[49]

Data-Enabled Talent Management System. The outcomes of the various boards (e.g., CPME, promotion) are the results of activities to the left of the actual board. A data-enabled talent management system would allow the DAF to set goals and develop metrics for outreach, recruiting, career development, advancement and promotion, and retention. Metrics are critical for accountability and tracking progress. The 2011 Military Leadership Diversity Commission report specifies the following as characteristics of good metrics (p. 104):[50]

---

[47] Lisa S. Meredith, Carra S. Sims, Benjamin Saul Batorsky, Adeyemi Theophilus Okunogbe, Brittany L. Bannon, and Craig A. Myatt, *Identifying Promising Approaches to U.S. Army Institutional Change: A Review of the Literature on Organizational Culture and Climate*, Santa Monica, Calif.: RAND Corporation, RR-1588-A, 2017, p. 34.

[48] Meredith et al., 2017, p. 35.

[49] Public Law 116-283, William M. (Mac) Thornberry National Defense Authorization Act for Fiscal Year 2021, January 1, 2021, Section 551.

[50] Military Leadership Diversity Commission, *From Representation to Inclusion: Diversity Leadership for the 21st-Century Military: Final Report*, Arlington, Va., March 15, 2011.

- developed with an end state in mind and systematically linked to strategic goals
- clearly stated to be easily understood and communicated
- value added by providing information on key aspects of performance
- actionable to drive improvement
- tracked over time
- verifiable.

Outreach, Recruiting, and Classification. For the DAF, our team added specialty classification to the framework originally developed for the Coast Guard. The latest DAF Disparity Review, prepared by SAF/IGS, reported that the operational career fields are still the least racially and ethnically diverse in the DAF.[51] The research literature on military recruiting suggests that eligibility requirements determine the number of eligible youths, while outreach shapes awareness, propensity to serve, and the degree to which the military services capitalize on eligible personnel in different underrepresented racial groups. Lim et al., 2014, demonstrated how DAF leadership diversity depends on all these areas of the military personnel life cycle (pp. 4–5). Eligibility requirements determine the population eligible to serve. Recruiting determines whether accession cohorts mirror the eligible population. Promotions and retention determine whether they all progress through higher grades at equal rates. And choice of a career field can strongly influence retention and promotion. Together, these factors ultimately determine the REG makeup of the highest levels of military leadership.

Deliberate Development. According to AFI 36-2670, the DTs are responsible for ensuring that all career field members are provided with appropriate development opportunities.[52] The DTs provide career vectors at five mandatory trigger points: O-4 selection, IDE outplacement, squadron command outplacement (except judge advocate generals/chaplains), O-5 selection, and SDE outplacement. As noted in the directive, additional trigger points may be added at DT discretion for specific career field development (i.e., at the five-year point, to provide an assignment vector prior to the O-4 board). Each DT's responsibilities include reviewing the demographic makeup of the functional community and identifying potential barriers to all airmen and guardians reaching their highest potential. The DT will conduct gap and barrier analyses to address any negative trends (p. 22). The barrier analysis will require the DTs to identify key assignments and opportunities needed by members of their respective communities to help ensure that those officers are competitive during the board process.

Inclusive Culture. Culture change depends on altering behaviors and beliefs. Members of the organization must understand what is expected of them and how to exhibit the new behaviors. Training may be used to communicate expectations and new behaviors.[53] Organizational culture

---

[51] IG DAF, 2020.

[52] Air Force Instruction 36-2670, Total Force Development, June 25, 2020, p. 20.

[53] In 2017, RAND analysts Meredith et al. identified training as one of several drivers that can bring about organizational culture and climate changes for the U.S. Army. The others are goals, accountability, resources, and engagement.

is often seen as tapping into the underlying "why" of organizational behavior (e.g., values, attitudes), while climate is seen more as the "what" of organizations (e.g., policies, rewards, and punishments).[54] While changing the organizational climate deals with the employees' perceptions of current practices, policies, and implementation (and is closely related to behaviors), the underlying culture must be changed as well, since it permeates all organizational activities and behaviors and sets the stage for climates to emerge.[55]

We offer the Lim et al. framework as an organizing construct that might facilitate the management and coordination of DAF's DEI effort for maximum effectiveness and efficiency.

Recommendations Summary

The qualitative and quantitative data-informed recommendations presented in Chapter 5 are grouped into three categories and include considerations for implementing the suggested changes.

First, there are *adjustments needed for future DE boards*. Research shows that people of different backgrounds may hear or read the same information but understand it differently.[56] Often, leaders during organizational change make the mistake of not communicating enough or not communicating in the correct way.[57] Drawing on board member feedback, Chapter 5 recommends the following changes before the next CPME boards:

- Communicate DEI goals, guidance, and intent to CPME board members and SRs.
- Review the IDE DA process.
- After making the recommended changes for future CPME boards, DAF should keep the REG data unmasked for the next CPME board and analyze the results to determine whether the changes are having the desired effect.

The second category of recommendations emphasizes a systemic approach to *leverage other aspects of human capital development and management cycles* to advance DEI. As shown in Figure 6.1, changes to human capital activities must occur prior to the CPME boards if there are to be meaningful changes in the boards' outcomes. These changes should extend to preaccession activities, such as developing, implementing, and evaluating a long-term strategic plan for

---

[54] For some reviews, see Cheri Ostroff, Angelo J. Kinicki, and Rabiah S. Muhammad, "Organizational Culture and Climate," *Industrial and Organizational Psychology*, Vol. 12, 2012; and B. M. Schneider, M. G. Ehrhart, and W. H. Macey, "Perspectives on Organizational Climate and Culture," in S. Zedeck, ed., *APA Handbook of Industrial and Organizational Psychology*, Vol. 1, Building and Developing the Organization, Washington, D.C.: American Psychological Association, 2011.

[55] Meredith et al., 2017, p. 2.

[56] Martha Farnsworth Riche, Amanda Kraus, April K. Hodari, and Jasen P. DePasquale, *Literature Review: Empirical Evidence Supporting the Business-Case Approach to Work Force Diversity*, Alexandria, Va.: CNA Corporation, CNA Research Memorandum D0011482.A2, 2005.

[57] For examples, see Martha Farnsworth Riche and Amanda Kraus, *Approaches to and Tools for Successful Diversity Management: Results from 360-Degree Diversity Management Case Studies*, Alexandria, Va.: CNA Corporation, CNA Research Memorandum D0020315, 2009.

outreach to, and recruiting from, untapped locations with high-potential women and racial or ethnic minorities. Once a person is recruited, the DAF is already implementing initiatives that should aid in specialty matching, which ideally would help officers excel. The DAF is updating the data and barrier analysis training provided to training career field managers and DTs. These and other changes should lead to improved diversity outcomes. The following recommendations in Chapter 5 are meant to complement DAF's ongoing initiatives:

- Establish REG applicant recruiting goals for the four commissioning sources.
- Establish REG operational career-field designation goals at commissioning.
- Update officer development and talent management guidance to squadron commanders, SRs, and DTs.
- Implement comprehensive rater training.

The third category of recommendations offers considerations with respect to *strategic communications and cultural change*. Changing from being blind to unblind with respect to REG is a cultural adjustment for the DAF. The complexity of culture makes it challenging to understand what specific aspects might challenge or conflict with the change that an organization is considering. The critical question that must be answered is why the change is necessary. That question prompted the following recommendations:

- Employ an enterprise strategic communications and change management approach.
- Address DAF cultural norms (blind versus unblind).

In closing, as America becomes more diverse, so will the talent pool that the DAF hopes to tap. To remain competitive, the DAF needs a diverse mix of officers with the ability to lead an increasingly diverse organization.

Appendix A. Developmental Education Board Process

This appendix describes the background of how DE boards developed, the process that the boards follow, and how that process has evolved.

The role of selecting officers for DE and other fellowships was held by promotion boards and assignment teams prior to about 2007, when DTs came into being. DTs were created in 2008 and were given the ability to rank and choose the DE selects from the central promotion board along with *candidates* (all other officers not selected for DE at the promotion board). The DT then forwarded its *primary* list (all last-look CSB selects, along with the other selects and candidates of its choice) and *alternate* list (another list usually 50 percent to 80 percent as long as the primary list), each with three vector schools, to the DE Designation Board, which de-conflicted the vectors and notified officers of their assigned school. As declinations and ops deferments came back from the field, the Developmental Education Designation Board (DEDB, made up of six colonels at AFPC) would replace those officers with members of the Alternate list from that same DT.

In 2014, a CPME board was held, motivated by the notions that the DTs' parochial interests had too large an influence on a process that ultimately drives the composition of DAF senior leadership and that a central board was needed to apply an enterprise perspective to evaluating officers for future leadership potential.

The CPME board is a *nonstatutory* board, meaning that its proceedings do not have to be destroyed within a specific time after the board, and the DAF retains greater autonomy in how the board is conducted.

In 2021, 9,899 officers were eligible for the Line of the Air Force (LAF) (including JAG) SDE or IDE boards, from which the SRs nominated 2,998 officers to fill 735 allocated DE slots (Figure A.1). In addition, 367 of 2,222 eligible officers in medical service categories were nominated to fill 23 DE slots, and 70 of 93 eligible chaplains were nominated to fill six DE slots. Logistically, that equates to scoring 22 records an hour in IDE and 19 records an hour in SDE.

Figure A.1. Numbers of Candidates Eligible, Nominated, and Selected for IDE/SDE

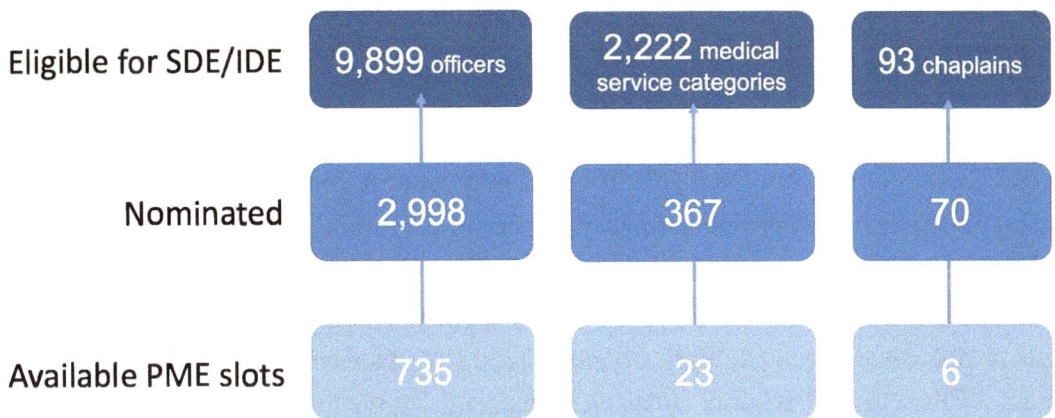

Eligibility

Yeargroups

Officers in accession yeargroups 2009–2011 were eligible for the 2021 LAF IDE board. Yeargroup 2009 officers had their last look, while yeargroup 2011 officers had their first look.

Officers in yeargroups 2001–2005 were eligible for the 2021 LAF SDE board. CPME boards prior to 2019 considered only four yeargroups (1998–2001 in 2018), but the 2019 CPME board was broadened to include one additional early yeargroup, to ultimately allow last-look officers to still have one year between the CPME board and their IPZ Colonel board. That allows last-look CPME designated officers to be sitting students rather than just designated when they meet their IPZ Colonel board. Yeargroups 2002 and 2003 both had their first look in 2019, their second in 2020, and their third in 2021 and face their last look in 2022. The 2023 CPME board will once again consider only four yeargroups: 2004–2007.

Obligations

To be nomination-eligible for the CPME board, officers not in their last look must also have had 12 months on station as of June 30, 2021, or 24 months on June 1, 2021, if in a Joint Duty Assignment; have had an expected return no later than December 31, 2021, if overseas; and no approved retirement/separation date in the system.

Nomination

The form for nominating officers was formerly Air Force Form 3849, but it has been incorporated into the MyVector portal and is now called the ODP-DE. Any officer on an SR's Master Eligibility List (MEL) who also meets the obligations listed above can be nominated, but

SRs' nominations are constrained to only 30 percent of the officers on the MEL. SRs requesting Deliberate Development credit for an officer who has already completed a PME-equivalent program must nominate that officer, choose the Deliberate Development option, and stratify him/her, but the officer will not count against the SR's 30-percent nomination constraint.

Operational Deferment

Officers selected for school at a CPME board may request deferral to the next academic year and have a guaranteed seat, provided their trajectory of performance is maintained. At the IDE level, designation to 11 schools guarantees that specific school the following year, while designation to any of the other 49 guarantees only a slot to IDE, but not specifically to the same school as previously designated. Similarly, at SDE, a slot at seven schools is guaranteed, while slots at any of the other 47 schools must *re-compete* among the available schools. Generally, large service-owned schools are guaranteed, while smaller specialized, Joint, and foreign school slots are not. Ops-deferred officers previously designated to re-compete schools must be re-nominated but do not count against the SR's nomination constraint. Ops-deferred officers previously designated to guaranteed schools are removed from consideration and not seen by the board but receive a guaranteed priority seat to that school to which they were previously designated.

Stratification

SRs must stratify their eligible officers on the ODP-DE. MyVector prevents scoring more than one officer at the same stratification number and fills in the number of officers on the MEL automatically as the numerator, so speeding within MyVector is not possible.

"Definitely Attend" Allocation

In addition to stratifying officers, in 2019 the DAF for the first time empowered SRs to designate one or more of their eligible officers to DA DE regardless of their board ranking. In 2019, commanders at seven special categories of command earned one DA outright,[58] while all others earned a DA only with 20 or more eligible officers. In 2020 the program allowed Wing CCs/Upper SML to receive a second DA if they had 30 eligibles, three with 50 eligibles, and four with 100 or more eligibles, while all other SRs earned a second DA if they had 50 eligibles and a third DA with 100 eligibles. In 2021, Wing CCs and Upper SML kept the same allocation rules while the other six special categories reverted to just one DA outright, as they had in 2019.

---

[58] The seven special categories are Wing Commanders (CCs) and Senior Material Leaders (SML), Major Command CCs, SAF/HAF two-digits, Numbered Air Force CCs, units above management level, Combatant Commanders, and Air Force Materiel Command Center CCs.

As a result, the ratio of DAs to nominations increased from 11.9 percent in 2019 to 15.4 percent in 2020 to 16.4 percent in 2021.

Scoring and Rank Ordering

Each board member evaluates each record, assigning a score between 6 and 10 points in half-point increments. The scores of all ten members are summed for each record, resulting in a total score between 60 and 100.

Split Resolution

Unsurprisingly, panel members sometimes disagree on the quality of a record by a significant margin, so the board room staff seek to resolve splits of more than 2 points between panel members. About twice a day during the board, board room administrators will pause the scoring process to highlight records for which the highest and lowest score were more than 1.5 points (for IDE) or 2 points (for SDE) apart. In many cases, both the highest- and lowest-score panel members will moderate their scores toward the mean, while sometimes only a single outlier will resolve the split by moderating his or her score. After several split resolution sessions, it becomes clear who the low- and high-mean scorers are, and this exerts a moderating influence on those members to try to score in the same range as the rest of the panel.

Tie-Breaking

After all scoring and split resolution is complete, the board must address the issue of tied scores, since in a range of only 40 points, there are just 81 distinct final scores possible. With 1,600 or more records, ties of over 100 records are not uncommon among the middle scores. As an alternative to painstakingly rescoring the records in each tie, the board room administrators use panel member score distribution to add fidelity to the relatively granular original scale. A personnel analyst in AFPC Analysis Branch standardizes all individual scores by panel member, resolving more than 99 percent of tied scores. The remaining unresolved ties return to the board, whose panel members rank all records involved in the tie, and the resulting sum of rankings determines the final order of merit.

Selected Changes from 2020 to 2021

Time Period Considered

The DAF reduced the number of years of OPRs and training reports available to panels in 2021, from the full officer record of performance reports to just the most recent five years. This was done to (1) reduce the number of screen flips needed to evaluate a record, saving time and enabling the board to evaluate more records without exceeding the two weeks designated for the board, and (2) focus the board on the most recent performance, masking earlier performance trajectories—both positive and negative—that might not have been sustained in the past five years.

One challenge noted by multiple panel members was keeping track of different frameworks of scoring officers from diverse career fields. To allow for more-consistent ranking within a career field, in 2021 the records were presented to panel members in DT and AFSC order. As members discuss what is important in each AFSC, they can return to all the records in that AFSC and consistently apply that new knowledge to all the scored records. Such a task would be harder if it involved reaching back to a record that had been scored several days earlier. Since scoring records consistently from the same AFSC is made easier, it can also be done faster, leading to more time to review and discuss scores, as well as less resistance to using a full ten members to score all records rather than breaking into three-member panels as promotion boards do.

Further detail can be obtained from the following PSDMs at the myPers website.

- PSDM 19-17, "CY19 IDE SDE DEDB Nom Procedural Memo for AY20-21."
- PSDM 19-98, "CY20 IDE SDE DEDB Nom Procedural Memo for AY21-22 (Corrected copy—10 Dec 2019)."
- PSDM 20-104, "CY21 IDE SDE DEDB Nom Procedural Memo for AY22-23."

Appendix B. Unmasking Trends in Developmental Education Selection

The DAF leadership has asserted that attracting, recruiting, developing, and retaining a diverse force while ensuring a culture of inclusion is a strategic and operational imperative.[59] Speaking directly to airmen after the death of George Floyd, Chief of Staff General Charles Q. Brown, Jr.—the first African American to serve as service chief of any military branch—spoke about his long, hard battle to become the leader of the DAF:

> I'm thinking about my Air Force career where I was often the only African American in my squadron, or as a senior officer the only African American in the room.[60]

A 2020 DAF IG Independent Racial Disparity Review found that Black officers have been "overrepresented in professional military education (PME) nominations but underrepresented in designations to attend [DAs]" for IDE since 2015.[61] In 2019, the DA process was implemented, providing every wing CC, the SML, and a few additional SRs with the opportunity for direct input into which officers were guaranteed an IDE slot.[62]

Several propositions have been made over the years to increase DEI at various points along the military career lifecycle.[63] As discussed in the main body of this report, the DAF instituted a significant procedural change to the 2021 DE selection board—no longer masking REG information in the officers' records—as part of its broader DEI initiative. During our qualitative interviews, it became apparent that senior DAF leaders are sharply divided on the issue of blind selection procedures. During the data analysis conducted for this study, we found that unmasking REG data did not have a significant effect on the 2021 IDE and SDE board outcomes (see Chapter 3). However, given that the majority of both IDE and SDE board members explicitly

---

[59] AFI 36-7001, 2019. Research has shown that more diverse militaries have greater trust with the citizenry and are more effective at accomplishing their missions, while armed forces with high rates of inequalities perform more poorly on the battlefield. For more information, see Jason Lyall, *Divided Armies: Inequality and Battlefield Performance in Modern War*, Princeton, N.J., Princeton University Press, 2020.

[60] Charles Q. Brown, Jr., "What I'm Thinking About," YouTube video, Pacific Air Forces, June 5, 2020.

[61] IG DAF, 2020, pp. 3, 52–56. On page 54 of the report, data are provided for 2015–2020 IDE/SDE Nomination/Designation rates. These data show that Black officers are consistently below the average designation rate for IDE and SDE compared with their White counterparts, even though they exceed the average nomination rate for all officers between 2016 and 2020.

[62] Currently, DAs are used only for IDE. According to IG DAF, 2020 (p. 55), Deputy Chief of Staff of the Air Force, Manpower, Personnel and Services, is working on building a similar DA process for SDE, in which SRs can designate an officer to attend SDE using a DA. The intent is for this process to allow for SDE DAs in approximately two years.

[63] Alan M. Osur, *Separate and Unequal: Race Relations in the AAF During World War II*, Maxwell Air Force Base, Ala.: Air Force History and Museums Program, 2000.

chose to not consider REG data during the process, this finding does not allow us to make definitive conclusions regarding the potential utility of unmasking.

In his award-winning book, preeminent sociologist Eduardo Bonilla-Silva changed the way that many social analysts talk about the impact of colorblindness, stating that

> Colorblind racial ideology creates a façade of racial inclusion by suggesting that in a post–Civil Rights era, everyone has an equal opportunity to succeed, and if differences in outcomes across racial groups continue to exist, these differences are best explained through culture [and] natural occurrences. . . . [64]

The underlying logic of colorblind ideology is quite simple: "if people or institutions do not notice race, then they cannot act in a racially biased manner."[65] However, as this appendix shows, evidence suggests that colorblindness may not achieve its supposed benefits, regardless of its laudable goal.

Most of the participants in the 2020 and 2021 IDE and SDE selection boards favored REG data being masked on performance reports, claiming that being blind is the only way to ensure a fair process so that unconscious biases do not impact the outcome and individuals are scored solely based on quality performance indicators such as stratification, deployments, leadership opportunities, and graduating from prestigious training schools.[66] Other participants favored unmasking REG data in the 2021 board process under certain conditions. For example, some senior leaders suggested that REG data should be unmasked only if the DAF provides guidance on how to consider it, others claimed that unmasking REG data allows for consideration of "the whole person," and some felt that it was a useful discriminator in tie-breaker situations. Table B.1 outlines the 2020 and 2021 IDE and SDE board members' perceptions of blinding in the selection process.

---

[64] Candis Watts Smith and Sara Mayorga-Gallo, "The New Principle-Policy Gap: How Diversity Ideology Subverts Diversity Initiatives," *Sociological Perspectives*, Vol. 60, No. 5, 2017, p. 891, citing Eduardo Bonilla-Silva, *Racism Without Racists: Color-Blind Racism and the Persistence of Racial Inequality in the United States*, 4th ed., Lanham, Md.: Rowman & Littlefield, [2003] 2014.

[65] Evan P. Apfelbaum, Michael I. Norton, and Samuel R. Sommers, "Racial Color Blindness: Emergence, Practice, and Implications," *Current Directions in Psychological Science*, Vol. 21, No. 3, 2012.

[66] Specifically, 13 of the 15 2021 board members and five of the 13 2020 board members interviewed did not believe that REG data should be visible during scoring. Four of the 13 2020 board members were either unsure or agnostic as to whether REG data should be visible. Also of note is the senior leader perspective that we gained from interviews with Command Selection Board members. Six of the eight panel members interviewed believed that REG data should be unmasked in both the CSB and CPME processes. Based on these breakdowns, senior Air Force leaders are more attuned to the potential benefits of unmasking REG data in selection proceedings than the O-6 and O-7 airmen who constitute the IDE and SDE boards.

Table B.1. Perceptions For and Against Blind IDE and SDE Selection Processes

Arguments for Masked REG Data (blind)	Arguments for Unmasked REG Data (aware)
• If performance is the most important criterion in scoring, then REG data are not necessary. • Consideration of REG data means or suggests the institution of demographic quotas. • Combatting unconscious bias requires masking REG data in the records, so some participants prefer that all person-centered information (i.e., REG data, names, pronouns, etc.) be removed from reports. • Masking REG data levels the playing field and ensures a fair process. • REG data create an opportunity for drag in decisionmaking and are distracting without directive guidance. • The only value that could stem from unmasking REG data is to address racial disparities, but there is a lack of certainty about whether that is the intent. • Consideration of REG data is the definition of racism and sexism. • Consideration of and access to REG data in records is illegal under Equal Opportunity and civil rights law.	• If performance is the most important selection criterion, and we cannot assume that everyone had equitable developmental opportunities to the left of the board, then REG data are necessary to contextualize performance, and board guidance will need to be amended; as senior DAF leaders, it is necessary for us to think beyond performance. • In tie-breaker situations in which two records are almost identical, REG data can be the deciding factor to further the DAF's stated DEI goals. • REG data are another piece of information for consideration that adds further context (e.g., consideration of "the whole person"). • Inclusion of REG data allows for statistical analysis of past IDE and SDE selections to identify unconscious bias and barriers to DEI. • REG data allow the board to identify trends in scoring based on demographics.

SOURCE: RAND thematic analysis of 2020 and 2021 IDE and SDE board member perceptions of masking and unmasking REG data.
NOTE: Insights are ordered in descending frequency from top to bottom.

While DAF senior leaders are split on blinding, there is robust literature that clearly lays out the perceived benefits and unintended consequences of blinding, as well as the potential benefits of unmasking REG information that are not currently being considered in the mainstream DAF debate on this issue. Before moving on to a discussion of the perceived benefits and unintended consequences of blinding concepts, it is important to note that concerns arose during some interviews about a perceived increase in airmen declining to respond when asked to identify their REG. However, according to our analysis, there has not been an increase in "decline to respond" (DTR) when they were asked to provide demographic information (see Figure B.1).

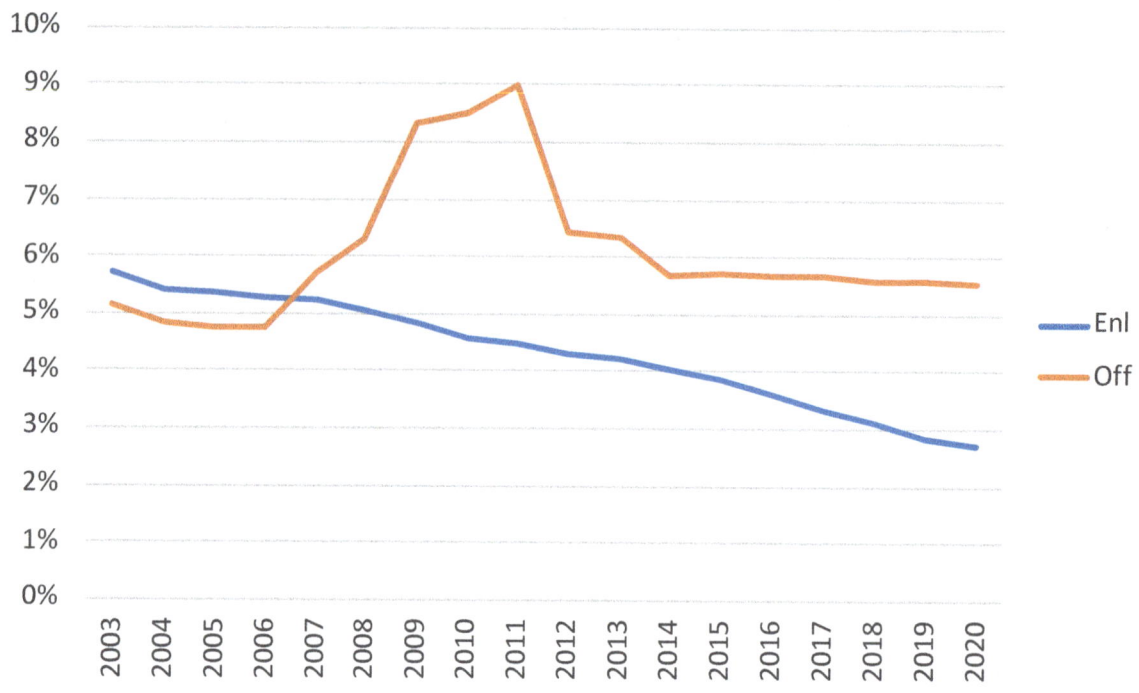

As Figure B.1 shows, for officers, DTR peaked around 2011 and plateaued at around 6 percent since 2014. Enlisted DTRs have steadily declined since at least 2003.[67] This perception of recent increases in airmen electing to not identify their demographic information may be explained, at least in part, by the ability to select multiple ethno-racial categories. Upon further analysis of the data, the rise in officers' DTRs between 2007 and 2011 may be attributed to a system glitch rather than the DTR being enforced from 2010 to the present.

In his book *The Great Demographic Illusion*, Richard Alba argues that Americans are under the spell of a distorted and polarizing minority-majority narrative that obscures a more transformative trend in rising numbers of young Americans from ethno-racially mixed families. Inclusion of multirace reporting both in the 2000 Census and within the DAF adds further context to the discussion on blinding.

Perceived Benefits and Unintended Consequences of Blinding Concepts

Blinding concepts—the notion "that because race *should not* matter in shaping individuals' life chances, then it *does not* matter"[68]—are not new and manifest in a variety of settings for

---

[67] This dataset includes both airmen and guardians, since guardians were not moved to a separate field until February 2021, which is after the end of the timeline represented in Figure B.1.

[68] Smith and Mayorga-Gallo, 2017, p. 890.

different reasons.[69] One of the most cited reasons for the use of blinding concepts is to reduce the impact of unconscious bias and subjectivity on the outcome and increase equality. *Blind review* (i.e., review in which the authors are not identified to reviewers and vice versa) is perceived as fairer and more objective.[70] It is possible that double-blind peer review processes may reduce the incidence of nepotism and institutional biases. Studies have shown that "authors familiar to reviewers, either through personal connection or the author's prominence in the field, are more likely to have their papers or grants accepted than unfamiliar authors."[71] The underlying logic of blinding is that it can prevent prejudice and discrimination. Apfelbaum, Norton, and Sommers, 2012, characterizes this intuition as "if people or institutions do not even notice race, then they cannot act in a racially biased manner."[72] This sentiment was echoed, almost exactly, by multiple interview participants in this study.

Color and gender blindness are aspirational at best and harmful at worst. Blinding sentiments may be well-meaning, but there is little evidence to support their efficacy in leveling the playing field. Masking REG information does not necessarily reduce the impact of bias on selection processes, has little impact on objective assessment of quality, and may even perpetuate prejudice over time. While it may seem intuitive that masking identifying information can reduce bias, studies have shown that both masked and unmasked reviews are equivalent in quality and have marginal impact on the influence of unconscious bias.[73] Studies have also shown that

---

[69] Eric D. Knowles, Brian S. Lowery, Caitlin M. Hogan, and Rosalind M. Chow, "On the Malleability of Ideology: Motivated Construals of Color Blindness," *Journal of Personality and Social Psychology*, Vol. 96, 2009.

[70] Joanna M. Setchell, "Editorial: Double-Blind Peer Review and the Advantages of Data Sharing," *International Journal of Primatology*, Vol. 36, 2015; Martin Enserink, "Few Authors Choose Anonymous Peer Review, Massive Study of Nature Journals Shows," *Nature*, September 22, 2017; Adrian Mulligan, Louise Hall, and Ellen Raphael, "Peer Review in a Changing World: An International Study Measuring the Attitudes of Researchers," *Journal of the American Society for Information Science and Technology*, 2012; Laura E. Hirshfield, "A Case for Double-Blind Review," *Academic Medicine*, Vol. 95, No. 11, 2020; Zosia Kmietowicz, "Double Blind Peer Reviews Are Fairer and More Objective, Say Academics," *BMJ*, 2008.

[71] Amelia R. Cox and Robert Montgomerie, "The Case For and Against Double-Blind Reviews," *PeerJ*, 2019, citing Ulf Sandström and Martin Hällsten, "Persistent Nepotism in Peer-Review," *Scientometrics*, Vol. 74, No. 2, 2008; Andrew Tomkins, Min Zhang, and William D. Heavlin, "Reviewer Bias in Single- Versus Double-Blind Peer Review," *Proceedings of the National Academy of Sciences*, Vol. 114, No. 48, 2017; and Kanu Okike, Kevin T. Hug, Mininder S. Kocher, and Seth F, Leopold, "Single-Blind vs Double-Blind Peer Review in the Setting of Author Prestige," *JAMA*, Vol. 316, No. 2, 2016. Note that the main findings of Amber E. Budden, Tom Tregnza, Lonnie W. Arssen, Julia Koricheva, Roosa Leimu, and Christopher J. Lortie, "Double-Blind Review Favours Increased Representation of Female Authors," *Trends in Ecology and Evolution*, Vol. 23, No. 1, 2008, that double-blind review increases the acceptance of female authorship, were challenged by other researchers, including Thomas J. Webb, Bob O'Hara, and Robert P. Freckleton, "Does Double-Blind Review Benefit Female Authors?" *Trends in Ecology and Evolution*, Vol. 23, No. 7, 2008.

[72] Apfelbaum, Norton, and Sommers, 2012, p. 205.

[73] Newcombe and Bouton, 2009; Mengyi Sun, Jainabou Barry Danfa, and Misha Teplitskiy, "Does Double-Blind Peer Review Reduce Bias? Evidence From a Top Computer Science Conference," *arXiv*, 2021; Tony Bazi, "Peer Review: Single-Blind, Double-Blind, or All the Way Blind?" *International Urogynecology Journal*, Vol. 31, 2020; Susan van Rooyen, Fiona Godlee, Stephen Evans, Richard Smith, and Nick Black, "Effect of Blinding and Unmasking on the Quality of Peer Review: A Randomized Trial," *JAMA: Journal of the American Medical*

blinding concepts can have a range of detrimental effects, such as limiting the ability to identify racism and perceive microaggressions, reduced willingness to remedy disparities, lower empathy in therapists, greater apathy to racism, and less willingness to support diversity initiatives.[74] In the hiring context, blind resume screening has been shown to statistically increase adverse effects for minority candidates because interrupted or nonstandard work history is not easily attenuated.[75] Thus, the absence of explicit and direct discussion on the role of REG data in selection processes can result in lower selection rates of racial and ethnic minorities and women—especially considering the unintended consequences of current interpretations of Equal Opportunity laws—and may perpetuate prejudice by discouraging action to alleviate disparities.[76]

Association, Vol. 280, 1998; Fiona Godlee, Catharine R. Gale, and Christopher N. Martyn, "Effect on the Quality of Peer Review of Blinding Reviewers and Asking Them to Sign Their Reports: A Randomized Control Trial," *JAMA: Journal of the American Medical Association*, Vol. 280, No. 3, 1998; Amy C. Justice, Mildred K. Cho, Margaret A. Winker, Jesse A. Berlin, and Drummond Rennie, "Does Masking Author Identity Improve Peer Review Quality? A Randomized Controlled Trial," *JAMA: Journal of the American Medical Association*, Vol. 280, 1998; C. Le Goues, Y. Brun, S. Apel, E. Berger, S. Khurshid, and Y. Smaragdakis, "Effectiveness of Anonymization in Double-Blind Review," *Communications of the ACM*, Vol. 61, No. 6, 2018; Emily A. Largent and Richard T. Snodgrass, "Blind Peer Review by Academic Journals," Chapter 5 of Christopher G. Robertson and Aaron Kesselheim, eds., *Blinding as a Solution to Bias: Strengthening Biomedical Science, Forensic Science, and Law*, 1st ed., Cambridge, Mass.: Academic Press, 2016; Smir Haffar, Fateh Bazerbachi, and M. Hassan Murad, "Peer Review Bias: A Critical Review," *Mayo Clinic Proceedings*, Vol. 94, No. 4, 2019.

[74] Victoria C. Plaut, Kecia M. Thomas, Kyneshawau Hurd, and Celina A. Romano, "Do Color Blindness and Multiculturalism Remedy or Foster Discrimination and Racism?" *Current Directions in Psychological Science*, 2018, citing H. A. Neville, R. L. Lilly, G. Duran, R. M. Lee, and L. Browne, "Construction and Initial Validation of the Color-Blind Racial Attitudes Scale (CoBRAS)," *Journal of Counseling Psychology*, Vol. 47, No. 1, 2000; Axinja Hachfeld, Adam Hahn, Sascha Schroeder, Yvonne Anders, and Mareike Kunter, "Should Teachers Be Colorblind? How Multicultural and Egalitarian Beliefs Differentially Relate to Aspects of Teachers' Professional Competence for Teaching in Diverse Classrooms," *Teaching and Teacher Education*, Vol. 48, 2015; Evan P. Apfelbaum, Kristin Pauker, Samuel R. Sommers, and Nalini Ambady, "In Blind Pursuit of Racial Equality?" *Psychological Science*, Vol. 21, 2010; L. R. Offermann, T. E. Basford, R. Graebner, S. Jaffer, S. B. D. Graaf, and S. E. Kaminsky, "See No Evil: Color Blindness and Perceptions of Subtle Racial Discrimination in the Workplace," *Cultural Diversity & Ethnic Minority Psychology*, Vol. 20, 2014; Derald Wing Sue, Christina M. Capodilupo, Gina C. Torino, Jennifer M. Bucceri, Aisha M. B. Holder, Kevin L. Nadal, and Marta Esquilin, "Racial Microaggressions in Everyday Life: Implications for Clinical Practice," *American Psychologist*, Vol. 62, 2007; O. R. Aragón, J. F. Dovidio, and M. J. Graham, "Colorblind and Multicultural Ideologies Are Associated with Faculty Adoption of Inclusive Teaching Practices," *Journal of Diversity in Higher Education*, Vol. 10, 2017; A. W. Burkard and S. Knox, "Effect of Therapist Color-Blindness on Empathy and Attributions in Cross-Cultural Counseling," *Journal of Counseling Psychology*, Vol. 51, 2004; Brandesha M. Tynes and Suzanne L. Markoe, "The Role of Color-Blind Racial Attitudes in Reactions to Racial Discrimination on Social Network Sites," *Journal of Diversity in Higher Education*, Vol. 3, 2010; Germine H. Awad, Kevin Cokley, and Joseph Ravitch, "Attitudes Toward Affirmative Action: A Comparison of Color-Blind Versus Modern Racist Attitudes," *Journal of Applied Social Psychology*, Vol. 35, 2006.

[75] Luc Behaghel, Bruno Crépon, and Thomas Le Barbanchon, "Unintended Effects of Anonymous Resumes," *American Economic Journal: Applied Economics*, Vol. 7, No. 3, 2015.

[76] Victoria C. Plaut, Flannery G. Garnett, Laura E. Buffardi, and Jeffrey Sanchez-Burks, "'What About Me?' Perceptions of Exclusion and Whites' Reactions to Multiculturalism," *Journal of Personality and Social Psychology*, Vol. 101, 2011; Knowles et al., 2009; Richard P. Eibach and Thomas Keegan, "Free at Last? Social Dominance, Loss Aversion, and White and Black Americans' Differing Assessments of Racial Progress," *Journal of*

Because reviewers, hiring committees, and selection boards can infer REG data from information provided within the submission or from the record itself, unmasking REG information can reveal the potential impact of bias on the outcome that would otherwise be hidden.[77] In the context of secondary education, evidence shows how blinding approaches can hinder students' critical thinking skills, negatively influence perceptions of personal identity and trust, and affect cognitive growth.[78] The potential benefits of unmasking REG data in developmental education selection boards range from reducing levels of racial prejudice to encouraging consideration of individuals holistically. Studies have found that gender blindness reduces bias in men's evaluations of and behavior toward female leaders that do not fit within typical gender stereotypes (e.g., instead of being considered "emotional" or "angry," women are attributed the masculine equivalent trait of "passionate" when their gender is unknown).[79]

While gender blinding strategies have shown promising results for reducing gender bias in certain contexts, such as orchestra auditions and leadership evaluations, the same is not true in all contexts or for racial and ethnic minorities in any context.[80] The reason that women benefit from blinding strategies, while racial and ethnic minorities do not, appears to be linked to the difference in how gender versus racial and ethnic stereotypes consciously or unconsciously

Personality and Social Psychology, Vol. 90, No. 3, 2006; Plaut et al., 2018; Behaghel, Crépon, and Le Barbanchon, 2015; Helen A. Neville, Miguel E. Gallardo, and Derald Wing Sue, "Introduction: Has the United States Really Moved Beyond Race?" in *The Myth of Racial Color Blindness: Manifestations, Dynamics, and Impact*, Washington, D.C.: American Psychological Association, 2016; Helen A. Neville, Germine H. Awad, James E. Brooks, Michelle P. Flores, and Jamie Bluemel, "Color-Blind Racial Ideology: Theory, Training, and Measurement in Psychology," *American Psychologist*, Vol. 68, No. 6, 2013; Carey S. Ryan, Jennifer S. Hunt, Joshua A. Weible, Charles R. Peterson, and Juan F. Casas, "Multicultural and Colorblind Ideology, Stereotypes, and Ethnocentrism Among Black and White Americans," *Group Processes and Intergroup Relations*, Vol. 10, No. 4, 2007; Lisa Rosenthal and Sheri R. Levy, "The Colorblind, Multicultural, and Polyculture Ideological Approaches to Improving Intergroup Attitudes and Relations," *Social Issues and Policy Review*, Vol. 4, No. 1, 2010; Luke J. Lara, "Faculty of Color Unmask Color-Blind Ideology in the Community College Faculty Search Process," *Community College Journal of Research and Practice*, Vol. 43, No. 10–11, 2019; Deborah Son Holoien and J. Nicole Shelton, "You Deplete Me: The Cognitive Costs of Colorblindness on Ethnic Minorities," *Journal of Experimental Social Psychology*, Vol. 48, 2012.

[77] Cox and Montgomerie, 2019. Also see Sun, Danfa, and Teplitskiy, 2021.

[78] Sheri A. Castro-Atwater, "Color-Blind Racial Ideology in K–12 Schools," in Helen A. Neville, Miguel E. Gallardo, and Derald Wing Sue, eds., *The Myth of Racial Color Blindness: Manifestations, Dynamics, and Impact*, Washington, D.C.: American Psychological Association, 2016.

[79] Ashley E. Martin and Katherine W. Phillips, "Blind to Bias: The Benefits of Gender-Blindness for STEM Stereotyping," *Journal of Experimental Social Psychology*, Vol. 82, 2019, p. 305.

[80] Seval Gündemir, Seval, Ashley E. Martin, and Astrid C. Homan, "Understanding Diversity Ideologies from the Target's Perspective: A Review and Future Directions," *Frontiers in Psychology*, Vol. 10, No. 282, 2019; Martin and Phillips, 2019. Also see Stefanie K. Johnson and Jessica F. Kirk, "Dual-Anonymization Yields Promising Results for Reducing Gender Bias: A Naturalistic Field Experiment of Applications for Hubble Space Telescope Time," *Publications of the Astronomical Society of the Pacific*, March 2020; Leigh S. Wilton, Jessica J. Good, Corinne A. Moss-Racusin, and Diana T. Sanchez, "Communicating More Than Diversity: The Effect of Institutional Diversity Statements on Expectations and Performance as a Function of Race and Gender," *Cultural Diversity and Ethnic Minority Psychology*, Vol. 21, No. 3, 2015. Also see Claudia Goldin and Cecelia Rouse, "Orchestrating Impartiality: The Impact of 'Blind' Auditions on Female Musicians," *American Economic Review*, Vol. 90, No. 4, 2000.

emerge. For example, masking a woman's gender during a performance evaluation obscures any inclination to perceive strong female leaders as "angry," while masking a black female leader's race and ethnicity in her performance record takes away the opportunity to positively associate her "blackness" with her leadership. While the former is a positive result, the latter impairs the ability to drive long-term cultural change and short-term representation gains.

If it is indeed the DAF's goal to increase minority representation in senior leadership positions, then it is critical that the DAF provide selection board members with REG data so they may begin the process of positively associating minority status with leadership potential. Given that, in the context of IDE and SDE selection processes, it is difficult to measure potential objectively beyond minimum universal requirements; subjective measures of being officer material carry more weight in considerations of patterns of performance.[81] IDE and SDE board members could contextualize the information within a service member's record and consider the whole person—including how an officer's REG might have negatively affected their ability to receive mentorship—which requires availability of REG data. Otherwise, board members are assuming that all service members have equal access to development opportunities to the left of the board, while the 2020 IG Racial Disparity Report found otherwise.[82]

Granted, as this appendix has shown, perceptions do not always translate to reality; however, it takes only a stroll down hallways with photos of DAF leadership to notice the stark reality that few racial and ethnic minorities make it to the top. Thus, increasing awareness and understanding of this reality using common data analysis would support current and future DAF talent management reforms and improve DAF-wide DEI initiatives. This requires that DAF provide guidance to board members that contextualizes the role of REG data in selections and effectively communicates the department's intent when unmasking demographic data, which will require a cultural and narrative shift. Whether senior leaders favor or oppose unmasking REG data in the DE process, their position acknowledges neither the potential for unintended consequences of masking nor the potential benefits that unmasking REG data could provide to the DAF.

Equal Opportunity Law and the Use of Race-Conscious Policies

Considering REG data during selection processes—especially in all developmental opportunities to the left of the board—is necessary to meet the DAF's operational need and mission imperative. This would not be the first time that the U.S. military unmasked REG information to increase DEI. The military used race-conscious policies to integrate the armed forces and to make reforms in response to racial reckoning during the Vietnam War.[83] At

---

[81] Not being viewed as a disruptor or "making waves" has historically been a defining feature in determining whether a female ought to be promoted. See Robert Knowles, "The Intertwined Fates of Affirmative Action and the Military," *Loyola University Chicago Law Journal*, Vol. 45, No. 4, 2014, pp. 1069–1070.

[82] IG DAF, 2020.

[83] Knowles, 2014, pp. 1031–1032.

present, the DAF is addressing racial disparities identified by the IG. Clearly, considering the "whole person" is in line with both current needs and past actions.[84]

The military has a history of vested interest in admission policies of colleges and universities, given that service-oriented ROTC programs are important sources for recruitment into the officer corps.[85] Specifically, the military's use of affirmative, race-conscious policies to integrate the armed forces was key in the Supreme Court's 2003 decision in *Grutter v. Bollinger* that

> narrowly tailored use of race in admissions decisions to further a compelling interest in obtaining the educational benefits that flow from a diverse student body is not prohibited by the Equal Protection Clause, Title VI, or §1981.[86]

The Department of Defense's new Office for Diversity, Equity, and Inclusion's mission to ensure that the department can meet the mission and readiness imperative of a diverse Total Force is aligned with its historical use of race-conscious policies and current interpretation of equal opportunity law.

In recent decades, the more selective colleges have altered admissions practices to promote greater diversity. The race-conscious admissions program at Harvard College, the undergraduate college of Harvard University, has served as a model for admissions programs at private and public universities across the country since roughly 1978, when the Supreme Court of the United States decided *Regents of the University of California v. Bakke*.[87] Since then, the Supreme Court has twice affirmed the constitutionality of race-conscious admissions programs based on Harvard's model, in which Harvard considers race as part of its holistic consideration of an applicant's traits and characteristics.[88] These strategies have been pursued as a means of

---

[84] Military leaders filed amicus briefs in support of affirmative admission policies for colleges and universities because they believe that it is important that officers' racial and ethnic profile reflects the enlisted members and can be considered the floor aim point for the percentage of diversity to target. Since the military asks its service members to potentially make the ultimate sacrifice in defense of the nation's interests, it is reasonable to require that those applying the direct leadership of war-making capabilities be reflective of the diversity of the force. The amici also recounted the military's successful use of affirmative race-conscious policies to integrate the armed forces and reform itself amid the Vietnam War era's racial reckoning. For more information on the U.S. armed forces' successful use of race-conscious policies, see Knowles, 2014, pp. 1031–1032. Also see Teri A. Kirby and Cheryl R. Kaiser, "Person-Message Fit: Racial Identification Moderates the Benefits of Multicultural and Colorblind Diversity Approaches," *Personality and Social Psychology*, Vol. 47, No. 6, 2021.

[85] Knowles, 2014, p. 1040.

[86] *Grutter v. Bollinger*, 539 U.S. 306, 307, 2003.

[87] Nancy L. Zisk, "The Future of Race-Conscious Admissions Programs and Why the Law Should Continue to Protect Them," *Northeastern University Law Review*, Vol. 12, No. 1, 2020, p. 58.

[88] Because the justices were unable to produce a majority decision, they left unsettled why the medical school's policy could not survive the court's scrutiny. This uncertainty left the lower courts without clear guidance on the permissibility of race-conscious admissions policies structured differently than the one struck down in *Bakke*. In the 40-plus years since *Regents of the University of California v. Bakke*, when the court first addressed those programs' constitutionality, the justices have remained divided over when or whether such programs can survive constitutional scrutiny. And a major point of disagreement among the justices is how strictly to review those policies and what the government or other state entity must do to justify its use of "benign" racial classifications. In recent decisions, the court has reviewed such classifications under a seemingly "elastic" regime of strict scrutiny, accepting those

expanding access to selective higher education for talented students from racially and economically marginalized backgrounds.

The tension between the strictness of the court's scrutiny and the court's approval of race-conscious admissions policies led the court to adjust its framework for scrutinizing similar policies over the years.[89] First, the court now requires public universities that adopt affirmative action admissions policies to explain in increasingly "concrete and precise" terms what diversity-related educational goals those policies serve and why the university has chosen to pursue them. Anything less, the court has held, would fail to present an interest sufficiently compelling under strict scrutiny. Second, the court also now expects universities to prove that their policies achieve those "concrete and precise goals" in an appropriately "flexible" way, as most clearly exemplified by the Harvard plan that Justice Powell singled out in *Bakke*.

The framework produced five hallmarks of an appropriately tailored affirmative action policy resulting in criteria that have guided lower courts in assessing other affirmative action plans.[90]

- *No quotas.* The use of racial quotas is the clearest violation of the requirement that a policy be narrowly tailored.
- *Individualized consideration.* An appropriately tailored program must remain flexible enough to ensure that each applicant is evaluated as an individual and does not make an applicant's race or ethnicity the defining feature of their application.
- *Serious, good-faith consideration of race (more or more flexible alternatives).* A university is to provide evidence that it undertook "serious, good faith consideration of workable race-neutral alternatives" before resorting to its choice of a race-conscious plan and that those alternatives either did not suffice to meet its approved educational goals or would have required some sacrifice of its "reputation for academic excellence."
- *No undue harm.* A race-conscious admissions policy must not unduly burden individuals who are not members of the favored racial and ethnic groups.
- *Ongoing review.* Race-conscious admissions policies must be limited in time. The end could come in the form of an explicit "durational limit," such as a sunset provision. Alternatively, it could come because of periodic reviews to determine whether racial preferences are still necessary to achieve student body diversity. Regardless of the approach that a university chooses to pursue, it has an ongoing obligation to engage in constant deliberation and continued reflection regarding its admissions policies and the role that race plays in them, or whether it should continue to play one at all.

---

classifications only where they have been narrowly tailored to serve compelling government interests. See Back, Christine J. Back and J. D. S. Hsin, "'Affirmative Action' and Equal Protection in Higher Education," Congressional Research Service, 2019, pp. 21–24, for more discussion.

[89] Back and Hsin, 2019, pp. 33–38.

[90] Back and Hsin, 2019, pp. 36–38. The diversity rationale emerged with the court's first encounter with a voluntary affirmative action policy in *Bakke*. Justice Powell explained what interests clearly would not be compelling enough to satisfy strict scrutiny. Powell was also clear about what interest he believed would satisfy strict scrutiny—namely, student body diversity. In *Bakke*, Powell set out the basic theory for why diversity could justify an affirmative action policy, at least "in the context of a university's admissions program." See Back and Hsin, 2019, p. 28, for more discussion.

When considering these five hallmarks of an appropriately tailored affirmative action policy, the DAF's use of REG data in IDE and SDE selection processes could affirm each. However, DAF should strategically and deliberately communicate the unintended consequences of blinding and the potential benefits of unmasking REG data during DE selection board processes to DAF senior leaders. To reap the benefits of unmasking, a DAF-wide change management approach is necessary to modify DAF cultural norms concerning blinding, synchronize actions to reduce real and perceived disparities across the force, and increase equity in selections to produce a more inclusive and diverse force. Specifically, providing clear scoring guidance and examples of how IDE and SDE board members could consider REG data during selection processes would facilitate the beginnings of such a change management approach. As Professor Patricia J. Williams stated in *Seeing a Color-Blind Future: The Paradox of Race*, "[we need] something more than the 'I think therefore it is' school of idealism. 'I don't think about color, therefore [race and ethnicity] problems don't exist.' If only it were so easy."[91]

---

[91] Patricia J. Williams, "The Emperor's New Clothes," Chapter One in *Seeing a Color-Blind Future: The Paradox of Race*, New York: Noonday Press, 1997.

Appendix C. IDE and SDE Model Analysis

This appendix of Chapter 3 reports the statistically significant officer attributes that help explain the 2020 IDE and SDE board results. It also provides each characteristic and its distribution of nominees and REG groups.

IDE Analysis Model Estimates

This model used a linear regression of OOM on officer attributes from the 2020 data (Table C.1), and the results are used to predict the OOM in 2021 as if no change was made at the beginning of 2021.

Table C.1. Statistically Significant IDE Attributes

Attributes	Avg. IDE OOM Percentile of Nominees with Attribute	IDE Model Coefficient	Groups with Attribute					
			Nominees (%)	Female (%)	Black (%)	Hispanic (%)	Asian (%)	White (%)
Stratified #1 of 1	51	0.08	14	19	19	16	18	13
Stratified #1 of 2	66	0.21	3	5	7	4	0	3
Stratified #1 of (3 to 5)	77	0.28	4	4	1	6	3	4
Stratified #1 of (6 to 9)	79	0.28	3	3	2	1	3	3
Stratified #2 of (3 to 5)	58	0.14	4	5	4	3	2	4
Stratified in top 10% of at least 6	88	0.31	4	6	3	5	2	4
Stratified 11%–20% of at least 6 and not #1 of (6 to 9)	76	0.23	5	6	2	4	3	5
Stratified 21%–30% of at least 6	67	0.18	7	6	3	10	6	7
Stratified 31%–40% of at least 6	59	0.13	7	4	4	11	5	6
Stratified 61%–70% of at least 6	36	−0.07	6	6	3	5	6	7
Stratified 71% or worse of at least 6	29	−0.13	22	17	20	17	30	22
O-10 SR	82	0.15	2	2	4	0	0	2
O-9 SR	61	0.06	4	7	3	2	5	4
O-8 or O-7 SR	52	0.04	28	30	34	31	32	27
SR in AETC	42	−0.09	14	10	9	22	14	13
SR in PACAF	46	−0.06	6	9	4	6	11	6
Female SR, Male Nominee	45	−0.05	8	0	5	8	11	7

Attributes	Avg. IDE OOM Percentile of Nominees with Attribute	IDE Model Coefficient	Groups with Attribute					
			Nominees (%)	Female (%)	Black (%)	Hispanic (%)	Asian (%)	White (%)
Male SR, Female Nominee	56	0.03	12	75	25	15	17	11
SOC DG	61	0.04	11	10	5	6	5	13
SOS DG with visible TR	74	0.19	9	7	2	11	6	10
SOS DG with TR not visible	63	0.07	6	2	4	1	5	7
APZ to O-4	19	−0.20	1	0	0	3	3	0
1st IDE look	52	0.04	27	31	27	32	30	26
3rd IDE look	47	−0.06	35	28	29	23	30	37
DA	73	0.06	17	21	19	10	11	18
No Opportunity for a DA	47	−0.08	22	26	32	30	26	21
Weapons School Grad	69	0.13	10	5	7	12	6	10
Assignment Limitation	47	−0.04	18	22	20	25	18	17
Bad Assignment Availability Code in past 5 years	13	−0.19	1	0	2	0	0	1
Failed Fitness Test in past 5 years	35	−0.07	2	3	3	1	3	2
Served in OSD or JCS in past 5 years	52	0.18	1	1	1	0	2	0
Ever a 97XX Exec	62	0.06	7	12	6	14	9	7
Non-97XX Exec in past 5 years	57	0.07	36	42	23	39	29	37
Non-97XX Exec prior to past 5 years	50	0.04	12	16	17	15	20	11
Currently	41	−0.03	9	4	2	5	6	10

Attributes	Avg. IDE OOM Percentile of Nominees with Attribute	IDE Model Coefficient	Nominees (%)	Female (%)	Black (%)	Hispanic (%)	Asian (%)	White (%)
						Groups with Attribute		
Assistant Director of Operations								
Core 13M (Airfield Operations)	62	0.17	1	2	2	3	0	1
Core 14 (Intelligence)	54	0.07	10	18	13	10	8	9
Core 19Z (Special Warfare)	68	0.10	2	0	1	1	0	2
Core 31 (Security Forces)	67	0.15	2	1	1	0	2	2%
Ever held F, K, Q, or W DAFSC prefix	52	0.05	46	26	22	40	29	50
No MSM	46	−0.07	52	43	43	50	61	53
3 or more MSMs	74	0.09	2	3	5	1	3	2
2% or more words used are fear words	47.6	−0.04	34	26	27	26	29	35

NOTES: AETC = Air Education and Training Command; Avg. = average; DAFSC = Duty Air Force Specialty Code; Exec = executive; JCS = Joint Chiefs of Staff; OSD = Office of the Secretary of Defense; PACAF = Pacific Air Forces. Adjusted R2 = 0.57.

SDE Analysis Model Estimates

This model used a linear regression of OOM on officer attributes from the 2020 data (Table C.2), and the results are used to predict the SDE OOM in 2021 as if no changes had been made at the beginning of 2021.

Table C.2. Statistically Significant SDE Attributes

Attributes	Avg. SDE OOM Percentile of Nominees with Attribute	SDE Model Coefficient	Nominees (%)	Female (%)	Black (%)	Hispanic (%)	Asian (%)	White (%)
						Groups with Attribute		
Stratified #1 of 1	50	0.06	17	17	25	24	44	16
Stratified #1 of 2	65	0.17	6	5	7	7	3	6

Attributes	Avg. SDE OOM Percentile of Nominees with Attribute	SDE Model Coefficient	Groups with Attribute					
			Nominees (%)	Female (%)	Black (%)	Hispanic (%)	Asian (%)	White (%)
Stratified #1 of (3 to 5)	79	0.25	7	6	7	3	6	7
Stratified #1 of (6 to 9)	88	0.34	4	4	0	4	0	5
Stratified #2 of (3 to 5)	62	0.12	7	7	1	5	8	7
Stratified #4 of 5, 5 of 5, 4 of 4, or 3 of 3	31	−0.11	9	9	15	14	6	8
Stratified in top 10% of at least 6	88	0.32	1	1	1	1	0	1
Stratified 11%–20% of at least 6 and not #1 of (6 to 9)	76	0.23	2	2	1	0	0	2
Stratified 21%–30% of at least 6	72	0.20	4	6	2	1	8	4
Stratified 31%–40% of at least 6	60	0.11	4	3	0	3	6	5
Stratified 61%–70% of at least 6	36	−0.10	4	3	2	4	6	5
Stratified 71% or worse of at least 6	24	−0.17	15	16	11	14	8	16
O-10 SR	84	0.18	1	3	0	1	3	1
SR above the management level	91	0.29	0.5	0.5	0	0	0	0
SOC DG	59	0.05	15	21	11	8	6	17
Traditional ISS in-residence	59	0.09	44	42	32	46	28	45
Other IDE in-residence	60	0.08	13	13	11	7	11	14
BPZ to O-5	83	0.19	9	11	2	5	8	10
1st SDE look	39	−0.04	15	19	19	15	25	14
Last SDE look	45	−0.05	17	15	21	15	6	18
Age		−0.01						
HBCU graduate	39	−0.11	1	3	14	0	0	0
Never a commander	27	−0.18	21	19	16	28	25	21
Weapons School grad	61	0.06	11	4	5	5	8	13
Deployed in past 5 years	48	−0.02	36	27	28	27	36	37
Aide in past 5 years	82	0.09	2	3	1	3	0	2

Attributes	Avg. SDE OOM Percentile of Nominees with Attribute	SDE Model Coefficient	Groups with Attribute					
			Nominees (%)	Female (%)	Black (%)	Hispanic (%)	Asian (%)	White (%)
Served in OSD or JCS in past 5 years	58	0.04	6	6	10	8	11	6
Ever assigned to Headquarters Air Force	57	0.03	25	39	49	36	39	22
97XX Exec in past 5 years	58	0.06	9	9	12	14	0	9
Currently an instructor	28	−0.07	4	0	4	4	3	4
Ever a military instructor at USAFA	53	−0.09	2	4	5	3	3	1
AFGHAN HANDS assignment	71	0.19	0.6	0	1	1	3	0
Core 19Z (Special Warfare)	67	0.16	1	0	0	1	0	1
Decoration higher than an MSM	55	0.03	17	12	19	23	17	17

NOTES: Avg. = average; ISS = Intermediate Service School; JCS = Joint Chiefs of Staff; OSD = Office of the Secretary of Defense. Adjusted R^2 = 0.65.

Appendix D. Augmenting Regression Analysis with Textual Analysis

During a board selection process, raters supply comments about their nominees that are visible to the selection board. These comments provide additional information in support of the candidate and can contain subtle differences in language that are understood by both the rater and board as representing differences in rater support and enthusiasm for the candidate. Here, we employ text analysis to understand how (1) raters talk about candidates, and (2) these rater comments affect board selection.

NLP is a class of techniques for developing software for automatic or semiautomatic understanding and manipulation of human language. NLP is a branch of artificial intelligence that enables computers to understand and interpret human language. Many advances in NLP have been developed in recent years with various applications: language translation and transcription, personal assistant devices, and text classification for scientific applications. Here, we aim to use NLP to analyze comments supplied by raters of nominees of Developmental Educational Selection Boards. We explore three key questions:

- Do rater comments differ depending on the enthusiasm of the rater?
- Do comments substantially influence the board selection process?
- Do comments differ by race or gender of the nominee?

The challenge is to provide an NLP framework to identify aspects of a rater's comment that indicate both the rater's enthusiasm and success in convincing board members that the nominee should be selected over others. We also analyzed the comments for any indications that comments differ by the race of the nominee. Our research program for this report is a two-step process. First, we draw from expertise on our team to build algorithms that detect raters' tendencies in writing their comments. We built algorithms that detected the presence of *white space* in the comment box, a key sign that the rater is not enthusiastic about the candidate. We looked for other indicators of enthusiasm, such as the presence of an exclamation point, the use of the nominee's first or last name or nickname; the presence of positive or negative language in the rater's entire comment; the presence of strong "push language" in the rater's final sentence (a normal practice among enthusiastic raters); the number and quality of the listed rankings and stratifications mentioned in the rater comment; and the presence of the rater's signature in the comment box. All these factors were listed as potential contributors to both expressions of rater enthusiasm and factors that the board will understand and interpret as indicators of enthusiasm. The results of these initial analyses are described in more detail in Table D.1.

Table D.1. Text Features of Senior Rater Comments for IDE and SDE Boards

Question	Justification as a Measure of Enthusiasm	Justification as a Measure of Strategy	Measure	Correlation with SR Ranking	Correlation with Board Selection	Takeaway
Is the SR comment unique?	SRs may put minimal effort into candidate comments when they are not enthusiastic.	A board may infer the SR is signaling that the nominee is not a good candidate.	Within-rater uniqueness of comment	No	None	SRs almost never do this.
Did the SR use expressive punctuation?	SRs may use exclamation points to express enthusiasm.	A board may consider an expressive tone as indication of a nominee's value.	Presence of an exclamation point in the comment	Yes	None	SRs often include exclamation points to express enthusiasm, but it did not affect board selection.
How long was the comment?	SRs may be more verbose to express enthusiasm.	A board may see white space in a comment box as an indication of low enthusiasm.	1) Length in characters; 2) length in characters divided by rater average	Yes	Yes	White space in the comment box was a major predictor of both the SR's ranking and board selection.
Did the SR mention the nominee's name or nickname?	SRs may express familiarity or informal relationship signals to telegraph enthusiasm.	A board may see indicators of friendship or familiarity with leadership as an indicator of confidence.	Binary mention of first name, last name, and/or nickname	Yes	No	SRs used names to establish familiarity for their highest-ranked nominees, but this feature did not appear to sway the board in its selection process.
Did the SR include their signature in the comment?	Signature verifies that the SR is making the comment.	A board may wonder whether the SR is making the comment.	Binary presence of signature in comment	Yes	No	SRs used signatures, but this did not appear to sway the board.
What stratifications did the rater mention in the comment?	SRs may express enthusiasm by searching for and mentioning rankings earned by the candidate.	Board members may be swayed by a history of impressive awards otherwise not listed in the candidate's record.	Rankings and ranking importance as considered by RAND researcher with Air Force experience	Yes	Yes	Mentioning stratifications appears to influence board decisions in both directions: High stratifications work in the nominee's favor, while low stratifications

Question	Justification as a Measure of Enthusiasm	Justification as a Measure of Strategy	Measure	Correlation with SR Ranking	Correlation with Board Selection	Takeaway
						appear to work against the nominee's advancement by the board.
Did the rater express positive sentiment in their comment?	SRs may use expressive, positive language to express enthusiasm.	Boards may implicitly or explicitly interpret positive language as a positive sign for a nominee.	$\dfrac{pos_{rn}}{mean(pos_r)}$	Yes	No	Raters used positive language to signal enthusiasm, but this language did not have an impact on board selection.
Did the rater express negative sentiment in their comment?	SRs may use negative language to indicate a candidate's value.	Boards may implicitly or explicitly interpret negative language in determining a candidate's value.	$\dfrac{neg_{rn}}{mean(neg_r)}$	Yes	Yes	Raters employ negative language to describe a good candidate, using aggressive-sounding language such as "crush " or "defeat" (i.e., an enemy).
Did the rater express neutral sentiment in their comment?	SRs may be neutral on a candidate to express low enthusiasm.	The board may interpret a neutral sentiment as an indicator of low enthusiasm.	$\dfrac{pos_{rn} + neg_{rn}}{mean(pos_r + neg_r)}$	Yes	No	Low neutrality had no effect on board selection outside of the use of language.
Did the rater use strong "push language" in their comment?	SRs may use specific terms that indicate enthusiasm.	The board may interpret specific words as positive or negative.	Binary inclusion of specific terms ("recommend," "send")	Yes	Yes	While many words were associated with an SR's ranking, only the word "perfect" seemed to affect the board's decision.

The next step of the research process was to go beyond expert-guided algorithm construction to a more automated detection of text features that may affect the board selection process. Using all rater comments from the previous five years (i.e., those visible to the board), we attempted to do this with a two-step process. First, we matched each comment against a pretrained sentiment analysis dataset from the NRC Word-Emotion Association Lexicon.[92] This lexicon consists of ten separate sentiment types built from a massive effort of human input: trust, fear, negative sentiment, sadness, anger, surprise, positive, disgust, joy, and anticipation. Each comment was assigned a score for the use of these sentiments. To find any clusters of keywords beyond these sentiments, we applied Principal Component Analysis (PCA) to N-grams of the comment set. Each comment was assigned a 0/1 value for the use of each word found in the entire comment set (words were represented by binary columns across rows representing comments). We then assigned each comment a score corresponding to their representation in each of the first three clusters found using PCA. Once each comment was given a score for each sentiment and each cluster, we entered the scores into a random forest model predicting the race of the nominee. The idea is to determine whether certain sentiments or "latent" features of the comments are associated with one race or gender. The models did poorly in predicting the race or gender of the nominees, suggesting that on average, the comments provided for nominees differed very little by the race or gender of the nominee. A second set of analyses used the same scores but, instead, predicted the combined race of the nominee and the rater; this model did very well, explaining about a third of the variation found in the data. In other words, while nominees were not rated differently according to their race, the nominees' supporting comments did differ by whether the race of the rater matched the race of the nominee. While random forest models are quite useful for prediction, they unfortunately are less useful for explaining why a variable is predicted. In this case, we are not able to determine how the race combination of the rater and ratee matters (e.g., whether White raters comment differently on their Black nominees versus White nominees). Future work could explore this in more detail.

Conclusion

Our analysis found several features of rater comments that influence the board selection process. We are confident that many of these features are intentional strategies used by raters to make a stronger case for their candidates. Some strategies apparently used by raters (e.g., the inclusion of names, nicknames, or signatures) backfired and negatively affected their candidates when presented to the board. Some raters used strategies that made no difference, such as most of the "push" language used in closing remarks. Others were able to successfully influence their board's decision by using strong language that is typically negative in other contexts ("crush" or "defeat"), using the full character set available to them (excluding white space in their comments), and including stratifications not otherwise listed in the candidate's record. While raters' strategies varied in their success, it is clear that selection boards pay attention to SR comments and allow them to inform their decisions about which candidates get selected. We also

---

[92] Saif M. Mohammad and Peter D. Turney, "Crowdsourcing a Word–Emotion Association Lexicon," *Computational Intelligence*, Vol. 29, No. 3, 2013.

found that rater comments did not differ by the race of the nominee, on average, but we did determine that comments depended on the race combination of the rater and ratee.

On the General Use of NLP in Understanding Board Certification

Here, we showed two different approaches for the use of NLP methods for understanding the board certification process. First, we used *expert human input* to build algorithms that detect the tendencies and strategies found in raters' comments. Second, we used *sentiment analysis* and *latent factors using PCA* to detect any unconscious behavior exhibited by the raters and not detected by humans experienced with the process. The first strategy worked with humans familiar with the process; the second strategy worked with automated methods to determine what may have been missed by the experts. Both strategies are vitally important aspects of NLP. While our research began with human input and then moved on to more automated methods, other RAND research has attempted to reverse the order of these approaches, with similar results.[93] While the goal of this project was to find text features that differed according to race or gender, any other goal (such as predicting the board's score itself, regardless whether it differs by race) should use a similar approach. Though NLP methods cannot think in the same way that a human can, they can be used in this way to achieve clearly defined goals, such as those outlined in this report.

---

[93] David Schulker, Nelson Lim, Luke J. Matthews, Geoffrey E. Grimm, Anthony Lawrence, and Perry Shameem Firoz, *Can Artificial Intelligence Help Improve Air Force Talent Management? An Exploratory Application*, Santa Monica, Calif.: RAND Corporation, RR-A812-1, 2021.

Appendix E. Look-Alike Analysis

This appendix of Chapter 4 provides some of the technical details of the analyses conducted, as well as the full results of the analyses presented in the report.

Purpose of Look-Alike Analyses: Exploring Cause and Effect

The evaluation of the impact of the rule changes in the CPME board process is designed to assess cause and effect: whether the new rules really led to changes in board ranking and that the changes are not explained by the characteristics of the different groups being compared. The ability to draw conclusions about cause and effect has traditionally hinged upon randomly assigning individuals to a treatment or control group, administering a treatment or change to the treatment group, and then comparing the outcomes to the control group. Properly implemented, random assignment allows estimation of causal effects because it ensures, in the long run, that any differences between the treatment (e.g., Black) and comparison groups (e.g., White) aside from group assignment before the CPME rule changes are due to chance.

However, in many cases, such as this evaluation, random assignments are not possible: Service members cannot be randomly assigned to be White or Black or to be a man or a woman to assess whether the CPME board ranking process leads to any disparity. In cases such as these, we can use look-alike analysis—a method to make the characteristics of Black and White groups or men and women equivalent except for their race, gender, or other target characteristic—to test a hypothesis about cause and effect.[94] This method mimics randomization when direct randomization is not possible.

One such approach to causality, the Rubin Causal Model,[95] defines causal effect as the true impact of race or gender on a given outcome. In this case, we explore the causal effect on CPME board rankings—that is, what the board ranking of Black service members would have been if they had been White and what the board ranking would have been for those service members in 2021 had the changes in the board process not been implemented (i.e., the same process as in 2020).

---

[94] William R. Shadish, Thomas D. Cook, and Donald T. Campbell, *Experimental and Quasi-Experimental Designs for Generalized Causal Inference*, Boston, Mass.: Houghton Mifflin, 2002.

[95] P. W. Holland, "Statistics and Causal Inference," *Journal of the American Statistical Association*, Vol. 81, No. 396, 1986; Donald B. Rubin, "Estimating Causal Effects of Treatments in Randomized and Nonrandomized Studies," *Journal of Educational Psychology*, Vol. 66, No. 5, 1974.

Methodology: Doubly Robust Estimation

For both IDE and SDE evaluation, a set of characteristics has been considered as potential factors that can explain observed differences between men and women or between White and minority groups. They include the officers' commission source, OOM, experience, background, technical abilities, assignment history, performance, awards, and career field characteristics. These characteristics will be used to examine whether unexplained differences in the board ranking outcomes exist after accounting for the characteristics. The significant characteristics of interest for this comparison will be those that may be influential to the board ranking process or correlated with positive ranking outcomes. We specifically consider all such metrics that are available in the observed officers' personnel records.

To evaluate how the recent changes affected the outcomes of IDE and SDE boards, we use a statistical technique in the Rubin Causal Model framework known as *doubly robust regression*.[96] The doubly robust estimation combines two statistical methods: the propensity score methods and more traditional regression methods.[97] Both methods are aimed at removing potential confounding factors from the comparison of the board ranking between men and women or between the different race groups. The process involves three steps.

In the first step for the men and women comparison, we set the sample of women as the group of interest (target group) and create a comparison group of men that looks as similar as possible to the group of women in all the relevant career, qualifications, and demographic characteristics. This is accomplished by modeling the probability that an officer in the DE selection pool, with a given set of observed characteristics, is a woman (compared with being a man). These estimated probabilities, called propensity scores, are then used to weight the sample of men in the dataset, such that men with characteristics more like women, or those with the higher propensity scores, receive a higher weight in the analyses. When gender differences exist among these characteristics, dissimilar men provide little predictive power regarding the CPME board ranking decisions of women, and their "full" inclusion in the analysis risks a disproportionate leverage on the range of characteristic values that are rarer among women when conducting a traditional regression analysis. The end result of the weighting process is a comparison group of men that looks as similar as possible to the observed women on the distribution of each characteristic of interest.

---

[96] Heejung Bang and James M. Robins, "Doubly Robust Estimation and Missing Data and Causal Inference Models," *Biometrics*, Vol. 61, No. 4, 2005; Joseph D. Y. Kang and Joseph L. Schafer, "Demystifying Double Robustness: A Comparison of Alternative Strategies for Estimating a Population Mean from Incomplete Data," *Statistical Science*, Vol. 22, No. 4, 2007.

[97] Paul R. Rosenbaum and Donald B. Rubin, "The Central Role of the Propensity Score in Observational Studies for Causal Effects," *Biometrika*, Vol. 70, No. 1, 1983.

We estimated propensity scores using generalized boosted models,[98] a flexible nonparametric technique that iteratively captures the relationship between a set of characteristics and gender with less bias than traditional linear or logistic regression.[99] We estimated propensity scores separately for each gender, as well as for the race comparison where the White group is compared with Black, Asian, and Hispanic groups separately to optimize each comparison. However, even when using the propensity score weights, there is always the possibility of small differences in characteristics remaining between the comparison group and the women.

In the second step of the analysis, the doubly robust estimation method reduced the potential bias caused by any of these remaining differences using a regression model. In the case of the CPME board ranking, we used a weighted linear regression to estimate the board ranking, where male observations (or the comparison group) were weighted as per the propensity scoring process discussed above (and women or the group of interest each received a weight of one full observation). For the top-tier ranking (being in the top 25 percent of the class), a logistic model was used instead of the linear model to estimate the likelihood of being in the top tier. In the model, we again controlled for the observed demographic and career characteristics and included an indicator for gender. If the estimated regression coefficient for gender differed from zero in this weighted regression model (i.e., was statistically significant), that indicated that the demographic and career characteristics being considered did not fully explain why the board ranking outcomes of women differ from those of men.

For the logistic regressions, the coefficient represents the log-odd of being in the top tier and did not cleanly inform the magnitude of a significant difference in terms of proportion of being ranked in the top tier. So, for ease of interpretation, we used a prediction method (a recycling method) to estimate the likelihood of top-tier ranking of each member of a group and computed the average within the group as the overall model-adjusted proportion of the top ranked for that group for comparison, since after application of the propensity score weights, the distribution of the groups being compared were very similar. To do so, we first recoded the observations of women as men and observed their estimated outcomes from the prediction in the fitted model, along with the standard errors of those estimates. Note that recoding the women in the dataset as men produced the hypothetical set of men that we are interested in (those with the exact same demographic and career characteristics observed among the women), and their estimated outcomes were an estimate of the female counterfactual outcomes. If the weighted logistic regression model indicated that a significant difference in gender top-tier rates still existed after accounting for the relevant characteristics, an estimate of the magnitude of that difference was

---

[98] G. Ridgeway, D. Madigan, and T. Richardson, "Boosting Methodology for Regression Problems," in D. Heckerman and J. Whittaker, eds., *Proceedings of Artificial Intelligence and Statistics '99*, 1999.

[99] D. F. McCaffrey, G. Ridgeway, and A. R. Morral, "Propensity Score Estimation with Boosted Regression for Evaluating Causal Effects in Observational Studies," *Psychological Methods*, Vol. 9, No. 4, 2004; Anastasios A. Tsiatis and Marie Davidian, "Comment: Demystifying Double Robustness: A Comparison of Alternative Strategies for Estimating a Population Mean from Incomplete Data," *Statistical Science*, Vol. 22, No. 4, 2007.

obtained by comparing the observed proportion of women in the top-tier group to the estimated proportion of the hypothetical comparison group of men in such top-tier group, i.e., by comparing the rate of women in the top tier to the estimated female counterfactual rate.

In the final step of the analysis, we compared the estimate of the disparity in the 2020 board ranking to the estimate of the disparity in 2021. If the new rules had been effective, any observed disparity in 2020 would have disappeared by 2021.

IDE Analyses

Men and Women Comparisons

For the analysis comparing men to women, the report presented an abbreviated table of the significant difference in characteristics between men and women. Tables E.1a and E.1b report these for all characteristics used in the models:

Table E.1a. IDE Comparison of Gender of Unweighted Characteristic of the Sample and Their Propensity Score Weighted Estimates in 2020

Distribution by GENDER		2020 Sample Distribution					
		Unweighted Estimates			Propensity Score Weighted Estimates		
Label	Levels	Men	Women	p-value	Men	Women	p-value
Race group	(%, n) Asian	4.11	5.92	**0.006**	5.15	5.92	0.970
	(%, n) Black	4.39	7.32		8.38	7.32	
	(%, n) Hispanic	2.76	3.83		3.93	3.83	
	(%, n) NoResponse	4.61	6.62		5.69	6.62	
	(%, n) OtherRace	3.61	6.27		5.16	6.27	
	(%, n) White	80.51	70.03		71.69	70.03	
DA	(%, n) No	85.4	76.31	**0.000**	76.92	76.31	0.865
	(%, n) Yes	14.6	23.69		23.08	23.69	
No DA chance: Some SRs were not allowed to award DAs. 1=Yes, 0=No	(%, n) No	76.97	77.7	0.787	77.43	77.7	0.939
	(%, n) Yes	23.03	22.3		22.57	22.3	
DG from: USAFA, Reserve Officer Training Corps, or OTS: 1=Yes, 0=No	(%, n) No	88.09	88.85	0.717	89.84	88.85	0.704
	(%, n) Yes	11.91	11.15		10.16	11.15	
DG from SOS	(%, n) No	83.77	90.94	**0.002**	90.39	90.94	0.823
	(%, n) Yes	16.23	9.06		9.61	9.06	
Promoted Above the Zone to Major	(%, n) No	98.51	100	**0.038**	99.23	100	0.135
	(%, n) Yes	1.49	0		0.77	0	
Weapons School Graduate	(%, n) No	89.16	94.08	**0.011**	94.1	94.08	0.990
	(%, n) Yes	10.84	5.92		5.9	5.92	
Number of MSM awarded	(%, n) 0	53.22	39.72	**0.000**	44.74	39.72	0.618
	(%, n) 1	35.93	40.07		38.13	40.07	
	(%, n) 2	8.65	15.68		12.82	15.68	
	(%, n) 3+	2.2	4.53		4.31	4.53	
Number of times an individual has met the IDE CPME board	(%, n) 1st	29.2	38.33	**0.008**	27.83	38.33	**0.031**
	(%, n) 2nd	39.19	32.75		38.71	32.75	
	(%, n) Last	31.61	28.92		33.46	28.92	
AETC: Member currently assigned to Air Education and Training Command	(%, n) No	86.53	91.99	**0.011**	91.79	91.99	0.933
	(%, n) Yes	13.47	8.01		8.21	8.01	
PACAF: Member currently assigned to Pacific Air Force 1=Yes, 0=No	(%, n) No	93.69	94.08	0.806	94.23	94.08	0.939
	(%, n) Yes	6.31	5.92		5.77	5.92	
SR's Rank (Grade)	(%, n) 4-star general	1.06	3.14	**0.000**	3.2	3.14	0.716
	(%, n) 3-stars	3.61	6.97		6.63	6.97	
	(%, n) 2-stars	13.54	15.33		20.17	15.33	
	(%, n) 1-star	17.43	24.04		18.97	24.04	
	(%, n) Colonel	58.82	46.34		46.13	46.34	
	(%, n) Senior Executive Service	4.82	3.48		4.04	3.48	

Distribution by GENDER		2020 Sample Distribution					
		Unweighted Estimates			Propensity Score Weighted Estimates		
Label	Levels	Men	Women	p-value	Men	Women	p-value
	(%, n) All Other	0.71	0.7		0.86	0.7	
Member has one of many possible assignment limitations.	(%, n) No	83.7	78.4	**0.030**	77.47	78.4	0.791
	(%, n) Yes	16.3	21.6		22.53	21.6	
Member had a bad Assignment Availability Code within the 5 years prior to the CPME board.	(%, n) No	99.29	99.65	0.488	99.16	99.65	0.445
	(%, n) Yes	0.71	0.35		0.84	0.35	
Member failed the fitness test within the 5 years prior to the CPME board.	(%, n) No	96.81	97.91	0.320	98.13	97.91	0.854
	(%, n) Yes	3.19	2.09		1.87	2.09	
Member had an Unfavorable Information File within the 5 years prior to the CPME board.	(%, n) No	99.5	99.65	0.739	99.54	99.65	0.838
	(%, n) Yes	0.5	0.35		0.46	0.35	
Member has been an aide (administrative assistant) to a high-ranking officer.	(%, n) No	98.87	97.21	**0.031**	96.06	97.21	0.449
	(%, n) Yes	1.13	2.79		3.94	2.79	
Member held a job in the Joint Chiefs of Staff or Office of Secretary of Defense within the 5 years prior to the CPME board.	(%, n) No	99.15	99.3	0.793	98.86	99.3	0.581
	(%, n) Yes	0.85	0.7		1.14	0.7	
Member was the Executive Officer for a high-ranking official within the 5 years prior to the CPME board.	(%, n) No	95.11	89.2	**0.000**	89.82	89.2	0.811
	(%, n) Yes	4.89	10.8		10.18	10.8	
Member was the Executive Officer for a high-ranking official earlier than 5 years prior to the CPME board.	(%, n) No	99.36	99.65	0.559	99.32	99.65	0.580
	(%, n) Yes	0.64	0.35		0.68	0.35	
Member was the Executive Officer for a lower-ranking official within the 5 years prior to the CPME board.	(%, n) No	65.13	57.49	**0.014**	58.95	57.49	0.726
	(%, n) Yes	34.87	42.51		41.05	42.51	
Member was the Executive Officer for a lower-ranking official earlier than 5 years prior to the CPME board.	(%, n) No	86.46	83.97	0.267	84.21	83.97	0.940
	(%, n) Yes	13.54	16.03		15.79	16.03	
Core ID: 13M=Airfield Operations 14=Intelligence 19Z=Special Warfare 31=Security Forces	(%, n) 13M	0.71	1.39	**0.000**	0.87	1.39	0.074
	(%, n) 14	6.59	15.33		9.18	15.33	
	(%, n) 19Z						
	(%, n) 31	2.13	1.39		3.03	1.39	
	(%, n) 63	4.82	3.83		6.63	3.83	
	(%, n) Other	85.75	78.05		80.28	78.05	
Member has one of the following Duty AFSC Prefixes: Prefix F, K, Q, W.	(%, n) No	51.31	72.13	**0.000**	71.86	72.13	0.945
	(%, n) Yes	48.69	27.87		28.14	27.87	

110

Table E.1b. IDE Comparison of Gender of Unweighted Characteristic of the Sample and Their Propensity Score Weighted Estimates in 2021

Distribution by GENDER		2021 Sample Distribution					
		Unweighted Estimates			Propensity Score Weighted Estimates		
Label	Levels	Men	Women	p-value	Men	Women	p-value
Race group	(%, n) Asian	3.63	6.84	**0.000**	7	6.84	0.998
	(%, n) Black	4.91	11.41		10.65	11.41	
	(%, n) Hispanic	2.72	2.28		2.14	2.28	
	(%, n) NoResponse	4.91	5.7		5.52	5.7	
	(%, n) OtherRace	3.55	4.18		3.58	4.18	
	(%, n) White	80.29	69.58		71.11	69.58	
DA	(%, n) No	83.84	79.09	0.061	79.05	79.09	0.993
	(%, n) Yes	16.16	20.91		20.95	20.91	
No DA chance: Some SRs were not allowed to award DAs. 1=Yes, 0=No	(%, n) No	78.63	74.14	0.110	73.75	74.14	0.918
	(%, n) Yes	21.37	25.86		26.25	25.86	
DG from: USAFA, Reserve Officer Training Corps, or OTS: 1=Yes, 0=No	(%, n) No	88.29	90.49	0.304	90.81	90.49	0.901
	(%, n) Yes	11.71	9.51		9.19	9.51	
DG from SOS	(%, n) No	83.38	90.49	**0.004**	89.72	90.49	0.769
	(%, n) Yes	16.62	9.51		10.28	9.51	
Promoted above the Zone to Major	(%, n) No	99.17	100	0.138	99.29	100	0.170
	(%, n) Yes	0.83	0		0.71	0	
Weapons School Graduate	(%, n) No	89.05	95.06	**0.003**	94.83	95.06	0.906
	(%, n) Yes	10.95	4.94		5.17	4.94	
Number of MSM awarded	(%, n) 0	53.93	43.35	**0.018**	46.8	43.35	0.747
	(%, n) 1	33.84	41.44		36.9	41.44	
	(%, n) 2	10.12	12.17		13.51	12.17	
	(%, n) 3+	2.11	3.04		2.79	3.04	
Number of times an individual has met the IDE CPME board	(%, n) 1st	26.13	31.18	**0.032**	26.04	31.18	0.103
	(%, n) 2nd	37.54	40.68		37.18	40.68	
	(%, n) Last	36.33	28.14		36.78	28.14	
AETC: Member currently assigned to Air Education and Training Command	(%, n) No	85.42	89.73	0.065	89.74	89.73	0.997
	(%, n) Yes	14.58	10.27		10.26	10.27	
PACAF: Member currently assigned to Pacific Air Force 1=Yes, 0=No	(%, n) No	94.11	91.25	0.083	91.08	91.25	0.943
	(%, n) Yes	5.89	8.75		8.92	8.75	
SR's rank (grade)	(%, n) 4-star general	1.51	1.9	**0.012**	1.77	1.9	0.948
	(%, n) 3-stars	3.1	7.22		6.67	7.22	
	(%, n) 2-stars	10.12	12.55		12.1	12.55	
	(%, n) 1-star	16.92	17.49		16.84	17.49	
	(%, n) Colonel	63.75	55.51		56.43	55.51	
	(%, n) Senior Executive Service	3.47	4.94		4.78	4.94	

111

Distribution by GENDER		2021 Sample Distribution					
		Unweighted Estimates			Propensity Score Weighted Estimates		
Label	Levels	Men	Women	p-value	Men	Women	p-value
	(%, n) All Other	1.13	0.38		1.4	0.38	
Member has one of many possible assignment limitations.	(%, n) No	82.78	77.57	**0.045**	76.72	77.57	0.819
	(%, n) Yes	17.22	22.43		23.28	22.43	
Member had a bad Assignment Availability Code within the 5 years prior to the CPME board.	(%, n) No	99.17	100	0.138	98.72	100	0.066
	(%, n) Yes	0.83	0		1.28	0	
Member failed the fitness test within the 5 years prior to the CPME board.	(%, n) No	97.66	97.34	0.756	97.59	97.34	0.857
	(%, n) Yes	2.34	2.66		2.41	2.66	
Member had an Unfavorable Information File within the 5 years prior to the CPME board.	(%, n) No	99.02	100	0.107	99.14	100	0.132
	(%, n) Yes	0.98	0		0.86	0	
Member has been an aide (administrative assistant) to a high-ranking officer.	(%, n) No	99.24	98.86	0.527	98.92	98.86	0.948
	(%, n) Yes	0.76	1.14		1.08	1.14	
Member held a job in the Joint Chiefs of Staff or Office of Secretary of Defense within the 5 years prior to the CPME board.	(%, n) No	99.4	99.24	0.770	99.37	99.24	0.861
	(%, n) Yes	0.6	0.76		0.63	0.76	
Member was the Executive Officer for a high-ranking official within the 5 years prior to the CPME board.	(%, n) No	94.18	89.35	**0.004**	90.17	89.35	0.760
	(%, n) Yes	5.82	10.65		9.83	10.65	
Member was the Executive Officer for a high-ranking official earlier than 5 years prior to the CPME board.	(%, n) No	99.47	98.48	0.076	99.48	98.48	0.260
	(%, n) Yes	0.53	1.52		0.52	1.52	
Member was the Executive Officer for a lower-ranking official within the 5 years prior to the CPME board.	(%, n) No	65.03	57.79	**0.026**	59.07	57.79	0.769
	(%, n) Yes	34.97	42.21		40.93	42.21	
Member was the Executive Officer for a lower-ranking official earlier than 5 years prior to the CPME board.	(%, n) No	88.6	83.65	**0.025**	84.01	83.65	0.912
	(%, n) Yes	11.4	16.35		15.99	16.35	
Core ID: 13M=Airfield Operations 14=Intelligence 19Z=Special Warfare 31=Security Forces	(%, n) 13M	0.76	1.52	**0.000**	1.34	1.52	**0.002**
	(%, n) 14	7.85	18.25		9.02	18.25	
	(%, n) 19Z	1.96	0		2.2	0	
	(%, n) 31	2.42	0.76		3.43	0.76	
	(%, n) 63	3.78	6.46		6.53	6.46	
	(%, n) Other	83.23	73		77.48	73	
Member has one of the following Duty AFSC Prefixes: Prefix F, K, Q, W.	(%, n) No	50	74.14	**0.000**	72.97	74.14	0.763
	(%, n) Yes	50	25.86		27.03	25.86	

Racial and Ethnic Groups Comparisons

For the analysis comparing White to Black, Asian, and Hispanic, the report presented the table of the significant difference in characteristics between men and women. Tables E.2a through E.2d report these for all characteristics used in the models:

Table E.2a. IDE Comparison of Racial and Ethnic Groups of Unweighted Characteristics in 2020 Before Propensity Score Weighting

Distribution by Race and Ethnicity		2020 Observed Estimates				
Label	Levels	Asian	Black	Hispanic	White	P-value
Gender female: 1=Yes, 0=No	(%, n) No	77.33	74.7	78	84.97	**0.006**
	(%, n) Yes	22.67	25.3	22	15.03	
DA: 1=Yes, 0=No	(%, n) No	85.33	79.52	86	84.67	0.113
	(%, n) Yes	14.67	20.48	14	15.33	
No DA chance: Some SRs were not allowed to award DAs: 1=Yes, 0=No	(%, n) No	70.67	66.27	54	79.21	**0.000**
	(%, n) Yes	29.33	33.73	46	20.79	
DG from: USAFA, Reserve Officer Training Corps, or OTS: 1=Yes, 0=No	(%, n) No	92	91.57	92	87.43	0.444
	(%, n) Yes	8	8.43	8	12.57	
DG from SOS: 1=Yes, 0=No	(%, n) No	90.67	96.39	98	82.95	**0.000**
	(%, n) Yes	9.33	3.61	2	17.05	
Promoted above the Zone to Major: 1=Yes, 0=No	(%, n) No	96	97.59	96	99.4	**0.000**
	(%, n) Yes	4	2.41	4	0.6	
Weapons School graduate: 1=Yes, 0=No	(%, n) No	92	95.18	92	89.3	0.479
	(%, n) Yes	8	4.82	8	10.7	
Number of MSM awarded. Visible to the CPME board	(%, n) 0	56	44.58	40	51.76	0.712
	(%, n) 1	29.33	42.17	42	36.2	
	(%, n) 2	12	9.64	14	9.5	
	(%, n) 3+	2.67	3.61	4	2.54	
Number of times an individual has met the IDE CPME board	(%, n) 1st	36	34.94	22	30.59	0.635
	(%, n) 2nd	28	30.12	42	38.89	
	(%, n) Last	36	34.94	36	30.52	
AETC: Member currently assigned to Air Education and Training Command: 1=Yes, 0=No	(%, n) No	93.33	90.36	88	87.06	0.423
	(%, n) Yes	6.67	9.64	12	12.94	
PACAF: Member currently assigned to Pacific Air Force: 1=Yes, 0=No	(%, n) No	96	96.39	94	93.34	0.783
	(%, n) Yes	4	3.61	6	6.66	
SR's Rank (grade): O-10=4-star general, O-9=3-stars, O-8=2-stars, O-7=1-star, O-6=Colonel, SES=Senior Executive Service, Other=All other SRs. SESs are Civil Service equivalents of General Officers.	(%, n) 4-star general	4	1.2	4	1.12	**0.000**
	(%, n) 3-stars	4	7.23	4	3.89	
	(%, n) 2-stars	12	20.48	18	13.84	
	(%, n) 1-star	16	27.71	12	18.4	
	(%, n) Colonel	54.67	36.14	46	58.19	
	(%, n) Senior Executive Service	8	6.02	16	4.04	
	(%, n) All Other	1.33	1.2	0	0.52	
Member has one of many possible assignment limitations.	(%, n) No	86.67	75.9	82	83.47	0.319
	(%, n) Yes	13.33	24.1	18	16.53	
Member had a bad Assignment Availability Code within the 5 years prior to the CPME board	(%, n) No	100	96.39	100	99.48	**0.017**
	(%, n) Yes	0	3.61	0	0.52	
Member failed the fitness test within the 5 years prior to the CPME board.	(%, n) No	97.33	95.18	100	97.01	0.759
	(%, n) Yes	2.67	4.82	0	2.99	

113

Distribution by Race and Ethnicity		2020 Observed Estimates				
Label	Levels	Asian	Black	Hispanic	White	P-value
Member had an Unfavorable Information File within the 5 years prior to the CPME board.	(%, n) No	98.67	100	100	99.63	**0.048**
	(%, n) Yes	1.33	0	0	0.37	
Member has been an aide (administrative assistant) to a high-ranking officer.	(%, n) No	97.33	95.18	100	98.8	**0.047**
	(%, n) Yes	2.67	4.82	0	1.2	
Member held a job in the Joint Chiefs of Staff or Office of Secretary of Defense within the 5 years prior to the CPME board.	(%, n) No	100	100	98	99.33	0.060
	(%, n) Yes	0	0	2	0.67	
Member was the Executive Officer for a high-ranking official within the 5 years prior to the CPME board.	(%, n) No	90.67	92.77	90	94.47	0.448
	(%, n) Yes	9.33	7.23	10	5.53	
Member was the Executive Officer for a high-ranking official earlier than 5 years prior to the CPME board.	(%, n) No	100	97.59	100	99.4	0.274
	(%, n) Yes	0	2.41	0	0.6	
Member was the Executive Officer for a lower-ranking official within the 5 years prior to the CPME board.	(%, n) No	64	54.22	78	63.87	0.154
	(%, n) Yes	36	45.78	22	36.13	
Member was the Executive Officer for a lower-ranking official earlier than 5 years prior to the CPME board.	(%, n) No	82.67	85.54	84	86.46	0.932
	(%, n) Yes	17.33	14.46	16	13.54	
Core ID: 13M=Airfield Operations 14=Intelligence 19Z=Special Warfare 31=Security Forces	(%, n) 13M	0	3.61	0	0.6	**0.011**
	(%, n) 14	5.33	2.41	14	8.3	
	(%, n) 19Z					
	(%, n) 31	1.33	1.2	0	2.24	
	(%, n) 63	4	12.05	6	4.26	
	(%, n) Other	89.33	80.72	80	84.59	
Member has one of the following Duty AFSC Prefixes: Prefix F, K, Q, W.	(%, n) No	61.33	72.29	64	53.03	**0.011**
	(%, n) Yes	38.67	27.71	36	46.97	

Table E.2b. IDE Comparison of Racial and Ethnic Groups of Characteristics in 2020 Weighted with Propensity Score for Balancing

Distribution by Race and Ethnicity		Propensity Score Weight Adjusted Estimates (means or %)								
Label	Levels	Asian	White Weighted	p-value	Black	White Adjusted	p-value	Hispanic	White Adjusted	p-value
Gender female: 1=Yes, 0=No	(%, n) No	77.33	79.46	0.757	74.7	76.41	0.801	78	76.95	0.902
	(%, n) Yes	22.67	20.54		25.3	23.59		22	23.05	
DA: 1=Yes, 0=No	(%, n) No	85.33	87	0.772	79.52	82.54	0.627	86	87.35	0.845
	(%, n) Yes	14.67	13		20.48	17.46		14	12.65	
No DA chance: Some SRs were not allowed to award DAs: 1=Yes, 0=No	(%, n) No	70.67	69.35	0.863	66.27	63.38	0.703	54	54.06	0.995
	(%, n) Yes	29.33	30.65		33.73	36.62		46	45.94	
DG from: USAFA, Reserve Officer Training Corps, or OTS: 1=Yes, 0=No	(%, n) No	92	92.94	0.830	91.57	91.89	0.941	92	92.7	0.898
	(%, n) Yes	8	7.06		8.43	8.11		8	7.3	
DG from SOS: 1=Yes, 0=No	(%, n) No	90.67	91.32	0.892	96.39	96	0.900	98	96.88	0.727
	(%, n) Yes	9.33	8.68		3.61	4		2	3.12	
Promoted above the Zone to Major: 1=Yes, 0=No	(%, n) No	96	98.26	0.421	97.59	99.25	0.405	96	98.57	0.442
	(%, n) Yes	4	1.74		2.41	0.75		4	1.43	
Weapons School graduate: 1=Yes, 0=No	(%, n) No	92	93.53	0.724	95.18	94.6	0.868	92	93.7	0.746
	(%, n) Yes	8	6.47		4.82	5.4		8	6.3	
Number of MSM awarded. Visible to the CPME board	(%, n) 0	56	48.87	0.547	44.58	44.64	0.997	40	44.68	0.887
	(%, n) 1	29.33	40.1		42.17	41.28		42	42.51	
	(%, n) 2	12	8.05		9.64	10.67		14	10.82	
	(%, n) 3+	2.67	2.97		3.61	3.41		4	2	
Number of times an individual has met the IDE CPME board	(%, n) 1st	36	31.92	0.442	34.94	31.79	0.764	22	25.47	0.847
	(%, n) 2nd	28	37.94		30.12	35.55		42	36.53	
	(%, n) Last	36	30.14		34.94	32.65		36	37.99	
AETC: Member currently assigned to Air Education and Training Command: 1=Yes, 0=No	(%, n) No	93.33	92.9	0.919	90.36	90.32	0.993	88	89.76	0.783
	(%, n) Yes	6.67	7.1		9.64	9.68		12	10.24	
PACAF: Member currently assigned to Pacific Air Force: 1=Yes, 0=No	(%, n) No	96	96.32	0.919	96.39	96.39	0.998	94	94.36	0.939
	(%, n) Yes	4	3.68		3.61	3.61		6	5.64	
SR's rank (grade): O-10=4-star general, O-9=3-stars, O-8=2-stars, O-7=1-star, O-6=Colonel, SES=Senior Executive Service, Other=All other SRs. SESs are Civil Service equivalents of General Officers.	(%, n) 4-star general	4	2.43	0.995	1.2	0.92	0.981	4	3.55	0.749
	(%, n) 3-stars	4	2.66		7.23	4.44		4	3.92	
	(%, n) 2-stars	12	13.39		20.48	20.9		18	9.89	
	(%, n) 1-star	16	15.07		27.71	26.74		12	20.49	
	(%, n) Colonel	54.67	57.8		36.14	41.41		46	48.51	
	(%, n) Senior Executive Service	8	7.74		6.02	5.02		16	11.82	
	(%, n) All Other	1.33	0.92		1.2	0.57		0	1.82	
Member has one of many possible assignment limitations.	(%, n) No	86.67	86.83	0.977	75.9	76.64	0.913	82	81.08	0.907
	(%, n) Yes	13.33	13.17		24.1	23.36		18	18.92	

115

Distribution by Race and Ethnicity		Propensity Score Weight Adjusted Estimates (means or %)								
Label	Levels	Asian	White Weighted	p-value	Black	White Adjusted	p-value	Hispanic	White Adjusted	p-value
Member had a bad Assignment Availability Code within the 5 years prior to the CPME board	(%, n) No	100	99.64	0.601	96.39	99.54	0.165	100	99.48	0.608
	(%, n) Yes	0	0.36		3.61	0.46		0	0.52	
Member failed the fitness test within the 5 years prior to the CPME board.	(%, n) No	97.33	97.83	0.847	95.18	96.29	0.730	100	98.45	0.377
	(%, n) Yes	2.67	2.17		4.82	3.71		0	1.55	
Member had an Unfavorable Information File within the 5 years prior to the CPME board.	(%, n) No	98.67	99.45	0.631	100	99.8	0.686	100	99.47	0.606
	(%, n) Yes	1.33	0.55		0	0.2		0	0.53	
Member has been an aide (administrative assistant) to a high-ranking officer.	(%, n) No	97.33	98.42	0.654	95.18	96.72	0.624	100	98.88	0.454
	(%, n) Yes	2.67	1.58		4.82	3.28		0	1.12	
Member held a job in the Joint Chiefs of Staff or Office of Secretary of Defense within the 5 years prior to the CPME board.	(%, n) No	100	98.68	0.318	100	99.21	0.417	98	97.54	0.877
	(%, n) Yes	0	1.32		0	0.79		2	2.46	
Member was the Executive Officer for a high-ranking official within the 5 years prior to the CPME board.	(%, n) No	90.67	92.13	0.755	92.77	92.5	0.948	90	91.32	0.824
	(%, n) Yes	9.33	7.87		7.23	7.5		10	8.68	
Member was the Executive Officer for a high-ranking official earlier than 5 years prior to the CPME board.	(%, n) No	100	99.25	0.451	97.59	99.25	0.405	100	99.56	0.638
	(%, n) Yes	0	0.75		2.41	0.75		0	0.44	
Member was the Executive Officer for a lower-ranking official within the 5 years prior to the CPME board.	(%, n) No	64	64.7	0.930	54.22	54.52	0.970	78	77.32	0.936
	(%, n) Yes	36	35.3		45.78	45.48		22	22.68	
Member was the Executive Officer for a lower-ranking official earlier than 5 years prior to the CPME board.	(%, n) No	82.67	83.38	0.910	85.54	85.36	0.975	84	86.1	0.772
	(%, n) Yes	17.33	16.62		14.46	14.64		16	13.9	
Core ID: 13M=Airfield Operations 14=Intelligence 19Z=Special Warfare 31=Security Forces	(%, n) 13M	0	0.32	0.799	3.61	1.45	0.127	0	0.67	0.560
	(%, n) 14	5.33	8.03		2.41	10.09		14	8.23	
	(%, n) 31	1.33	3.29		1.2	3.53		0	3.67	
	(%, n) 63	4	5.74		12.05	5.9		6	4.69	
	(%, n) Other	89.33	82.62		80.72	79.03		80	82.75	
Member has one of the following Duty AFSC Prefixes: Prefix F, K, Q, W.	(%, n) No	61.33	63.15	0.822	72.29	72.15	0.984	64	63.89	0.991
	(%, n) Yes	38.67	36.85		27.71	27.85		36	36.11	

Table E.2c. IDE Comparison of Race Groups of Unweighted Characteristics in 2021 Before Propensity Score Weighting

Distribution by Race and Ethnicity			2021 Observed Race and Ethnicity Differences					
Label	Levels		Asian	Black	Hispanic	White	Total	P-value
Gender female: 1=Yes, 0=No	(%, n)	No	72.73	68.42	85.71	85.31	83.43	**0.000**
	(%, n)	Yes	27.27	31.58	14.29	14.69	16.57	
DA: 1=Yes, 0=No	(%, n)	No	89.39	81.05	85.71	82.26	83.05	0.395
	(%, n)	Yes	10.61	18.95	14.29	17.74	16.95	
No DA chance: Some SRs were not allowed to award DAs: 1=Yes, 0=No	(%, n)	No	74.24	68.42	59.52	79.45	77.88	**0.004**
	(%, n)	Yes	25.76	31.58	40.48	20.55	22.12	
DG from: USAFA, Reserve Officer Training Corps, or OTS: 1=Yes, 0=No	(%, n)	No	95.45	94.74	95.24	87.08	88.66	**0.012**
	(%, n)	Yes	4.55	5.26	4.76	12.92	11.34	
DG from SOS: 1=Yes, 0=No	(%, n)	No	89.39	93.68	92.86	83.07	84.56	**0.010**
	(%, n)	Yes	10.61	6.32	7.14	16.93	15.44	
Promoted above the Zone to Major: 1=Yes, 0=No	(%, n)	No	96.97	100	92.86	99.6	99.31	**0.000**
	(%, n)	Yes	3.03	0	7.14	0.4	0.69	
Weapons School graduate: 1=Yes, 0=No	(%, n)	No	93.94	92.63	90.48	89.57	90.04	0.811
	(%, n)	Yes	6.06	7.37	9.52	10.43	9.96	
Number of MSM awarded. Visible to the CPME board	(%, n) 0		60.61	43.16	28.57	53.29	52.17	**0.035**
	(%, n) 1		25.76	35.79	47.62	34.91	35.1	
	(%, n) 2		10.61	15.79	21.43	9.63	10.46	
	(%, n) 3+		3.03	5.26	2.38	2.17	2.27	
Number of times an individual has met the IDE CPME board	(%, n) 1st		30.3	27.37	28.57	26.48	26.97	0.558
	(%, n) 2nd		39.39	43.16	35.71	37	38.06	
	(%, n) Last		30.3	29.47	35.71	36.52	34.97	
AETC: Member currently assigned to Air Education and Training Command: 1=Yes, 0=No	(%, n)	No	86.36	90.53	80.95	86.28	86.14	0.633
	(%, n)	Yes	13.64	9.47	19.05	13.72	13.86	
PACAF: Member currently assigned to Pacific Air Force: 1=Yes, 0=No	(%, n)	No	89.39	95.79	95.24	93.74	93.64	0.219
	(%, n)	Yes	10.61	4.21	4.76	6.26	6.36	
SR's rank (grade). O-10=4-star general, O-9=3-stars, O-8=2-stars, O-7=1-star, O-6=Colonel, SES=Senior Executive Service, Other=All other SRs. SESs are Civil Service equivalents of General Officers.	(%, n) 4-star general		0	4.21	0	1.61	1.58	0.156
	(%, n) 3-stars		4.55	3.16	2.38	3.69	3.78	
	(%, n) 2-stars		12.12	15.79	9.52	9.79	10.52	
	(%, n) 1-star		19.7	17.89	28.57	17.01	17.01	
	(%, n) Colonel		60.61	50.53	47.62	63.48	62.38	
	(%, n) Senior Executive Service		3.03	6.32	11.9	3.37	3.72	
	(%, n) All Other		0	2.11	0	1.04	1.01	
Member has one of many possible assignment limitations.	(%, n)	No	81.82	80	64.29	82.66	81.92	0.076
	(%, n)	Yes	18.18	20	35.71	17.34	18.08	
Member had a bad Assignment Availability Code within the 5 years prior to the CPME board	(%, n)	No	100	97.89	100	99.44	99.31	0.407
	(%, n)	Yes	0	2.11	0	0.56	0.69	
Member failed the fitness test within the 5 years prior to the CPME board.	(%, n)	No	96.97	96.84	97.62	97.67	97.61	0.992
	(%, n)	Yes	3.03	3.16	2.38	2.33	2.39	

117

Distribution by Race and Ethnicity			2021 Observed Race and Ethnicity Differences					
Label	Levels		Asian	Black	Hispanic	White	Total	P-value
Member had an Unfavorable Information File within the 5 years prior to the CPME board.	(%, n)	No	100	98.95	100	99.2	99.18	0.518
	(%, n)	Yes	0	1.05	0	0.8	0.82	
Member has been an aide (administrative assistant) to a high-ranking officer.	(%, n)	No	100	97.89	97.62	99.36	99.18	0.417
	(%, n)	Yes	0	2.11	2.38	0.64	0.82	
Member held a job in the Joint Chiefs of Staff or Office of Secretary of Defense within the 5 years prior to the CPME board.	(%, n)	No	98.48	98.95	100	99.6	99.37	**0.010**
	(%, n)	Yes	1.52	1.05	0	0.4	0.63	
Member was the Executive Officer for a high-ranking official within the 5 years prior to the CPME board.	(%, n)	No	92.42	93.68	78.57	94.22	93.38	**0.003**
	(%, n)	Yes	7.58	6.32	21.43	5.78	6.62	
Member was the Executive Officer for a high-ranking official earlier than 5 years prior to the CPME board.	(%, n)	No	98.48	100	100	99.2	99.31	0.733
	(%, n)	Yes	1.52	0	0	0.8	0.69	
Member was the Executive Officer for a lower-ranking official within the 5 years prior to the CPME board.	(%, n)	No	71.21	76.84	61.9	62.84	63.83	0.050
	(%, n)	Yes	28.79	23.16	38.1	37.16	36.17	
Member was the Executive Officer for a lower-ranking official earlier than 5 years prior to the CPME board.	(%, n)	No	80.3	83.16	85.71	88.68	87.78	0.205
	(%, n)	Yes	19.7	16.84	14.29	11.32	12.22	

Core ID:
    13M=Airfield Operations
    14=Intelligence
    19Z=Special Warfare
    31=Security Forces
	(%, n)	13M	0	2.11	2.38	0.8	0.88	**0.047**

	(%, n)	14	7.58	12.63	11.9	9.63	9.58	
	(%, n)	19Z	0	1.05	0	1.77	1.64	
	(%, n)	31	1.52	1.05	0	2.33	2.14	
	(%, n)	63	6.06	13.68	2.38	3.77	4.22	
	(%, n)	Other	84.85	69.47	83.33	81.7	81.54	
Member has one of the following Duty AFSC Prefixes: Prefix F, K, Q, W.	(%, n)	No	71.21	77.89	73.81	50	54	**0.000**
	(%, n)	Yes	28.79	22.11	26.19	50	46	

Table E.2d. IDE Comparison of Racial and Ethnic Groups of Characteristics in 2021 Weighted with Propensity Score for Balancing

Distribution by Race and Ethnicity		Propensity Score Weight-Adjusted Estimates (means or %)								
Label	Levels	Asian	White Weighted	p-value	Black	White Adjusted	p-value	Hispanic	White Adjusted	p-value
Gender female: 1=Yes, 0=No	(%, n) No	72.73	73.6	0.912	68.42	69.75	0.845	85.71	82.09	0.654
	(%, n) Yes	27.27	26.4		31.58	30.25		14.29	17.91	
DA: 1=Yes, 0=No	(%, n) No	89.39	90.22	0.877	81.05	81.25	0.972	85.71	86.17	0.952
	(%, n) Yes	10.61	9.78		18.95	18.75		14.29	13.83	
No DA chance: Some SRs were not allowed to award DAs: 1=Yes, 0=No	(%, n) No	74.24	76.84	0.734	68.42	68.8	0.956	59.52	61.72	0.839
	(%, n) Yes	25.76	23.16		31.58	31.2		40.48	38.28	
DG from: USAFA, Reserve Officer Training Corps, or OTS: 1=Yes, 0=No	(%, n) No	95.45	95.64	0.959	94.74	94.38	0.915	95.24	90.96	0.442
	(%, n) Yes	4.55	4.36		5.26	5.62		4.76	9.04	
DG from SOS: 1=Yes, 0=No	(%, n) No	89.39	89.88	0.929	93.68	93.06	0.863	92.86	88.37	0.484
	(%, n) Yes	10.61	10.12		6.32	6.94		7.14	11.63	
Promoted above the Zone to Major: 1=Yes, 0=No	(%, n) No	96.97	99.64	0.251	100	99.66	0.570	92.86	99.74	0.101
	(%, n) Yes	3.03	0.36		0	0.34		7.14	0.26	
Weapons School graduate: 1=Yes, 0=No	(%, n) No	93.94	93.35	0.892	92.63	92.92	0.939	90.48	92.13	0.791
	(%, n) Yes	6.06	6.65		7.37	7.08		9.52	7.87	
Number of MSM awarded. Visible to the CPME board	(%, n) 0	60.61	48.93	0.601	43.16	43.99	0.719	28.57	45.72	0.381
	(%, n) 1	25.76	35.43		35.79	40.95		47.62	39.91	
	(%, n) 2	10.61	12.49		15.79	11.92		21.43	11.78	
	(%, n) 3+	3.03	3.15		5.26	3.13		2.38	2.58	
Number of times an individual has met the IDE CPME board.	(%, n) 1st	30.3	24.96	0.770	27.37	25.33	0.560	28.57	26.03	0.961
	(%, n) 2nd	39.39	40.34		43.16	37.86		35.71	38.04	
	(%, n) Last	30.3	34.7		29.47	36.8		35.71	35.93	
AETC: Member currently assigned to Air Education and Training Command 1=Yes, 0=No	(%, n) No	86.36	87.45	0.856	90.53	90.25	0.949	80.95	83.83	0.732
	(%, n) Yes	13.64	12.55		9.47	9.75		19.05	16.17	
PACAF: Member currently assigned to Pacific Air Force 1=Yes, 0=No	(%, n) No	89.39	88.41	0.860	95.79	95.56	0.939	95.24	93.91	0.790
	(%, n) Yes	10.61	11.59		4.21	4.44		4.76	6.09	
SR's rank (grade). O-10=4-star general, O-9=3-stars, O-8=2-stars, O-7=1-star, O-6=Colonel, SES=Senior Executive Service, Other=All other SRs. SESs are Civil Service equivalents of General Officers.	(%, n) 4-star general	0	0.83	0.967	4.21	4.18	0.996	0	1.26	0.804
	(%, n) 3-stars	4.55	3.79		3.16	3.44		2.38	4.06	
	(%, n) 2-stars	12.12	11.69		15.79	14.78		9.52	14.85	
	(%, n) 1-star	19.7	18.73		17.89	19.59		28.57	22.25	
	(%, n) Colonel	60.61	59.25		50.53	51.31		47.62	51.54	
	(%, n) Senior Executive Service	3.03	5.08		6.32	5.81		11.9	5.16	
	(%, n) All Other	0	0.64		2.11	0.89		0	0.88	
Member has one of	(%, n) No	81.82	82.37	0.936	80	79.89	0.985	64.29	69.68	0.603

119

Distribution by Race and Ethnicity		Propensity Score Weight-Adjusted Estimates (means or %)								
Label	Levels	Asian	White Weighted	p-value	Black	White Adjusted	p-value	Hispanic	White Adjusted	p-value
many possible assignment limitations.	(%, n) Yes	18.18	17.63		20	20.11		35.71	30.32	
Member had a bad Assignment Availability Code within the 5 years prior to the CPME board	(%, n) No	100	99.47	0.553	97.89	99.54	0.320	100	99.62	0.687
	(%, n) Yes	0	0.53		2.11	0.46		0	0.38	
Member failed the fitness test within the 5 years prior to the CPME board.	(%, n) No	96.97	97.07	0.972	96.84	97.06	0.931	97.62	97.04	0.869
	(%, n) Yes	3.03	2.93		3.16	2.94		2.38	2.96	
Member had an Unfavorable Information File within the 5 years prior to the CPME board.	(%, n) No	100	99.29	0.492	98.95	98.85	0.948	100	99.33	0.594
	(%, n) Yes	0	0.71		1.05	1.15		0	0.67	
Member has been an aide (administrative assistant) to a high-ranking officer.	(%, n) No	100	99.55	0.584	97.89	99.47	0.347	97.62	99.48	0.481
	(%, n) Yes	0	0.45		2.11	0.53		2.38	0.52	
Member held a job in the Joint Chiefs of Staff or Office of Secretary of Defense within the 5 years prior to the CPME board.	(%, n) No	98.48	99.68	0.487	98.95	99.38	0.748	100	99.45	0.631
	(%, n) Yes	1.52	0.32		1.05	0.62		0	0.55	
Member was the Executive Officer for a high-ranking official within the 5 years prior to the CPME board.	(%, n) No	92.42	93.6	0.795	93.68	93.43	0.942	78.57	81.56	0.735
	(%, n) Yes	7.58	6.4		6.32	6.57		21.43	18.44	
Member was the Executive Officer for a high-ranking official earlier than 5 years prior to the CPME board.	(%, n) No	98.48	98.76	0.896	100	98.64	0.254	100	99.41	0.617
	(%, n) Yes	1.52	1.24		0	1.36		0	0.59	
Member was the Executive Officer for a lower-ranking official within the 5 years prior to the CPME board.	(%, n) No	71.21	72.97	0.825	76.84	77.44	0.922	61.9	63.33	0.894
	(%, n) Yes	28.79	27.03		23.16	22.56		38.1	36.67	
Member was the Executive Officer for a lower-ranking official earlier than 5 years prior to the CPME board.	(%, n) No	80.3	82.65	0.734	83.16	82.65	0.927	85.71	86.82	0.884
	(%, n) Yes	19.7	17.35		16.84	17.35		14.29	13.18	
Core ID: 13M=Airfield Operations 14=Intelligence 19Z=Special Warfare	(%, n) 13M	0	0.76	0.796	2.11	0.72	0.508	2.38	0.99	0.731
	(%, n) 14	7.58	9.48		12.63	13.13		11.9	10.07	
	(%, n) 19Z	0	1.69		1.05	1.53		0	1.59	
	(%, n) 31	1.52	3.43		1.05	3.01		0	2.7	
	(%, n) 63	6.06	5.59		13.68	6.4		2.38	5.97	

Distribution by Race and Ethnicity		Propensity Score Weight-Adjusted Estimates (means or %)								
Label	Levels	Asian	White Weighted	p-value	Black	White Adjusted	p-value	Hispanic	White Adjusted	p-value
31=Security Forces	(%, n) Other	84.85	79.06		69.47	75.21		83.33	78.69	
Member has one of the following Duty AFSC Prefixes: Prefix F, K, Q, W	(%, n) No	71.21	69.78	0.860	77.89	77.53	0.952	73.81	67.77	0.546
	(%, n) Yes	28.79	30.22		22.11	22.47		26.19	32.23	

SDE Analyses

Men and Women Comparisons

For the SDE analysis comparing men with women, the report presented an abbreviated table of the significant difference in characteristics between men and women. The tables below report these for all characteristics used in the models:

Table E.3a. SDE Comparison of Gender of Unweighted Characteristic of the Sample and Their Propensity Score Weighted Estimates in 2020

Distribution by Gender			2020 Sample Distribution						
			Unweighted Estimates				Propensity Score Weighted Estimates		
Label	Levels		Men	Women	p-value		Men	Women	p-value
Traditional ISS In-Residence: 1=Yes, 0=No	(%, n) No		56.2	60.34	0.297		61.2	60.34	0.870
	(%, n) Yes		43.8	39.66			38.8	39.66	
SDE completed by correspondence: 1=Yes, 0=No	(%, n) No		65.12	60.89	0.269		62.45	60.89	0.768
	(%, n) Yes		34.88	39.11			37.55	39.11	
Selected for SDE by the central promotion board: 1=Yes, 0=No	(%, n) No		86.78	88.27	0.580		89.48	88.27	0.722
	(%, n) Yes		13.22	11.73			10.52	11.73	
DG from: USAFA, Reserve Officer Training Corps, or OTS	(%, n) No		86.86	84.92	0.476		86.13	84.92	0.750
	(%, n) Yes		13.14	15.08			13.87	15.08	
DG from SOS	(%, n) No		83.97	92.74	**0.002**		90.31	92.74	0.419
	(%, n) Yes		16.03	7.26			9.69	7.26	
Promoted APZ to lieutenant colonel: 1=Yes, 0=No	(%, n) No		98.43	97.21	0.241		97.19	97.21	0.993
	(%, n) Yes		1.57	2.79			2.81	2.79	
Promoted BPZ to lieutenant colonel: 1=Yes, 0=No	(%, n) No		89.83	91.06	0.610		90.42	91.06	0.837
	(%, n) Yes		10.17	8.94			9.58	8.94	
Weapons School graduate	(%, n) No		87.85	97.21	**0.000**		94.94	97.21	0.278
	(%, n) Yes		12.15	2.79			5.06	2.79	
Never a commander: 1=Yes, 0=No	(%, n) No		79.01	74.86	0.208		73.71	74.86	0.807

Distribution by Gender		2020 Sample Distribution						
		Unweighted Estimates				Propensity Score Weighted Estimates		
Label	Levels	Men	Women	p-value		Men	Women	p-value
	(%, n) Yes	20.99	25.14			26.29	25.14	
Stratified in the top 10% by an SR with at least 6 nominees	(%, n) No	98.35	98.88	0.592		98.1	98.88	0.551
	(%, n) Yes	1.65	1.12			1.9	1.12	
Stratified in the top 20% by an SR with at least 6 nominees	(%, n) No	94.13	93.85	0.883		95	93.85	0.645
	(%, n) Yes	5.87	6.15			5	6.15	
Stratified in the top 30% by an SR with at least 6 nominees	(%, n) No	95.37	96.65	0.440		96.38	96.65	0.893
	(%, n) Yes	4.63	3.35			3.62	3.35	
Stratified in the top 40% by an SR with at least 6 nominees	(%, n) No	94.71	96.65	0.269		95.18	96.65	0.491
	(%, n) Yes	5.29	3.35			4.82	3.35	
Stratified in the top 50% by an SR with at least 6 nominees	(%, n) No	93.72	95.53	0.343		95.38	95.53	0.947
	(%, n) Yes	6.28	4.47			4.62	4.47	
Stratified in the top 80% by an SR with at least 6 nominees	(%, n) No	83.14	84.36	0.684		83.94	84.36	0.916
	(%, n) Yes	16.86	15.64			16.06	15.64	
An individual was stratified #1 by an SR with 2 nominees.	(%, n) No	93.8	94.97	0.540		94.52	94.97	0.852
	(%, n) Yes	6.2	5.03			5.48	5.03	
An individual was stratified #1 by an SR with 3 to 5 nominees.	(%, n) No	93.06	95.53	0.214		94.91	95.53	0.789
	(%, n) Yes	6.94	4.47			5.09	4.47	
SR grade: 4 stars	(%, n) No	99.26	97.77	0.053		98.56	97.77	0.588
	(%, n) Yes	0.74	2.23			1.44	2.23	
SR grade: O-9	(%, n) No	92.98	91.06	0.357		91.87	91.06	0.788
	(%, n) Yes	7.02	8.94			8.13	8.94	
SR grade: O-8 or O-7	(%, n) No	63.39	59.22	0.281		58.07	59.22	0.829
	(%, n) Yes	36.61	40.78			41.93	40.78	
Member is in Air Combat Command	(%, n) No	80.74	89.94	**0.003**		88.14	89.94	0.593
	(%, n) Yes	19.26	10.06			11.86	10.06	
Member is in Air Force Special Operations Command: 1=Yes, 0=No	(%, n) No	95.54	97.21	0.301		97.09	97.21	0.948
	(%, n) Yes	4.46	2.79			2.91	2.79	
Member is in Air Mobility Command: 1=Yes, 0=No	(%, n) No	91.32	94.41	0.161		93.7	94.41	0.779
	(%, n) Yes	8.68	5.59			6.3	5.59	
Ever assigned to Headquarters Air Force	(%, n) No	74.13	61.45	**0.000**		61.51	61.45	0.992
	(%, n) Yes	25.87	38.55			38.49	38.55	
Member has been an aide (administrative assistant) to a high-ranking officer within the 5 years prior to the CPME board.	(%, n) No	98.6	96.09	**0.016**		95.35	96.09	0.735
	(%, n) Yes	1.4	3.91			4.65	3.91	
Member was the Executive Officer for a lower-ranking official within the 5 years prior to the CPME board.	(%, n) No	90.25	86.59	0.132		88.82	86.59	0.530
	(%, n) Yes	9.75	13.41			11.18	13.41	
Member had a bad Assignment Availability Code within the 5 years prior to the CPME board	(%, n) No	99.67	100	0.441		99.85	100	0.610
	(%, n) Yes	0.33	0			0.15	0	

Distribution by Gender		2020 Sample Distribution						
		Unweighted Estimates				Propensity Score Weighted Estimates		
Label	Levels	Men	Women	p-value		Men	Women	p-value
Member failed Air Force Fitness Exam within past 5 years: 1=Yes, 0=No	(%, n) No	97.85	97.21	0.586		96.72	97.21	0.794
	(%, n) Yes	2.15	2.79			3.28	2.79	
Is a current instructor: 1=Yes, 0=No	(%, n) No	96.78	94.41	0.110		94.54	94.41	0.958
	(%, n) Yes	3.22	5.59			5.46	5.59	
Age	1. Mean (Std.)	41.28 (3.50)	40.89 (3.33)	0.162		40.82 (1.24)	40.89 (3.33)	0.698
	2. Mean (Std. Err.)	41.28 (0.10)	40.89 (0.25)			40.82 (0.10)	40.89 (0.25)	
Graduate of an HBCU	(%, n) No	98.84	96.09	**0.005**		95.39	96.09	0.750
	(%, n) Yes	1.16	3.91			4.61	3.91	
Graduate of a Hispanic-Serving Institution	(%, n) No	98.26	94.97	**0.005**		96.23	94.97	0.571
	(%, n) Yes	1.74	5.03			3.77	5.03	
Marital Status: 1=Married, 0=Not Married	(%, n) Not Married	4.63	26.82	**0.000**		24.53	26.82	0.629
	(%, n) Married	95.37	73.18			75.47	73.18	
Eliminated from pilot training: 1=Yes, 0=No	(%, n) No	93.64	94.97	0.489		92.9	94.97	0.420
	(%, n) Yes	6.36	5.03			7.1	5.03	
Core ID:. 21=Logistics	(%, n) No	90.25	91.06	0.731		91.29	91.06	0.941
	(%, n) Yes	9.75	8.94			8.71	8.94	
Core ID: 31=Security Forces	(%, n) No	97.19	97.77	0.660		98.16	97.77	0.797
	(%, n) Yes	2.81	2.23			1.84	2.23	
Core ID: 38=Manpower	(%, n) No	98.18	88.83	**0.000**		90.38	88.83	0.638
	(%, n) Yes	1.82	11.17			9.62	11.17	
Current Duty AFSC is 16XX: 1=Yes, 0=No	(%, n) No	93.88	92.18	0.382		90.2	92.18	0.517
	(%, n) Yes	6.12	7.82			9.8	7.82	

NOTE: Std. = standard; Err. = error.

Table E.3b. SDE Comparison of Gender of Unweighted Characteristic of the Sample and Their Propensity Score Weighted Estimates in 2021

Distribution by Gender		2021 Sample Distribution						
		Unweighted Estimates				Propensity Score Weighted Estimates		
Label	Levels	Men	Women	p-value		Men	Women	p-value
Traditional ISS In-Residence: 1=Yes, 0=No	(%, n) No	55.46	58.29	0.470		56.02	58.29	0.665
	(%, n) Yes	44.54	41.71			43.98	41.71	
Other IDE In-Residence: 1=Yes, 0=No	(%, n) No	87.59	86.63	0.714		86.47	86.63	0.963
	(%, n) Yes	12.41	13.37			13.53	13.37	
SDE completed by correspondence: 1=Yes, 0=No	(%, n) No	61.97	59.36	0.496		62.69	59.36	0.518
	(%, n) Yes	38.03	40.64			37.31	40.64	

123

Distribution by Gender		2021 Sample Distribution						
		Unweighted Estimates				Propensity Score Weighted Estimates		
Label	Levels	Men	Women	p-value		Men	Women	p-value
Selected for SDE by the central promotion board: 1=Yes, 0=No	(%, n) No	94.01	93.05	0.610		93.96	93.05	0.726
	(%, n) Yes	5.99	6.95			6.04	6.95	
DG from: USAFA, Reserve Officer Training Corps, or OTS	(%, n) No	85.74	78.61	**0.012**		81.72	78.61	0.461
	(%, n) Yes	14.26	21.39			18.28	21.39	
DG from SOS	(%, n) No	83.54	91.44	**0.005**		87.63	91.44	0.237
	(%, n) Yes	16.46	8.56			12.37	8.56	
Promoted APZ to lieutenant colonel: 1=Yes, 0=No	(%, n) No	97.98	97.33	0.568		97.68	97.33	0.832
	(%, n) Yes	2.02	2.67			2.32	2.67	
Promoted BPZ to lieutenant colonel: 1=Yes, 0=No	(%, n) No	91.29	89.3	0.380		89.58	89.3	0.933
	(%, n) Yes	8.71	10.7			10.42	10.7	
Weapons School graduate	(%, n) No	87.59	95.72	**0.001**		92.96	95.72	0.255
	(%, n) Yes	12.41	4.28			7.04	4.28	
Never a commander: 1=Yes, 0=No	(%, n) No	78.08	81.28	0.323		78.96	81.28	0.582
	(%, n) Yes	21.92	18.72			21.04	18.72	
Stratified in the top 10% by an SR with at least 6 nominees	(%, n) No	98.59	98.93	0.711		98.95	98.93	0.988
	(%, n) Yes	1.41	1.07			1.05	1.07	
Stratified in the top 20% by an SR with at least 6 nominees	(%, n) No	94.54	94.12	0.814		95.21	94.12	0.645
	(%, n) Yes	5.46	5.88			4.79	5.88	
Stratified in the top 30% by an SR with at least 6 nominees	(%, n) No	96.13	94.12	0.202		95.2	94.12	0.649
	(%, n) Yes	3.87	5.88			4.8	5.88	
Stratified in the top 40% by an SR with at least 6 nominees	(%, n) No	95.51	96.79	0.424		96.52	96.79	0.887
	(%, n) Yes	4.49	3.21			3.48	3.21	
Stratified in the top 50% by an SR with at least 6 nominees	(%, n) No	93.93	96.79	0.116		94.16	96.79	0.228
	(%, n) Yes	6.07	3.21			5.84	3.21	
Stratified in the top 80% by an SR with at least 6 nominees	(%, n) No	84.86	83.96	0.751		85.43	83.96	0.698
	(%, n) Yes	15.14	16.04			14.57	16.04	
An individual was stratified #1 by an SR with 2 nominees.	(%, n) No	93.57	95.19	0.397		93.33	95.19	0.449
	(%, n) Yes	6.43	4.81			6.67	4.81	
An individual was stratified #1 by an SR with 3 to 5 nominees.	(%, n) No	93.4	94.12	0.711		93.78	94.12	0.894
	(%, n) Yes	6.6	5.88			6.22	5.88	
SR grade: 4 stars	(%, n) No	99.56	97.33	**0.001**		99.65	97.33	0.076
	(%, n) Yes	0.44	2.67			0.35	2.67	
SR grade: O-9	(%, n) No	93.75	93.05	0.715		92.86	93.05	0.943
	(%, n) Yes	6.25	6.95			7.14	6.95	
SR grade: O-8 or O-7	(%, n) No	64.79	69.52	0.207		66.33	69.52	0.517
	(%, n) Yes	35.21	30.48			33.67	30.48	
Member is in Air Combat Command.	(%, n) No	80.28	87.7	**0.016**		85.07	87.7	0.467

124

Distribution by Gender		2021 Sample Distribution						
		Unweighted Estimates				Propensity Score Weighted Estimates		
Label	Levels	Men	Women	p-value		Men	Women	p-value
	(%, n) Yes	19.72	12.3			14.93	12.3	
Member is in Air Force Special Operations Command: 1=Yes, 0=No	(%, n) No	95.33	96.79	0.371		96.17	96.79	0.747
	(%, n) Yes	4.67	3.21			3.83	3.21	
Member is in Air Mobility Command: 1=Yes, 0=No	(%, n) No	91.55	89.84	0.442		90.3	89.84	0.884
	(%, n) Yes	8.45	10.16			9.7	10.16	
Ever assigned to Headquarters Air Force	(%, n) No	76.85	60.96	**0.000**		63.63	60.96	0.602
	(%, n) Yes	23.15	39.04			36.37	39.04	
Member has been an aide (administrative assistant) to a high-ranking officer within the 5 years prior to the CPME board.	(%, n) No	98.68	96.79	0.056		96.19	96.79	0.758
	(%, n) Yes	1.32	3.21			3.81	3.21	
Member was the Executive Officer for a lower-ranking official within the 5 years prior to the CPME board.	(%, n) No	90.14	90.37	0.921		89.53	90.37	0.791
	(%, n) Yes	9.86	9.63			10.47	9.63	
Member had a bad Assignment Availability Code within the 5 years prior to the CPME board.	(%, n) No	99.56	100	0.363		99.59	100	0.380
	(%, n) Yes	0.44	0			0.41	0	
Member failed Air Force Fitness Exam within last 5 years: 1=Yes, 0=No	(%, n) No	98.86	98.93	0.929		98.74	98.93	0.864
	(%, n) Yes	1.14	1.07			1.26	1.07	
Is a current instructor: 1=Yes, 0=No	(%, n) No	96.13	94.65	0.345		96.57	94.65	0.376
	(%, n) Yes	3.87	5.35			3.43	5.35	
Age	1. Mean (Std.)	41.23 (3.50)	40.51 (3.58)	**0.010**		40.61 (1.38)	40.51 (3.58)	0.623
	2. Mean (Std. Err.)	41.23 (0.10)	40.51 (0.26)			40.61 (0.11)	40.51 (0.26)	
Graduate of an HBCU	(%, n) No	99.21	97.33	**0.020**		97.54	97.33	0.898
	(%, n) Yes	0.79	2.67			2.46	2.67	
Graduate of a Hispanic-Serving Institution	(%, n) No	97.98	96.79	0.306		97.81	96.79	0.554
	(%, n) Yes	2.02	3.21			2.19	3.21	
Marital status: 1=Married, 0=Not married	(%, n) Not Married	5.55	23.53	**0.000**		18.62	23.53	0.255
	(%, n) Married	94.45	76.47			81.38	76.47	
Eliminated from pilot training: 1=Yes, 0=No	(%, n) No	92.69	95.19	0.214		92.77	95.19	0.334
	(%, n) Yes	7.31	4.81			7.23	4.81	
Core ID: 21=Logistics	(%, n) No	90.32	88.77	0.512		90.34	88.77	0.627
	(%, n) Yes	9.68	11.23			9.66	11.23	
Core ID: 31=Security Forces	(%, n) No	96.39	97.33	0.518		97.18	97.33	0.932
	(%, n) Yes	3.61	2.67			2.82	2.67	
Core ID: 38=Manpower	(%, n) No	97.8	89.3	**0.000**		91.11	89.3	0.566
	(%, n) Yes	2.2	10.7			8.89	10.7	
Current Duty AFSC is 16XX: 1=Yes, 0=No	(%, n) No	93.66	92.51	0.555		91.87	92.51	0.819
	(%, n) Yes	6.34	7.49			8.13	7.49	

Racial and Ethnic Groups Comparisons

For the analysis comparing the White group to Black, Asian, and Hispanic groups, the report presented an abbreviated table of the significant difference in characteristics between men and women. The tables below report these for all characteristics used in the models:

Table E.4a. SDE Comparison of Race Groups of Unweighted Characteristics in 2020 Before Propensity Score Weighting

Distribution by Race and Ethnicity		2020 Observed Estimates				
Label	Levels	Asian	Black	Hispanic	White	P-value
Traditional ISS In-Residence: 1=Yes, 0=No	(%, n) No	61.76	62.34	64.71	55.59	0.476
	(%, n) Yes	38.24	37.66	35.29	44.41	
Other IDE In-Residence: 1=Yes, 0=No	(%, n) No	100	100	100	100	
	(%, n) Yes					
SDE completed by correspondence: 1=Yes, 0=No	(%, n) No	64.71	53.25	74.51	64.41	0.150
	(%, n) Yes	35.29	46.75	25.49	35.59	
Selected for SDE by the central promotion board	(%, n) No	85.29	97.4	90.2	85.5	**0.003**
	(%, n) Yes	14.71	2.6	9.8	14.5	
DG from: USAFA, Reserve Officer Training Corps, or OTS: 1=Yes, 0=No	(%, n) No	88.24	90.91	92.16	86.04	0.407
	(%, n) Yes	11.76	9.09	7.84	13.96	
DG from SOS	(%, n) No	85.29	98.7	88.24	83.6	**0.008**
	(%, n) Yes	14.71	1.3	11.76	16.4	
Promoted APZ to lieutenant colonel: 1=Yes, 0=No	(%, n) No	97.06	98.7	98.04	98.38	0.966
	(%, n) Yes	2.94	1.3	1.96	1.62	
Promoted BPZ to lieutenant colonel	(%, n) No	88.24	97.4	94.12	88.83	**0.014**
	(%, n) Yes	11.76	2.6	5.88	11.17	
Weapons School graduate	(%, n) No	97.06	97.4	94.12	87.75	**0.037**
	(%, n) Yes	2.94	2.6	5.88	12.25	
Never a commander: 1=Yes, 0=No	(%, n) No	76.47	77.92	72.55	79.1	0.796
	(%, n) Yes	23.53	22.08	27.45	20.9	
Stratified in the top 10% by an SR with at least 6 nominees	(%, n) No	97.06	97.4	98.04	98.38	0.723
	(%, n) Yes	2.94	2.6	1.96	1.62	
Stratified in the top 20% by an SR with at least 6 nominees	(%, n) No	94.12	97.4	92.16	94.23	0.160
	(%, n) Yes	5.88	2.6	7.84	5.77	
Stratified in the top 30% by an SR with at least 6 nominees	(%, n) No	91.18	96.1	98.04	95.5	0.220
	(%, n) Yes	8.82	3.9	1.96	4.5	
Stratified in the top 40% by an SR with at least 6 nominees	(%, n) No	97.06	97.4	98.04	94.77	0.611
	(%, n) Yes	2.94	2.6	1.96	5.23	
Stratified in the top 50% by an SR with at least 6 nominees	(%, n) No	94.12	97.4	96.08	93.69	0.802
	(%, n) Yes	5.88	2.6	3.92	6.31	

Distribution by Race and Ethnicity		2020 Observed Estimates				
Label	Levels	Asian	Black	Hispanic	White	P-value
Stratified in the top 80% by an SR with at least 6 nominees	(%, n) No	91.18	85.71	88.24	82.07	0.205
	(%, n) Yes	8.82	14.29	11.76	17.93	
An individual was stratified #1 by an SR with 2 nominees.	(%, n) No	94.12	90.91	96.08	94.05	0.859
	(%, n) Yes	5.88	9.09	3.92	5.95	
An individual was stratified #1 by an SR with 3 to 5 nominees.	(%, n) No	88.24	93.51	98.04	93.24	0.230
	(%, n) Yes	11.76	6.49	1.96	6.76	
SR grade: O-10 (4 stars)	(%, n) No	97.06	98.7	98.04	99.1	0.657
	(%, n) Yes	2.94	1.3	1.96	0.9	
SR grade: O-9	(%, n) No	91.18	90.91	94.12	93.15	0.777
	(%, n) Yes	8.82	9.09	5.88	6.85	
SR grade: O-8 or O-7	(%, n) No	50	53.25	58.82	63.24	0.102
	(%, n) Yes	50	46.75	41.18	36.76	
Member is in Air Combat Command: 1=Yes, 0=No	(%, n) No	91.18	87.01	86.27	81.08	0.257
	(%, n) Yes	8.82	12.99	13.73	18.92	
Member is in Air Force Special Operations Command: 1=Yes, 0=No	(%, n) No	94.12	96.1	98.04	95.68	0.963
	(%, n) Yes	5.88	3.9	1.96	4.32	
Member is in Air Mobility Command: 1=Yes, 0=No	(%, n) No	88.24	93.51	90.2	91.26	0.411
	(%, n) Yes	11.76	6.49	9.8	8.74	
Ever assigned to Headquarters Air Force	(%, n) No	67.65	58.44	84.31	73.24	**0.028**
	(%, n) Yes	32.35	41.56	15.69	26.76	
Member has been an aide (administrative assistant) to a high-ranking officer within the 5 years prior to the CPME board.	(%, n) No	97.06	98.7	100	98.2	0.909
	(%, n) Yes	2.94	1.3	0	1.8	
Member was the Executive Officer for a lower-ranking official within the 5 years prior to the CPME board.	(%, n) No	85.29	89.61	94.12	89.64	0.859
	(%, n) Yes	14.71	10.39	5.88	10.36	
Member had a bad Assignment Availability Code within the 5 years prior to the CPME board.	(%, n) No	100	100	100	99.64	0.962
	(%, n) Yes	0	0	0	0.36	
Member failed Air Force Fitness Exam within past 5 years: 1=Yes, 0=No	(%, n) No	100	97.4	100	97.75	0.632
	(%, n) Yes	0	2.6	0	2.25	
Is a current instructor: 1=Yes, 0=No	(%, n) No	100	98.7	96.08	96.04	0.298
	(%, n) Yes	0	1.3	3.92	3.96	
Age	1. Mean (Std.)	40.47 (3.41)	43.55 (4.41)	41.33 (3.46)	41.07 (3.38)	**0.000**
Graduate of an HBCU	(%, n) No	100	84.42	100	99.55	**0.000**
	(%, n) Yes	0	15.58	0	0.45	
Graduate of a Hispanic-Serving Institution	(%, n) No	97.06	98.7	74.51	99.19	**0.000**
	(%, n) Yes	2.94	1.3	25.49	0.81	
Marital status: 1=Married, 0=Not married	(%, n) Not Married	8.82	16.88	7.84	6.31	**0.007**
	(%, n) Married	91.18	83.12	92.16	93.69	

127

Distribution by Race and Ethnicity		2020 Observed Estimates				
Label	Levels	Asian	Black	Hispanic	White	P-value
Eliminated from pilot training: 1=Yes, 0=No	(%, n) No	85.29	97.4	90.2	94.05	0.138
	(%, n) Yes	14.71	2.6	9.8	5.95	
Core ID: 21=Logistics	(%, n) No	91.18	85.71	86.27	90.9	0.596
	(%, n) Yes	8.82	14.29	13.73	9.1	
Core ID: 31=Security Forces	(%, n) No	100	98.7	94.12	97.12	0.528
	(%, n) Yes	0	1.3	5.88	2.88	
Core ID: 38=Manpower	(%, n) No	100	94.81	92.16	97.3	0.199
	(%, n) Yes	0	5.19	7.84	2.7	
Current Duty AFSC is 16XX: 1=Yes, 0=No	(%, n) No	91.18	94.81	86.27	94.05	0.348
	(%, n) Yes	8.82	5.19	13.73	5.95	

Table E.4b. SDE Comparison of Racial and Ethnic Groups of Characteristics in 2020 Weighted with Propensity Score for Balancing

Distribution by Race/Ethnicity		2020 Propensity Score Weight-Adjusted Estimates (means or %)								
Label	Levels	Asian	White Weighted	p-value	Black	White Adjusted	p-value	Hispanic	White Adjusted	p-value
Traditional ISS In-Residence: 1=Yes, 0=No	(%, n) No	61.76	64.2	0.844	62.34	61.34	0.902	64.71	70.51	0.548
	(%, n) Yes	38.24	35.8		37.66	38.66		35.29	29.49	
SDE completed by correspondence: 1=Yes, 0=No	(%, n) No	64.71	65.37	0.957	53.25	52.75	0.953	74.51	71.62	0.752
	(%, n) Yes	35.29	34.63		46.75	47.25		25.49	28.38	
Selected for SDE by the central promotion board	(%, n) No	85.29	86.33	0.908	97.4	94.23	0.337	90.2	91.82	0.784
	(%, n) Yes	14.71	13.67		2.6	5.77		9.8	8.18	
DG from: USAFA, Reserve Officer Training Corps, or OTS: 1=Yes, 0=No	(%, n) No	88.24	88.74	0.951	90.91	88.51	0.635	92.16	88.11	0.507
	(%, n) Yes	11.76	11.26		9.09	11.49		7.84	11.89	
DG from SOS	(%, n) No	85.29	85	0.974	98.7	94.75	0.174	88.24	88.11	0.985
	(%, n) Yes	14.71	15		1.3	5.25		11.76	11.89	
Promoted APZ to lieutenant colonel: 1=Yes, 0=No	(%, n) No	97.06	98.02	0.811	98.7	98.41	0.884	98.04	96.99	0.742
	(%, n) Yes	2.94	1.98		1.3	1.59		1.96	3.01	
Promoted BPZ to lieutenant colonel	(%, n) No	88.24	87.99	0.977	97.4	96.04	0.644	94.12	93.36	0.879
	(%, n) Yes	11.76	12.01		2.6	3.96		5.88	6.64	
Weapons School graduate	(%, n) No	97.06	93.78	0.532	97.4	93.84	0.290	94.12	92.37	0.735
	(%, n) Yes	2.94	6.22		2.6	6.16		5.88	7.63	
Never a commander: 1=Yes, 0=No	(%, n) No	76.47	74.19	0.835	77.92	83.82	0.371	72.55	74.91	0.795
	(%, n) Yes	23.53	25.81		22.08	16.18		27.45	25.09	
Stratified in the top 10%	(%, n) No	97.06	97.16	0.980	97.4	98.33	0.702	98.04	98.77	0.780

128

Distribution by Race/Ethnicity		2020 Propensity Score Weight-Adjusted Estimates (means or %)								
Label	Levels	Asian	White Weighted	p-value	Black	White Adjusted	p-value	Hispanic	White Adjusted	p-value
by an SR with at least 6 nominees	(%, n) Yes	2.94	2.84		2.6	1.67		1.96	1.23	
Stratified in the top 20% by an SR with at least 6 nominees	(%, n) No	94.12	93.96	0.979	97.4	94.17	0.329	92.16	93.81	0.755
	(%, n) Yes	5.88	6.04		2.6	5.83		7.84	6.19	
Stratified in the top 30% by an SR with at least 6 nominees	(%, n) No	91.18	93.15	0.775	96.1	96.28	0.956	98.04	97.54	0.870
	(%, n) Yes	8.82	6.85		3.9	3.72		1.96	2.46	
Stratified in the top 40% by an SR with at least 6 nominees	(%, n) No	97.06	95.15	0.697	97.4	96.7	0.803	98.04	96.88	0.719
	(%, n) Yes	2.94	4.85		2.6	3.3		1.96	3.12	
Stratified in the top 50% by an SR with at least 6 nominees	(%, n) No	94.12	92.82	0.837	97.4	94.8	0.415	96.08	95.02	0.802
	(%, n) Yes	5.88	7.18		2.6	5.2		3.92	4.98	
Stratified in the top 80% by an SR with at least 6 nominees	(%, n) No	91.18	89.09	0.783	85.71	85.32	0.947	88.24	83.56	0.512
	(%, n) Yes	8.82	10.91		14.29	14.68		11.76	16.44	
An individual was stratified #1 by an SR with 2 nominees.	(%, n) No	94.12	92.77	0.830	90.91	91.38	0.921	96.08	94.79	0.764
	(%, n) Yes	5.88	7.23		9.09	8.62		3.92	5.21	
An individual was stratified #1 by an SR with 3 to 5 nominees.	(%, n) No	88.24	89.56	0.869	93.51	92.86	0.877	98.04	95.28	0.449
	(%, n) Yes	11.76	10.44		6.49	7.14		1.96	4.72	
SR grade: O-10 (4 stars)	(%, n) No	97.06	99.19	0.550	98.7	99.04	0.851	98.04	99.48	0.538
	(%, n) Yes	2.94	0.81		1.3	0.96		1.96	0.52	
SR grade: O-9	(%, n) No	91.18	93	0.793	90.91	91.24	0.944	94.12	93.02	0.828
	(%, n) Yes	8.82	7		9.09	8.76		5.88	6.98	
SR grade: O-8 or O-7	(%, n) No	50	47.75	0.860	53.25	52.76	0.953	58.82	59.51	0.946
	(%, n) Yes	50	52.25		46.75	47.24		41.18	40.49	
Member is in Air Combat Command: 1=Yes, 0=No	(%, n) No	91.18	91.03	0.984	87.01	87.44	0.939	86.27	87.56	0.853
	(%, n) Yes	8.82	8.97		12.99	12.56		13.73	12.44	
Member is in Air Force Special Operations Command: 1=Yes, 0=No	(%, n) No	94.12	93.76	0.953	96.1	97.53	0.628	98.04	95.25	0.446
	(%, n) Yes	5.88	6.24		3.9	2.47		1.96	4.75	
Member is in Air Mobility Command: 1=Yes, 0=No	(%, n) No	88.24	89.15	0.910	93.51	94.68	0.767	90.2	88.85	0.831
	(%, n) Yes	11.76	10.85		6.49	5.32		9.8	11.15	
Ever assigned to Headquarters Air Force	(%, n) No	67.65	71.72	0.729	58.44	62.62	0.609	84.31	82.51	0.814
	(%, n) Yes	32.35	28.28		41.56	37.38		15.69	17.49	
Member has been an aide (administrative assistant) to a high-ranking officer within the 5 years prior to the CPME board.	(%, n) No	97.06	97.32	0.950	98.7	98.95	0.893	100	98.66	0.407
	(%, n) Yes	2.94	2.68		1.3	1.05		0	1.34	
Member was the Executive Officer for a lower-ranking official within the 5 years prior to the CPME board.	(%, n) No	85.29	87.79	0.776	89.61	90.14	0.916	94.12	93.47	0.897
	(%, n) Yes	14.71	12.21		10.39	9.86		5.88	6.53	

Distribution by Race/Ethnicity		2020 Propensity Score Weight-Adjusted Estimates (means or %)								
Label	Levels	Asian	White Weighted	p-value	Black	White Adjusted	p-value	Hispanic	White Adjusted	p-value
Member had a bad Assignment Availability Code within the 5 years prior to the CPME board.	(%, n) No	100	99.87	0.835	100	99.8	0.696	100	99.81	0.756
	(%, n) Yes	0	0.13		0	0.2		0	0.19	
Member failed Air Force Fitness Exam within past 5 years: 1=Yes, 0=No	(%, n) No	100	97.76	0.381	97.4	96.35	0.716	100	98.08	0.320
	(%, n) Yes	0	2.24		2.6	3.65		0	1.92	
Is a current instructor: 1=Yes, 0=No	(%, n) No	100	95.67	0.221	98.7	96.62	0.402	96.08	96.71	0.869
	(%, n) Yes	0	4.33		1.3	3.38		3.92	3.29	
Age	1. Mean (Std.)	40.47 (3.41)	40.44 (0.45)	0.875	43.55 (4.41)	43.40 (1.05)	0.566	41.33 (3.46)	41.05 (0.69)	0.169
Graduate of an HBCU	(%, n) No	100	99.59	0.708	84.42	90.15	0.306	100	98.53	0.385
	(%, n) Yes	0	0.41		15.58	9.85		0	1.47	
Graduate of a Hispanic-Serving Institution	(%, n) No	97.06	99.01	0.592	98.7	99.29	0.728	74.51	80.52	0.487
	(%, n) Yes	2.94	0.99		1.3	0.71		25.49	19.48	
Marital status: 1=Married, 0=Not married	(%, n) Not Married	8.82	7.27	0.824	16.88	13.31	0.551	7.84	7.82	0.996
	(%, n) Married	91.18	92.73		83.12	86.69		92.16	92.18	
Eliminated from pilot training: 1=Yes, 0=No	(%, n) No	85.29	87.05	0.842	97.4	95.94	0.623	90.2	90.73	0.930
	(%, n) Yes	14.71	12.95		2.6	4.06		9.8	9.27	
Core ID: 21=Logistics	(%, n) No	91.18	90.87	0.966	85.71	83.99	0.773	86.27	84.97	0.856
	(%, n) Yes	8.82	9.13		14.29	16.01		13.73	15.03	
Core ID: 31=Security Forces	(%, n) No	100	97.12	0.319	98.7	96.47	0.376	94.12	94.32	0.967
	(%, n) Yes	0	2.88		1.3	3.53		5.88	5.68	
Core ID: 38=Manpower	(%, n) No	100	97.42	0.346	94.81	94.09	0.851	92.16	93.72	0.768
	(%, n) Yes	0	2.58		5.19	5.91		7.84	6.28	
Current Duty AFSC is 16XX: 1=Yes, 0=No	(%, n) No	91.18	91.67	0.945	94.81	94.61	0.959	86.27	91.33	0.440
	(%, n) Yes	8.82	8.33		5.19	5.39		13.73	8.67	

Table E.4c. SDE Comparison of Racial and Ethnic Groups of Unweighted Characteristics in 2021 Before Propensity Score Weighting

Distribution by Race or Ethnicity		2021 Estimates (means or %)				
Label	Levels	Asian	Black	Hispanic	White	P-value
Traditional ISS In-Residence: 1=Yes, 0=No	(%, n) No	72.22	67.9	61.54	54.24	**0.012**
	(%, n) Yes	27.78	32.1	38.46	45.76	
Other IDE In-Residence: 1=Yes, 0=No	(%, n) No	88.89	88.89	92.31	86.47	0.370
	(%, n) Yes	11.11	11.11	7.69	13.53	

Distribution by Race or Ethnicity		2021 Estimates (means or %)				
Label	Levels	Asian	Black	Hispanic	White	P-value
SDE completed by correspondence: 1=Yes, 0=No	(%, n) No	66.67	58.02	63.46	61.25	0.440
	(%, n) Yes	33.33	41.98	36.54	38.75	
Selected for SDE by the central promotion board	(%, n) No	97.22	100	98.08	93.09	0.109
	(%, n) Yes	2.78	0	1.92	6.91	
DG from: USAFA, Reserve Officer Training Corps, or OTS: 1=Yes, 0=No	(%, n) No	94.44	88.89	90.38	83.54	0.230
	(%, n) Yes	5.56	11.11	9.62	16.46	
DG from SOS	(%, n) No	91.67	100	94.23	82.18	**0.000**
	(%, n) Yes	8.33	0	5.77	17.82	
Promoted APZ to lieutenant colonel: 1=Yes, 0=No	(%, n) No	94.44	93.83	98.08	98.25	0.090
	(%, n) Yes	5.56	6.17	1.92	1.75	
Promoted BPZ to lieutenant colonel	(%, n) No	91.67	97.53	98.08	90.26	0.135
	(%, n) Yes	8.33	2.47	1.92	9.74	
Weapons School graduate	(%, n) No	91.67	95.06	96.15	87.15	**0.022**
	(%, n) Yes	8.33	4.94	3.85	12.85	
Never a commander: 1=Yes, 0=No	(%, n) No	75	83.95	69.23	79.45	0.167
	(%, n) Yes	25	16.05	30.77	20.55	
Stratified in the top 10% by an SR with at least 6 nominees	(%, n) No	100	98.77	98.08	98.54	0.933
	(%, n) Yes	0	1.23	1.92	1.46	
Stratified in the top 20% by an SR with at least 6 nominees	(%, n) No	100	98.77	94.23	93.77	0.172
	(%, n) Yes	0	1.23	5.77	6.23	
Stratified in the top 30% by an SR with at least 6 nominees	(%, n) No	91.67	97.53	100	95.91	**0.030**
	(%, n) Yes	8.33	2.47	0	4.09	
Stratified in the top 40% by an SR with at least 6 nominees	(%, n) No	94.44	100	98.08	95.42	0.362
	(%, n) Yes	5.56	0	1.92	4.58	
Stratified in the top 50% by an SR with at least 6 nominees	(%, n) No	97.22	93.83	96.15	94.26	0.929
	(%, n) Yes	2.78	6.17	3.85	5.74	
Stratified in the top 80% by an SR with at least 6 nominees	(%, n) No	91.67	88.89	86.54	84.03	0.472
	(%, n) Yes	8.33	11.11	13.46	15.97	
An individual was stratified #1 by an SR with 2 nominees.	(%, n) No	97.22	92.59	94.23	93.96	0.672
	(%, n) Yes	2.78	7.41	5.77	6.04	
An individual was stratified #1 by an SR with 3 to 5 nominees.	(%, n) No	94.44	92.59	98.08	93.38	0.513
	(%, n) Yes	5.56	7.41	1.92	6.62	
SR grade: O-10 (4-stars)	(%, n) No	97.22	100	100	99.12	0.529
	(%, n) Yes	2.78	0	0	0.88	
SR grade: O-9	(%, n) No	83.33	90.12	96.15	94.74	**0.008**
	(%, n) Yes	16.67	9.88	3.85	5.26	
SR grade: O-8 or O-7	(%, n) No	61.11	64.2	57.69	65.82	0.819
	(%, n) Yes	38.89	35.8	42.31	34.18	

Distribution by Race or Ethnicity		2021 Estimates (means or %)				
Label	Levels	Asian	Black	Hispanic	White	P-value
Member is in Air Combat Command: 1=Yes, 0=No	(%, n) No	86.11	86.42	92.31	79.94	**0.040**
	(%, n) Yes	13.89	13.58	7.69	20.06	
Member is in Air Force Special Operations Command: 1=Yes, 0=No	(%, n) No	94.44	97.53	100	95.03	0.314
	(%, n) Yes	5.56	2.47	0	4.97	
Member is in Air Mobility Command: 1=Yes, 0=No	(%, n) No	91.67	93.83	92.31	91.04	0.959
	(%, n) Yes	8.33	6.17	7.69	8.96	
Ever assigned to Headquarters Air Force	(%, n) No	61.11	50.62	71.15	77.31	**0.000**
	(%, n) Yes	38.89	49.38	28.85	22.69	
Member has been an aide (administrative assistant) to a high-ranking officer within the 5 years prior to the CPME board.	(%, n) No	100	98.77	98.08	98.15	0.671
	(%, n) Yes	0	1.23	1.92	1.85	
Member was the Executive Officer for a lower-ranking official within the 5 years prior to the CPME board.	(%, n) No	88.89	83.95	88.46	90.75	0.339
	(%, n) Yes	11.11	16.05	11.54	9.25	
Member had a bad Assignment Availability Code within the 5 years prior to the CPME board	(%, n) No	100	100	100	99.61	0.809
	(%, n) Yes	0	0	0	0.39	
Member failed Air Force Fitness Exam within last 5 years: 1=Yes, 0=No	(%, n) No	100	95.06	100	99.12	**0.017**
	(%, n) Yes	0	4.94	0	0.88	
Is a current instructor: 1=Yes, 0=No	(%, n) No	97.22	96.3	96.15	95.81	0.985
	(%, n) Yes	2.78	3.7	3.85	4.19	
Age	1. Mean (Std.)	40.72 (3.58)	42.47 (4.64)	41.52 (3.30)	41.06 (3.48)	**0.009**
Graduate of an HBCU	(%, n) No	100	86.42	100	99.81	**0.000**
	(%, n) Yes	0	13.58	0	0.19	
Graduate of a Hispanic-Serving Institution	(%, n) No	97.22	100	76.92	98.83	**0.000**
	(%, n) Yes	2.78	0	23.08	1.17	
Marital status: 1=Married, 0=Not married	(%, n) Not Married	8.33	27.16	9.62	6.33	**0.000**
	(%, n) Married	91.67	72.84	90.38	93.67	
Eliminated from pilot training: 1=Yes, 0=No	(%, n) No	91.67	96.3	88.46	92.89	0.469
	(%, n) Yes	8.33	3.7	11.54	7.11	
Core ID: 21=Logistics	(%, n) No	97.22	86.42	88.46	89.78	0.188
	(%, n) Yes	2.78	13.58	11.54	10.22	
Core ID: 31=Security Forces	(%, n) No	100	95.06	96.15	96.3	0.629
	(%, n) Yes	0	4.94	3.85	3.7	
Core ID: 38 =Manpower	(%, n) No	97.22	95.06	90.38	96.88	0.192
	(%, n) Yes	2.78	4.94	9.62	3.12	
Current Duty AFSC is 16XX: 1=Yes, 0=No	(%, n) No	91.67	95.06	92.31	93.67	0.947
	(%, n) Yes	8.33	4.94	7.69	6.33	

Table E.4d. SDE Comparison of Racial and Ethnic Groups of Characteristics in 2021 Weighted with Propensity Score for Balancing

Distribution by Race and Ethnicity		2021 Propensity Score Weight-Adjusted Estimates (means or %)								
Label	Levels	Asian	White Weighted	p-value	Black	White Adjusted	p-value	Hispanic	White Adjusted	p-value
Traditional ISS In-Residence: 1=Yes, 0=No	(%, n) No	72.22	70.55	0.880	67.9	66.48	0.863	61.54	57.28	0.666
	(%, n) Yes	27.78	29.45		32.1	33.52		38.46	42.72	
Other IDE In-Residence: 1=Yes, 0=No	(%, n) No	88.89	88.34	0.943	88.89	87.94	0.866	92.31	90.8	0.787
	(%, n) Yes	11.11	11.66		11.11	12.06		7.69	9.2	
SDE completed by correspondence: 1=Yes, 0=No	(%, n) No	66.67	64.45	0.849	58.02	58.56	0.951	63.46	64.1	0.947
	(%, n) Yes	33.33	35.55		41.98	41.44		36.54	35.9	
Selected for SDE by the central promotion board	(%, n) No	97.22	96.17	0.809	100	97.26	0.134	98.08	94.69	0.362
	(%, n) Yes	2.78	3.83		0	2.74		1.92	5.31	
DG from: USAFA, Reserve Officer Training Corps, or OTS: 1=Yes, 0=No	(%, n) No	94.44	91.34	0.618	88.89	89.33	0.935	90.38	86.62	0.556
	(%, n) Yes	5.56	8.66		11.11	10.67		9.62	13.38	
DG from SOS	(%, n) No	91.67	90.06	0.819	100	96.88	0.110	94.23	90.77	0.511
	(%, n) Yes	8.33	9.94		0	3.12		5.77	9.23	
Promoted APZ to lieutenant colonel: 1=Yes, 0=No	(%, n) No	94.44	95.69	0.815	93.83	94.68	0.836	98.08	96.7	0.665
	(%, n) Yes	5.56	4.31		6.17	5.32		1.92	3.3	
Promoted BPZ to lieutenant colonel	(%, n) No	91.67	91.25	0.952	97.53	96.38	0.697	98.08	94.27	0.319
	(%, n) Yes	8.33	8.75		2.47	3.62		1.92	5.73	
Weapons School Graduate	(%, n) No	91.67	91.76	0.989	95.06	93.2	0.647	96.15	93.55	0.556
	(%, n) Yes	8.33	8.24		4.94	6.8		3.85	6.45	
Never a commander: 1=Yes, 0=No	(%, n) No	75	73.85	0.914	83.95	84.99	0.871	69.23	73.02	0.678
	(%, n) Yes	25	26.15		16.05	15.01		30.77	26.98	
Stratified in the top 10% by an SR with at least 6 nominees	(%, n) No	100	99.27	0.608	98.77	99.03	0.886	98.08	99.21	0.632
	(%, n) Yes	0	0.73		1.23	0.97		1.92	0.79	
Stratified in the top 20% by an SR with at least 6 nominees	(%, n) No	100	95.53	0.200	98.77	96.89	0.444	94.23	94.29	0.989
	(%, n) Yes	0	4.47		1.23	3.11		5.77	5.71	
Stratified in the top 30% by an SR with at least 6 nominees	(%, n) No	91.67	91.04	0.927	97.53	96.9	0.825	100	96.73	0.189
	(%, n) Yes	8.33	8.96		2.47	3.1		0	3.27	
Stratified in the top 40% by an SR with at least 6 nominees	(%, n) No	94.44	94.94	0.927	100	97.3	0.137	98.08	96.28	0.586
	(%, n) Yes	5.56	5.06		0	2.7		1.92	3.72	
Stratified in the top 50% by a senior rater with at least 6 nominees	(%, n) No	97.22	96.3	0.831	93.83	94.14	0.940	96.15	96.12	0.993
	(%, n) Yes	2.78	3.7		6.17	5.86		3.85	3.88	

Distribution by Race and Ethnicity		2021 Propensity Score Weight-Adjusted Estimates (means or %)								
Label	Levels	Asian	White Weighted	p-value	Black	White Adjusted	p-value	Hispanic	White Adjusted	p-value
Stratified in the top 80% by an SR with at least 6 nominees	(%, n) No	91.67	89.43	0.754	88.89	85.74	0.587	86.54	84.56	0.780
	(%, n) Yes	8.33	10.57		11.11	14.26		13.46	15.44	
An individual was stratified #1 by an SR with 2 nominees.	(%, n) No	97.22	95.48	0.702	92.59	93.77	0.793	94.23	93.76	0.922
	(%, n) Yes	2.78	4.52		7.41	6.23		5.77	6.24	
An individual was stratified #1 by an SR with 3 to 5 nominees.	(%, n) No	94.44	93.89	0.922	92.59	93.66	0.811	98.08	94.92	0.388
	(%, n) Yes	5.56	6.11		7.41	6.34		1.92	5.08	
SR grade: O-10 (4-stars)	(%, n) No	97.22	98.21	0.788	100	98.97	0.360	100	98.85	0.438
	(%, n) Yes	2.78	1.79		0	1.03		0	1.15	
SR grade: O-9	(%, n) No	83.33	85.86	0.775	90.12	92.65	0.613	96.15	95.39	0.849
	(%, n) Yes	16.67	14.14		9.88	7.35		3.85	4.61	
SR grade: O-8 or O-7	(%, n) No	61.11	58.21	0.808	64.2	65.44	0.883	57.69	54.8	0.772
	(%, n) Yes	38.89	41.79		35.8	34.56		42.31	45.2	
Member is in Air Combat Command: 1=Yes, 0=No	(%, n) No	86.11	87.24	0.892	86.42	81.87	0.473	92.31	88.58	0.527
	(%, n) Yes	13.89	12.76		13.58	18.13		7.69	11.42	
Member is in Air Force Special Operations Command: 1=Yes, 0=No	(%, n) No	94.44	93.42	0.860	97.53	97.23	0.915	100	96.3	0.162
	(%, n) Yes	5.56	6.58		2.47	2.77		0	3.7	
Member is in Air Mobility Command: 1=Yes, 0=No	(%, n) No	91.67	92.11	0.946	93.83	93.28	0.898	92.31	90.78	0.784
	(%, n) Yes	8.33	7.89		6.17	6.72		7.69	9.22	
Ever assigned to Headquarters Air Force	(%, n) No	61.11	65.51	0.709	50.62	56.94	0.471	71.15	73.49	0.795
	(%, n) Yes	38.89	34.49		49.38	43.06		28.85	26.51	
Member has been an aide (administrative assistant) to a high-ranking officer within the 5 years prior to the CPME board.	(%, n) No	100	97.35	0.326	98.77	99.3	0.761	98.08	98.77	0.785
	(%, n) Yes	0	2.65		1.23	0.7		1.92	1.23	
Member was the Executive Officer for a lower-ranking official within the 5 years prior to the CPME board.	(%, n) No	88.89	89.95	0.887	83.95	87.87	0.526	88.46	90.49	0.744
	(%, n) Yes	11.11	10.05		16.05	12.13		11.54	9.51	
Member had a bad Assignment Availability Code within the 5 years prior to the CPME board.	(%, n) No	100	99.9	0.849	100	99.95	0.844	100	99.71	0.697
	(%, n) Yes	0	0.1		0	0.05		0	0.29	

Distribution by Race and Ethnicity		2021 Propensity Score Weight-Adjusted Estimates (means or %)								
Label	Levels	Asian	White Weighted	p-value	Black	White Adjusted	p-value	Hispanic	White Adjusted	p-value
Member failed Air Force Fitness Exam within past 5 years: 1=Yes, 0=No	(%, n) No	100	98.95	0.538	95.06	97.99	0.382	100	99.13	0.500
	(%, n) Yes	0	1.05		4.94	2.01		0	0.87	
Is a current instructor: 1=Yes, 0=No	(%, n) No	97.22	95.65	0.727	96.3	96.2	0.977	96.15	95.55	0.880
	(%, n) Yes	2.78	4.35		3.7	3.8		3.85	4.45	
Age	1. Mean (Std.)	40.72 (3.58)	40.82 (0.61)	0.639	42.47 (4.64)	42.09 (0.96)	0.163	41.52 (3.30)	41.51 (0.78)	0.964
Graduate of an HBCU	(%, n) No	100	99.9	0.849	86.42	97.58	**0.027**	100	98.96	0.461
	(%, n) Yes	0	0.1		13.58	2.42		0	1.04	
Graduate of a Hispanic-Serving Institution	(%, n) No	97.22	98.28	0.771	100	98.47	0.264	76.92	82	0.534
	(%, n) Yes	2.78	1.72		0	1.53		23.08	18	
Marital status: 1=Married, 0=Not married	(%, n) Not Married	8.33	8.52	0.978	27.16	19.54	0.311	9.62	7.86	0.758
	(%, n) Married	91.67	91.48		72.84	80.46		90.38	92.14	
Eliminated from pilot training: 1=Yes, 0=No	(%, n) No	91.67	91.39	0.967	96.3	94.11	0.551	88.46	89.65	0.851
	(%, n) Yes	8.33	8.61		3.7	5.89		11.54	10.35	
Core ID: 21=Logistics	(%, n) No	97.22	93.06	0.421	86.42	85.13	0.833	88.46	86.4	0.757
	(%, n) Yes	2.78	6.94		13.58	14.87		11.54	13.6	
Core ID: 31=Security Forces	(%, n) No	100	97.25	0.317	95.06	94.22	0.830	96.15	94.15	0.642
	(%, n) Yes	0	2.75		4.94	5.78		3.85	5.85	
Core ID: 38=Manpower	(%, n) No	97.22	96.13	0.801	95.06	95.14	0.983	90.38	90.88	0.932
	(%, n) Yes	2.78	3.87		4.94	4.86		9.62	9.12	
Current Duty AFSC is 16XX: 1=Yes, 0=No	(%, n) No	91.67	91.37	0.965	95.06	95.55	0.895	92.31	93.39	0.835
	(%, n) Yes	8.33	8.63		4.94	4.45		7.69	6.61	

Appendix F. Board Member Interview Protocols

INTERVIEW PROTOCOL: 2020 DE BOARD MEMBERS

Provide Study Overview and Administer Consent

General Background/Ice Breaker Questions

We are going to begin with some background questions.

1. How many years of service have you provided since commissioning?
What is your core AFSC?
How many times have you served on a developmental education board?

   a. Have you served previously on any [or another] centralized board? If so, which boards and how many times?

Have you served as a Senior Rater?

   a. If yes, how many times?
   b. If yes, have you nominated officers for Developmental Education?
      i. If yes, have you awarded "DA" Definitely Attend recommendation(s)?
      ii. What criteria did you use in awarding your Definitely Attend(s)?

Knowledge and Communication of Board Guidance

How were you provided guidance related to the board selection process? Please describe.

   a. Were you provided guidance in writing prior to the board? What did this information include? When and how was this provided to you? Please describe.
   b. Were you provided guidance in-person at the start of the board? Please describe.
   c. If verbal guidance was provided, how did it differ, if at all, from the written guidance provided in the memorandum of instruction (MOI)?

After receiving the MOI guidance, was it clear to you how to apply it to scoring records?

   a. If not, what questions did you have about the guidance? Were you allowed the opportunity to ask clarifying questions about the board guidance prior to the board selection process? Did you receive the clarifying information you needed to apply the guidance to the board decision process?

What, if any, guidance did you receive related to the role of diversity, equity, and inclusion in the board selection process? Can describe it in your own words?

   a. Did you receive written guidance about diversity, equity, and inclusion?
   b. Did you receive any verbal guidance related to diversity, equity, and inclusion?
   c. If verbal guidance was provided, how did it differ, if at all, from the written guidance provided in the memorandum of instruction (MOI)?

d. Did you discuss the guidance related to diversity, equity, and inclusion, or the topic of diversity, equity, and inclusion in the board context more generally, with other board members? This can include informally, outside of the board process itself. If so, please describe.

Based on your experience, are there improvements that the Air Force should make in communicating the guidance to board members? If so, please describe.

a. Is there additional information about the guidance related to diversity, equity, and inclusion that you wish you had prior to the board process? If so, please describe?

Experience with 2020 Board Selection Process

How would you describe the profile of a competitive officer in the DE board process? What characteristics did officers tend to have who were competitive in the process or were most likely to be selected?
During the board process, what factors did you use to make decisions when scoring records?

a. What factors did you consider the deciding "tie breakers"?

We discussed earlier how guidance related to diversity, equity, and inclusion was *communicated* to you and other board members. I now would like to talk about the role, if any, that diversity, equity, and inclusion played in decisions that you made in the board selection process. To kick off this next set of questions, I'd like to read excerpts from the 2020 MOI from Lt Gen Kelly as a reminder of the language provided on diversity, equity, and inclusion:

MOI: "*. . . acknowledging diversity is a force multiplier, I need you to recognize officers who demonstrate initiative and display an ability to lead in our increasingly diverse DAF culture. Selection officers must be the highest performers who model our core values, foster inclusiveness, and champion dignity and respect while leveraging the contribution of our Total Force.*"

Addendum to MOI: "*To remain competitive, the Department must have members from the entire spectrum of qualified talent available. Accordingly, the DoD needs to make every effort to encourage service from individuals of all backgrounds by providing for the equal treatment and equitable considerations of all personnel considered for development.*"

How, if at all, did you apply this guidance about diversity, equity, and inclusion when scoring records?
We know the race/ethnicity and gender of the applicants wasn't officially made available to you but were you able to infer any demographics from the records or narratives (e.g., use of female pronouns)? Please explain.

Based on the MOI guidance (and any additional verbal guidance) you were provided on diversity, equity, and inclusion, how, if at all, was race/ethnicity and gender considered during the DE board selection process?

   a. If race/ethnicity or gender were able to be inferred from records, did you consider them at all in the selection process? If so, how so?

Imagine that all applicants' race/ethnicity and gender had all been intentionally visible to you during the board process. Based on the MOI guidance you were provided on diversity, equity, and inclusion, how, if at all, would race/ethnicity and gender have factored into your process for scoring records?

   a. Probe: How would you have weighted race/ethnicity and gender in the scoring process if you had access to this information?
      i. Would you have used race/ethnicity or gender as a factor equivalent to a quality indicator like an award or training?
   b. Probe: If you were considering two candidates with otherwise similar records but one was a racial/ethnic minority or female, how, if it at all, would you have considered race/ethnicity or gender as a "tie breaker" if you had access to this information?
      i. Would have you used race/ethnicity or gender as a form of "tie breaker" for otherwise similar records if you had access to this information? If so, please describe.

Based on your experience with the board process, are there improvements you think the Air Force should make regarding board guidance related to diversity, equity, and inclusion? If so, please describe.

   a. Do you believe the race/ethnicity and gender information should be visible to board members when scoring records? Please explain.

Closing Questions

Beyond unmasking race/ethnicity and gender during the 2021 DE board process, there were several other changes made to the board process. I want to get your input on some of those:

   a. [For IDE board members] Unmasked "Definitely Attend's" (DAs): How, if at all, would you have used this information when scoring records? Would it have been helpful to you? Please explain.
   b. Having only a 5-year window for officer records, focusing on recent performance: How, if at all, do you feel that would have affected the board process for you?
   c. Scoring by DTs: How, if at all, do you feel that would have affected the board process for you?

During the board process, how would you describe the level of difficulty of assessing records outside of your core AFSC? Was it more difficult to assess those outside of your core AFSC? Please explain.

   a. Were there any particularly strong AFSCs in the board process? Were there any particularly weak AFSCs in the board process?

Is there anything important for us to know about the DE selection process that we haven't asked you about or any key take-aways we should have for how the Air Force could better inform you about guidance for the board selection process or how diversity, equity, and inclusion can be integrated into the process?

INTERVIEW PROTOCOL: 2021 DE BOARD MEMBERS

Provide Study Overview and Administer Consent

General Background/Ice Breaker Questions

We are going to begin with some background questions.

1. How many years of service have you provided since commissioning?
What is your core AFSC?
How many times have you served on a developmental education board?

   a. Have you served previously on any [or another] centralized board? If so, which boards and how many times?

Have you served as a Senior Rater?

   a. If yes, how many times?
   b. If yes, have you nominated officers for Developmental Education?
      i. If yes, have you awarded "DA" Definitely Attend recommendation(s)?
      ii. What criteria did you use in awarding your Definitely Attend(s)?

Knowledge of Board Guidance

How were you provided information about the board guidance related to diversity, equity, and inclusion? Please describe.

   a. Were you provided information about the guidance in writing prior to the board? What did this information include? When and how was this provided to you? Please describe.
   b. Were you provided information about the guidance in-person at the start of the board? Please describe.
   c. If verbal guidance was provided, how did it differ, if at all, from the written guidance provided?
   d. [For participants who have served on a previous board(s)] Was the communication about board guidance significantly different on the previous boards you participated in?

After receiving the guidance, was it clear to you how to apply it to scoring a nominated officer's record?

   a. If not, what questions did you have about the guidance? Were you allowed the opportunity to ask clarifying questions about the board guidance prior to the board selection process? Did you receive the clarifying information you needed to apply the standards to the board decision process?
   b. Did you discuss the guidance related to diversity, equity, and inclusion, or the topic of diversity, equity, and inclusion in the board context more generally, with other board members? This can include informally, outside of the board process itself. If so, please describe.

Based on your experience, are there improvements that the Air Force should make in communicating the guidance to board members? If so, please describe.

    a. Is there additional information about the guidance related to diversity, equity, and inclusion that you wish you had prior to the board selection process? If so, please describe?

Experience with 2021 Board Selection Process

How would you describe the profile of competitive officer in the DE board process? What characteristics did officers tend to have who were competitive in the process or were most likely to be selected?

During the board process, what factors did you use to make decisions when scoring officers' records?

    a. What factors are considered the deciding "tie breakers"?

In your own words, what does the board guidance related to diversity, equity, and inclusion entail?

    a. How, if at all, did you apply this guidance about diversity, equity, and inclusion when scoring records?

During the board process, were you aware that race/ethnicity and gender were visible in all records?

    a. If you were <u>not</u> aware that race/ethnicity and gender was unmasked, were you able to infer demographics from the narratives (e.g., use of female pronouns)?

If you were aware that race/ethnicity and gender was unmasked (or could infer this information from narratives), how, if at all did you consider this information in the board process?

    a. Probe: How did you weight race/ethnicity and gender in the scoring process?

        i. Did you use race/ethnicity or gender as a factor equivalent to a quality indicator like an award or training?

    b. Probe: If you were considering two candidates with otherwise similar records but one was a racial/ethnic minority or female, how, if it at all, would you consider race/ethnicity or gender as a "tie breaker"?

        i. Did you use race/ethnicity or gender as a form of "tie breaker" for otherwise similar records? If so, please describe.

    c. Did you discuss (informally) how, if at all, you used or planned to use race/ethnicity or gender data with other board members? If so, please describe.

How, if at all, did the information provided in the unconscious bias video shown at the beginning of the board factor into the board process for you? Do you think this information affected your decisionmaking in the board process? If so, how?

    a. Was it clear to you how to apply the information provided about unconscious bias to the board process? Please explain.

141

Based on your experience with the board process, are there improvements you think the Air Force should make regarding the board guidance related to diversity, equity, and inclusion? If so, please describe.

   a. Do you believe that race/ethnicity and gender information should be visible to board members during the board process? Please explain.

I now have some questions about the other changes to the board guidance.

[For IDE board members] Was it useful to you to have "Definitely Attend" (DA) information unmasked? How, if at all, did you use this information in scoring records?

   a. Did you sense Senior Raters were using similar or different criteria in awarding their DA(s)?
   b. What is your sense of how, if at all, DAs impacted the board's order of merit?
      i. Any opinion on whether this impact was "good" or "bad" for the Air Force institutionally? Please explain.

What are your thoughts on having just a 5-year window for officer records, focusing on recent performance? How, if at all, do you feel that affected the board process?

What are your thoughts on scoring by DTs? How, if at all, do you feel that affected the board process?

During the board process, how would you describe the level of difficulty of assessing records outside of your core AFSC? Was it more difficult to assess those outside of your core AFSC? Please explain.

   a. Were there any particularly strong AFSCs in the board process? Where there any particularly weak AFSCs in the board process?

Closing Question

Is there anything important for us to know about the DE selection process that we haven't asked you about or any key take-aways we should have for how the Air Force could better inform you about guidance for the board selection process or how diversity, equity, and inclusion can be integrated into the process?

If needed for reference during discussion, from the 2021 MOI Addendum:

"To remain competitive, and acknowledging that diversity is both a force multiplier and essential within an all-volunteer force, you should look to select a diverse mix of officers who demonstrate initiative and display an ability to lead in our increasingly diverse Air Force organizations. In assessing diversity, you may consider the broad background and experiences of the candidates, including their demographics, education, experiences, source of military commission and training, prior enlistment and service experience, and any other factor. Diversity should not be interpreted as a mandate to apply weight solely based on a candidate's race, gender, or other demographic qualifier. Your assessment of each candidate must remain

individualized. The Air Force needs to make every effort to encourage service from individuals of all cultural backgrounds by providing for the equal treatment and equitable consideration of all personnel considered for development."

INTERVIEW PROTOCOL: CSB MEMBERS

Provide Study Overview and Administer Consent

Knowledge of Board Guidance

How were you provided information about the board guidance related to diversity, equity, and inclusion? Please describe.

- Were you provided information about the guidance in writing prior to the board? What did this information include? When and how was this provided to you? Please describe.
- Were you provided information about the guidance in-person at the start of the board? Please describe.
- If verbal guidance was provided, how did it differ, if at all, from the written guidance provided?

After receiving the guidance, was it clear to you how to apply it to scoring officers' records?

- If not, what questions did you have about the guidance? Were you allowed the opportunity to ask clarifying questions about the board guidance prior to the CSB process? Did you receive the clarifying information you needed to apply the standards to the CSB process?
- Did you discuss the guidance related to diversity, equity, and inclusion, or the topic of diversity, equity, and inclusion in the board context more generally, with other board members? This can include informally, outside of the board process itself. If so, please describe.

Based on your experience, are there improvements that the Air Force should make in communicating the guidance to board members? If so, please describe.

- Is there additional information about the guidance related to diversity, equity, and inclusion that you wish you had prior to the CSB process? If so, please describe?

Experience with 2021 Board Selection Process

In your own words, what does the board guidance related to diversity, equity, and inclusion entail?

- How, if at all, did you apply this guidance about diversity, equity, and inclusion when scoring records?

During the board process, were you aware that race/ethnicity and gender were visible in all records?

- If you were <u>not</u> aware that race/ethnicity and gender was unmasked, were you able to infer demographics from the narratives (e.g., use of female pronouns)?

If you were aware that race/ethnicity and gender was unmasked (or could infer this information from narratives), how, if at all did you consider this information in the CSB process?

- – Probe: How did you weight race/ethnicity and gender in the scoring process?
  - ▪ Did you use race/ethnicity or gender as a factor equivalent to a quality indicator like an award or training?
- – Probe: If you were considering two candidates with otherwise similar records but one was a racial/ethnic minority or female, how, if it at all, would you consider race/ethnicity or gender as a "tie breaker"?
  - ▪ Did you use race/ethnicity or gender as a form of "tie breaker" for otherwise similar records? If so, please describe.
- – Did you discuss (informally) how, if at all, you used or planned to use race/ethnicity or gender data with other board members? If so, please describe.
- – Once the board has the ranked list, can you describe the process for looking at the outcomes of the board in terms of diversity and how, or if, decisions are made to move a diverse candidate above the line to increase the diversity of the candidate pool?

Based on your experience with the CSB process, are there improvements you think the Air Force should make related to how diversity, equity, and inclusion is integrated into the CSB process? If so, please describe.

- – Do you believe that race/ethnicity and gender information should be visible to board members during the CSB process? Please explain.

Closing Questions

If you have served on boards in the past, do you have any thoughts on how the recent CSB compared in terms of DEI guidance provided or the role diversity, equity, and inclusion played in the process?

What role, if any, do you think diversity, equity, and inclusion should play in the developmental education selection process (IDE and SDE)?

- – Do you think race/ethnicity and gender information should be unmasked and visible to DE board members when they are scoring officers' records?
- – If so, how do you think board members should use race/ethnicity and gender information when they are scoring officers' records?
- – What guidance do you think should be provided to DE board members regarding DEI?

Is there anything important for us to know about the CSB process that we haven't asked you about or any key take-aways we should capture for how the Air Force could better inform you about guidance for the CSB process or how diversity, equity, and inclusion should or should not be integrated into the process?

- Any other final thoughts about the role of DEI in current officer management and selection processes more generally?
- Any other final thoughts about how the Air Force could improve demographic disparities in the force and increase the demographic diversity of Air Force senior leaders?

If needed for reference during discussion, from the CSB MOI:

Diversity and Inclusion: *To remain competitive, and acknowledging that diversity is both a force multiplier and essential within an all-volunteer force, you should look to select a diverse mix of officers who demonstrate initiative and display an ability to command in our increasingly diverse Air Force organizations. In assessing diversity, you may consider the broad background and experiences of the candidates, including their demographics, education, experiences, source or military commission and training, prior enlistment and service experience, and any other factor. Diversity should not be interpreted as a mandate to apply weight solely based on a candidate's race, gender, or other demographic qualifier. Your assessment of each candidate must remain individualized. The Air Force needs to make every effort to encourage service from individuals of all cultural backgrounds by providing for the equal treatment and equitable consideration of all personnel considered for command opportunities.*

Abbreviations

AAD	advanced academic degree
ACSC	Air Command and Staff College
AFI	Air Force Instruction
AFIT	Air Force Institute of Technology
AFPC	Air Force Personnel Center
AFROTC	Air Force Reserve Officer Training Corps
AFSC	Air Force Specialty Code
APZ	above the promotion zone
BPZ	below the promotion zone
CAF	Combat Air Forces
CC	commander
CPME	Central Professional Military Education
CSAF	Chief of Staff of the Air Force
CSB	Command Screening Board
DA	definitely attend
DAF	Department of the Air Force
DE	developmental education
DEDB	Developmental Education Designation Board
DEI	diversity, equity, and inclusion
DG	distinguished graduate
DP	Definitely Promote
DT	development team
DTR	decline to respond
HBCU	historically black college or university
IDE	intermediate developmental education
IG	Inspector General
IPZ	in the promotion zone
LAF	Line of the Air Force
MAF	Mobility Air Forces
MEL	Master Eligibility List
MLR	Management Level Review
MOI	memorandum of instruction
MSM	meritorious service medal
NDAA	National Defense Authorization Act

NLP	natural language processing
OOM	order-of-merit
OPR	Officer Performance Report
OTS	Officer Training School
PCA	Principal Component Analysis
PME	Professional Military Education
PSDM	Personnel Services Delivery Memorandum
REG	race, ethnicity, and gender
SAF/IGS	Air Force Inspector General
SDE	senior developmental education
SECAF	Secretary of the Air Force
SML	Senior Material Leaders
SOC	source of commission
SOS	Squadron Officer School
SR	senior rater
TR	training report
ULF	unit level flyer
USAFA	U.S. Air Force Academy

References

AFI—*See* Air Force Instruction.

"Air Force Announces IDE in-Residence Nomination Process Change," press release, Secretary of the Air Force, January 5, 2022. As of June 13, 2022:
https://www.af.mil/News/Article-Display/Article/2889834/air-force-announces-ide-in-residence-nomination-process-change/

Air Force Instruction 36-7001, Diversity and Inclusion, February 19, 2019.

Air Force Instruction 36-2670, Total Force Development, June 25, 2020.

Apfelbaum, Evan P., Michael I. Norton, and Samuel R. Sommers, "Racial Color Blindness: Emergence, Practice, and Implications," *Current Directions in Psychological Science*, Vol. 21, No. 3, 2012. As of June 15, 2022:
https://www.hbs.edu/ris/Publication%20Files/Racial%20Color%20Blindness_16f0f9c6-9a67-4125-ae30-5eb1ae1eff59.pdf

Apfelbaum, Evan P., Kristin Pauker, Samuel R. Sommers, and Nalini Ambady, "In Blind Pursuit of Racial Equality?" *Psychological Science*, Vol. 21, 2010, pp. 1587–1592. As of June 15, 2022:
https://www.jstor.org/stable/41062417?seq=1#metadata_info_tab_contents

Aragón, O. R., J. F. Dovidio, and M. J. Graham, "Colorblind and Multicultural Ideologies Are Associated with Faculty Adoption of Inclusive Teaching Practices," *Journal of Diversity in Higher Education*, Vol. 10, 2017, pp. 201–215. As of June 17, 2022:
http://web.b.ebscohost.com/ehost/pdfviewer/pdfviewer?vid=1&sid=53003a04-c880-4507-863b-2a724d6f7acc%40sessionmgr102

Awad, Germine H., Kevin Cokley, and Joseph Ravitch, "Attitudes Toward Affirmative Action: A Comparison of Color-Blind Versus Modern Racist Attitudes," *Journal of Applied Social Psychology*, Vol. 35, 2006, pp. 1384–1399. As of June 17, 2022:
https://onlinelibrary.wiley.com/doi/abs/10.1111/j.1559-1816.2005.tb02175.x

Back, Christine J., and J. D. S. Hsin, "'Affirmative Action' and Equal Protection in Higher Education," Congressional Research Service, 2019.

Bailey, Zinzi D., Nancy Krieger, Madina Agénor, Jasmine Graves, Natalia Linos, and Mary T. Bassett, "Structural Racism and Health Inequities in the USA: Evidence and Interventions," *The Lancet*, Vol. 389, No. 10077, 2017, pp. 1453–1463. As of May 20, 2022:
https://www.thelancet.com/pdfs/journals/lancet/PIIS0140-6736(17)30569-X.pdf

Bang, Heejung, and James M. Robins, "Doubly Robust Estimation and Missing Data and Causal Inference Models," *Biometrics*, Vol. 61, No. 4, 2005, pp. 962–972.

Barth, Billy, "Heritage Today: Unconscious Bias," video, U.S. Air Force, August 27, 2020. As of May 23, 2022:
https://www.airman.af.mil/HeritageToday/videoid/765005/dvpcc/false/#DVIDSVideoPlayer 33885

Bazi, Tony, "Peer Review: Single-Blind, Double-Blind, or All the Way Blind?" *International Urogynecology Journal*, Vol. 31, 2020. As of June 15, 2022:
https://link.springer.com/content/pdf/10.1007/s00192-019-04187-2.pdf

Behaghel, Luc, Bruno Crépon, and Thomas Le Barbanchon, "Unintended Effects of Anonymous Resumes," *American Economic Journal: Applied Economics*, Vol. 7, No. 3, 2015, pp. 1–27. As of June 17, 2022:
https://pubs.aeaweb.org/doi/pdfplus/10.1257/app.20140185

Brown, Charles Q., Jr., "What I'm Thinking About," YouTube video, Pacific Air Forces, June 5, 2020. As of June 14, 2022:
https://www.youtube.com/watch?v=mx0HnOTUkVI&t=2s

Budden, Amber E., Tom Tregnza, Lonnie W. Arssen, Julia Koricheva, Roosa Leimu, and Christopher J. Lortie, "Double-Blind Review Favours Increased Representation of Female Authors," *Trends in Ecology and Evolution*, Vol. 23, No. 1, 2008. As of June 15, 2022:
https://pubmed.ncbi.nlm.nih.gov/17963996/

Burkard, A. W., and S. Knox, "Effect of Therapist Color-Blindness on Empathy and Attributions in Cross-Cultural Counseling," *Journal of Counseling Psychology*, Vol. 51, 2004, pp. 387–397. As of June 17, 2022:
http://web.a.ebscohost.com/ehost/pdfviewer/pdfviewer?vid=1&sid=660b4851-8d3c-43c0-8330-25abfb95cc18%40sessionmgr4007

Castro-Atwater, Sheri A., "Color-Blind Racial Ideology in K–12 Schools," in Helen A. Neville, Miguel E. Gallardo, and Derald Wing Sue, eds., *The Myth of Racial Color Blindness: Manifestations, Dynamics, and Impact*, Washington, D.C.: American Psychological Association, 2016, pp. 207–225. As of June 17, 2022:
https://psycnet.apa.org/record/2015-24372-013

Cox, Amelia R., and Robert Montgomerie, "The Case For and Against Double-Blind Reviews," *PeerJ*, 2019, citing Sandström, Ulf, and Martin Hällsten, "Persistent Nepotism in Peer-Review," *Scientometrics*, Vol. 74, No. 2, 2008, pp. 175–189. As of June 15, 2022:
https://www.ncbi.nlm.nih.gov/pmc/articles/PMC6450368/pdf/peerj-07-6702.pdf

DeNisi, Angelo S., and Kevin R. Murphy, "Performance Appraisal and Performance Management: 100 Years of Progress?" *Journal of Applied Psychology*, Vol. 102, No. 3, 2017, pp. 421–433.

Department of Labor, "Affirmative Action Frequently Asked Question," fact sheet, Washington, D.C., January 7, 2021.

Eibach, Richard P., and Thomas Keegan, "Free at Last? Social Dominance, Loss Aversion, and White and Black Americans' Differing Assessments of Racial Progress," *Journal of Personality and Social Psychology*, Vol. 90, No. 3, 2006, pp. 453–467. As of June 17, 2022: https://psycnet.apa.org/record/2006-03946-008?doi=1

Enserink, Martin, "Few Authors Choose Anonymous Peer Review, Massive Study of Nature Journals Shows," *Nature*, September 22, 2017. As of June 15, 2022: https://www.sciencemag.org/news/2017/09/few-authors-choose-anonymous-peer-review-massive-study-nature-journals-shows

Godlee, Fiona, Catharine R. Gale, and Christopher N. Martyn, "Effect on the Quality of Peer Review of Blinding Reviewers and Asking Them to Sign Their Reports: A Randomized Control Trial," *JAMA: Journal of the American Medical Association*, Vol. 280, No. 3, 1998. As of June 15, 2022: https://psycnet.apa.org/record/1998-04896-003

Goldin, Claudia, and Cecelia Rouse, "Orchestrating Impartiality: The Impact of 'Blind' Auditions on Female Musicians," *American Economic Review*, Vol. 90, No. 4, 2000, pp. 715–741. As of June 17, 2022: https://gap.hks.harvard.edu/orchestrating-impartiality-impact-"blind"-auditions-female-musicians

Grutter v. Bollinger, 539 U.S. 306, 307, June 23, 2003. As of June 17, 2022: https://supreme.justia.com/cases/federal/us/539/306/case.pdf

Gündemir, Seval, Ashley E. Martin, and Astrid C. Homan, "Understanding Diversity Ideologies from the Target's Perspective: A Review and Future Directions," *Frontiers in Psychology*, Vol. 10, No. 282, 2019. As of June 17, 2022: https://www.frontiersin.org/articles/10.3389/fpsyg.2019.00282/full

Hachfeld, Axinja, Adam Hahn, Sascha Schroeder, Yvonne Anders, and Mareike Kunter, "Should Teachers Be Colorblind? How Multicultural and Egalitarian Beliefs Differentially Relate to Aspects of Teachers' Professional Competence for Teaching in Diverse Classrooms," *Teaching and Teacher Education*, Vol. 48, 2015, pp. 44–55. As of June 15, 2022: https://www.sciencedirect.com/science/article/pii/S0742051X1500027X

Haffar, Smir, Fateh Bazerbachi, and M. Hassan Murad, "Peer Review Bias: A Critical Review," *Mayo Clinic Proceedings*, Vol. 94, No. 4, 2019. As of June 15, 2022:
https://www.mayoclinicproceedings.org/article/S0025-6196(18)30707-9/fulltext

Hanover Research, *The Impact of Implicit Bias Training*, Arlington, Va., March 2019. As of June 13, 2022:
https://wasa-oly.org//WASA/images/WASA/6.0%20Resources/
Hanover/IMPLICIT%20BIAS%20TRAINING.pdf

Hanser, Lawrence M., Jennifer J. Li, Carra S. Sims, Norah Griffin, and Spencer R. Case, *Air Force Professional Military Education: Considerations for Change*, Santa Monica, Calif.: RAND Corporation, RR-A401-1, 2021. As of July 27, 2022:
https://www.rand.org/pubs/research_reports/RRA401-1.html

Hatzenbuehler, Mark L., Kate A. McLaughlin, Katherine M. Keyes, and Deborah S. Hasin, "The Impact of Institutional Discrimination on Psychiatric Disorders in Lesbian, Gay, and Bisexual Populations: A Prospective Study," *American Journal of Public Health*, Vol. 100, No. 3, 2010, pp. 452–459. As of May 20, 2022:
https://doi.org/10.2105/AJPH.2009.168815

Hirshfield, Laura E., "A Case for Double-Blind Review," *Academic Medicine*, Vol. 95, No. 11, 2020. As of June 15, 2022:
https://journals.lww.com/academicmedicine/Fulltext/2020/11000/A_Case_for_Double_Blind_Review.7.aspx

Holland, P. W., "Statistics and Causal Inference," *Journal of the American Statistical Association*, Vol. 81, No. 396, 1986, pp. 945–960.

Holoien, Deborah Son, and J. Nicole Shelton, "You Deplete Me: The Cognitive Costs of Colorblindness on Ethnic Minorities," *Journal of Experimental Social Psychology*, Vol. 48, 2012, pp. 562–565. As of June 17, 2022:
https://www.sciencedirect.com/science/article/pii/S002210311100240X

IG DAF—*See* Inspector General Department of the Air Force.

Inspector General Department of the Air Force, *Independent Racial Disparity Review (Report of Inquiry S8918P)*, Arlington, Va., December 2020. As of June 14, 2022:
https://www.af.mil/Portals/1/documents/ig/IRDR.pdf

Inspector General Department of the Air Force, *Report of Inquiry Addendum (S8918P): Disparity Review*, Arlington, Va., November 2021.

Johnson, Stefanie K., and Jessica F. Kirk, "Dual-Anonymization Yields Promising Results for Reducing Gender Bias: A Naturalistic Field Experiment of Applications for Hubble Space Telescope Time," *Publications of the Astronomical Society of the Pacific*, March 2020. As of June 17, 2022:
https://iopscience.iop.org/article/10.1088/1538-3873/ab6ce0/pdf

Justice, Amy C., Mildred K. Cho, Margaret A. Winker, Jesse A. Berlin, and Drummond Rennie, "Does Masking Author Identity Improve Peer Review Quality? A Randomized Controlled Trial," *JAMA: Journal of the American Medical Association*, Vol. 280, 1998. As of June 15, 2022:
https://jamanetwork.com/journals/jama/fullarticle/187758

Kang, Joseph D. Y., and Joseph L. Schafer, "Demystifying Double Robustness: A Comparison of Alternative Strategies for Estimating a Population Mean from Incomplete Data," *Statistical Science*, Vol. 22, No. 4, 2007, pp. 523–539.

Keller, Kirsten M., Kimberly Curry Hall, Miriam Matthews, Leslie Adrienne Payne, Lisa Saum-Manning, Douglas Yeung, David Schulker, Stefan Zavislan, and Nelson Lim, *Addressing Barriers to Female Officer Retention in the Air Force*, Santa Monica, Calif.: RAND Corporation, RR-2073-AF, 2018. As of May 20, 2022:
https://www.rand.org/pubs/research_reports/RR2073.html

Kirby, Teri A., and Cheryl R. Kaiser, "Person-Message Fit: Racial Identification Moderates the Benefits of Multicultural and Colorblind Diversity Approaches," *Personality and Social Psychology*, Vol. 47, No. 6, 2021. As of June 17, 2022:
https://www.ncbi.nlm.nih.gov/pmc/articles/PMC8107502/pdf/10.1177_0146167220948707.pdf

Kmietowicz, Zosia, "Double Blind Peer Reviews Are Fairer and More Objective, Say Academics," *BMJ*, 2008. As of June 15, 2022:
https://www.ncbi.nlm.nih.gov/pmc/articles/PMC2223019/

Knowles, Eric D., Brian S. Lowery, Caitlin M. Hogan, and Rosalind M. Chow, "On the Malleability of Ideology: Motivated Construals of Color Blindness," *Journal of Personality and Social Psychology*, Vol. 96, 2009, pp. 857–869. As of June 15, 2022:
https://socialecology.uci.edu/files/users/eknowles/knowles2009.pdf

Knowles, Robert, "The Intertwined Fates of Affirmative Action and the Military," *Loyola University Chicago Law Journal*, Vol. 45, No. 4, 2014. As of June 17, 2022:
https://lawecommons.luc.edu/cgi/viewcontent.cgi?article=1481&context=luclj

Lara, Luke, J., "Faculty of Color Unmask Color-Blind Ideology in the Community College Faculty Search Process," *Community College Journal of Research and Practice*, Vol. 43, No. 10–11, 2019. As of June 17, 2022: https://www.tandfonline.com/doi/pdf/10.1080/10668926.2019.1600608?needAccess=true

Largent, Emily A., and Richard T. Snodgrass, "Blind Peer Review by Academic Journals," Chapter 5 of Christopher G. Robertson and Aaron Kesselheim, eds., *Blinding as a Solution to Bias: Strengthening Biomedical Science, Forensic Science, and Law*, 1st ed., Cambridge, Mass.: Academic Press, 2016, pp. 84–87. As of June 15, 2022: https://www2.cs.arizona.edu/~rts/pubs/BlindingChapter.pdf

Le Goues, C., Y. Brun, S. Apel, E. Berger, S. Khurshid, and Y. Smaragdakis, "Effectiveness of Anonymization in Double-Blind Review," *Communications of the ACM*, Vol. 61, No. 6, 2018. As of June 15, 2022: https://cacm.acm.org/magazines/2018/6/228027-effectiveness-of-anonymization-in-double-blind-review/fulltext

Lim, Nelson, Kimberly Curry Hall, Kirsten M. Keller, David Schulker, Louis T. Mariano, Miriam Matthews, Lisa Saum-Manning, Devon Hill, Brandon Crosby, Leslie Adrienne Payne, Linda Cottrell, and Clara A. Aranibar, *Improving the Representation of Women and Racial/Ethnic Minorities Among U.S. Coast Guard Active-Duty Members*, Santa Monica, Calif.: RAND Corporation, RR-A362-2, 2021. As of May 20, 2022: https://www.rand.org/pubs/research_reports/RRA362-2.html

Lim, Nelson, Louis T. Mariano, Amy G. Cox, David Schulker, Lawrence M. Hanser, "Improving Demographic Diversity in the U.S. Air Force Officer Corps," Santa Monica, Calif.: RAND Corporation, RR-495-AF, 2014. As of June 13, 2022: https://www.rand.org/pubs/research_reports/RR495.html

Lyall, Jason, *Divided Armies: Inequality and Battlefield Performance in Modern War*, Princeton, N.J., Princeton University Press, 2020.

Martin, Ashley E., and Katherine W. Phillips, "Blind to Bias: The Benefits of Gender-Blindness for STEM Stereotyping," *Journal of Experimental Social Psychology*, Vol. 82, 2019.

McCaffrey, D. F., G. Ridgeway, and A. R. Morral, "Propensity Score Estimation with Boosted Regression for Evaluating Causal Effects in Observational Studies," *Psychological Methods*, Vol. 9, No. 4, 2004, pp. 403–425.

Meredith, Lisa S., Carra S. Sims, Benjamin Saul Batorsky, Adeyemi Theophilus Okunogbe, Brittany L. Bannon, and Craig A. Myatt, *Identifying Promising Approaches to U.S. Army Institutional Change: A Review of the Literature on Organizational Culture and Climate*, Santa Monica, Calif.: RAND Corporation, RR-1588-A, 2017. As of May 20, 2022: https://www.rand.org/pubs/research_reports/RR1588.html

Military Leadership Diversity Commission, *From Representation to Inclusion: Diversity Leadership for the 21st-Century Military: Final Report*, Arlington, Va., March 15, 2011. As of May 20, 2022:
https://www.hsdl.org/?abstract&did=11390

Mohammad, Saif M., and Peter D. Turney, "Crowdsourcing a Word–Emotion Association Lexicon," *Computational Intelligence*, Vol. 29, No. 3, 2013, pp. 436-465.

Mulligan, Adrian, Louise Hall, and Ellen Raphael, "Peer Review in a Changing World: An International Study Measuring the Attitudes of Researchers," *Journal of the American Society for Information Science and Technology*, 2012. As of June 15, 2022:
https://onlinelibrary.wiley.com/doi/full/10.1002/asi.22798

Newcombe, Nora S., and Mark E. Bouton, "Masked Reviews Are Not Fairer Reviews," *Perspectives on Psychological Science*, Vol. 4, No. 1, 2009. As of May 20, 2022:
https://www.jstor.org/stable/40212293?seq=1#metadata_info_tab_contents

Neville, Helen A., Germine H. Awad, James E. Brooks, Michelle P. Flores, and Jamie Bluemel, "Color-Blind Racial Ideology: Theory, Training, and Measurement in Psychology," *American Psychologist*, Vol. 68, No. 6, 2013. As of June 17, 2022:
https://psycnet.apa.org/record/2013-31242-001

Neville, Helen A., Miguel E. Gallardo, and Derald Wing Sue, "Introduction: Has the United States Really Moved Beyond Race?" in *The Myth of Racial Color Blindness: Manifestations, Dynamics, and Impact*, Washington, D.C.: American Psychological Association, 2016. As of June 17, 2022:
https://www.apa.org/pubs/books/The-Myth-of-Racial-Color-Blindness-Intro-Sample.pdf

Offermann, L. R., T. E. Basford, R. Graebner, S. Jaffer, S. B. D. Graaf, and S. E. Kaminsky, "See No Evil: Color Blindness and Perceptions of Subtle Racial Discrimination in the Workplace," *Cultural Diversity & Ethnic Minority Psychology*, Vol. 20, 2014, pp. 499–507. As of June 17, 2022:
https://psycnet.apa.org/record/2014-32907-001?doi=1

Okike, Kanu, Kevin T. Hug, Mininder S. Kocher, and Seth F, Leopold, "Single-Blind vs Double-Blind Peer Review in the Setting of Author Prestige," *JAMA*, Vol. 316, No. 2, 2016. As of June 15, 2022:
https://jamanetwork.com/journals/jama/fullarticle/2556112

Oliver, Mary Beth, "African American Men as 'Criminal and Dangerous': Implications of Media Portrayals of Crime on the "Criminalization" of African American Men," *Journal of African American Studies*, Vol. 7, No. 2, 2003, pp. 3–18.

Onyeador, Ivuoma N., Sa-kiera T. J. Hudson, and Neil A. Lewis, Jr., "Moving Beyond Implicit Bias Training: Policy Insights for Increasing Organizational Diversity," *Policy Insights from the Behavioral and Brain Sciences*, Vol. 8, No. 1, 2021, pp. 19–26.

Ostroff, Cheri, Angelo J. Kinicki, and Rabiah S. Muhammad, "Organizational Culture and Climate," *Industrial and Organizational Psychology*, Vol. 12, 2012, pp. 643–676. As of June 30, 2022:
https://doi.org/10.1002/9781118133880.hop212024

Osur, Alan M., *Separate and Unequal: Race Relations in the AAF During World War II*, Maxwell Air Force Base, Ala.: Air Force History and Museums Program, 2000. As of June 14, 2022:
https://media.defense.gov/2010/Sep/29/2001329784/-1/-1/0/SeparateAndUnequal.pdf

Plaut, Victoria C., Flannery G. Garnett, Laura E. Buffardi, and Jeffrey Sanchez-Burks, "'What About Me?' Perceptions of Exclusion and Whites' Reactions to Multiculturalism," *Journal of Personality and Social Psychology*, Vol. 101, 2011, pp. 337–353. As of June 17, 2022:
http://web.b.ebscohost.com/ehost/pdfviewer/pdfviewer?vid=1&sid=5dbbbfee-93ed-4dad-9611-b10245b17ad4%40pdc-v-sessmgr01

Plaut, Victoria C., Kecia M. Thomas, Kyneshawau Hurd, and Celina A. Romano, "Do Color Blindness and Multiculturalism Remedy or Foster Discrimination and Racism?" *Current Directions in Psychological Science*, 2018, citing H. A. Neville, R. L. Lilly, G. Duran, R. M. Lee, and L. Browne, "Construction and Initial Validation of the Color-Blind Racial Attitudes Scale (CoBRAS)," *Journal of Counseling Psychology*, Vol. 47, No. 1, 2000, pp. 59–70. As of June 15, 2022:
https://pubmed.ncbi.nlm.nih.gov/21534702/

Polanco-Santana, John C., Alessandra Storino, Sidhu P. Gangadharan, and Tara S. Kent, "Ethnic/Racial Bias in Medical School Performance Evaluation of General Surgery Residency Applicants," *Journal of Surgical Education*, Vol. 78, No. 5, September–October 2021, pp. 1524–1534. As of June 13, 2022:
https://www.sciencedirect.com/science/article/pii/S1931720421000489

Poos, Jackie M., Karel van den Bosch, and Christian P. Janssen, "Battling Bias: Effects of Training and Training Context," *Computers and Education*, Vol. 111, 2017, pp. 101–113.

Public Law 116-283, William M. (Mac) Thornberry National Defense Authorization Act for Fiscal Year 2021, January 1, 2021.

Riche, Martha Farnsworth, Amanda Kraus, April K. Hodari, and Jasen P. DePasquale, *Literature Review: Empirical Evidence Supporting the Business-Case Approach to Work Force Diversity*, Alexandria, Va.: CNA Corporation, CNA Research Memorandum D0011482.A2, 2005.

Riche, Martha Farnsworth, and Amanda Kraus, *Approaches to and Tools for Successful Diversity Management: Results from 360-Degree Diversity Management Case Studies*, Alexandria, Va.: CNA Corporation, CNA Research Memorandum D0020315, 2009.

Ridgeway, G., D. Madigan, and T. Richardson, "Boosting Methodology for Regression Problems," in D. Heckerman and J. Whittaker, eds., *Proceedings of Artificial Intelligence and Statistics '99*, 1999, pp. 152–161.

Rosenbaum, Paul R., and Donald B. Rubin, "The Central Role of the Propensity Score in Observational Studies for Causal Effects," *Biometrika*, Vol. 70, No. 1, 1983, pp. 41–55.

Rosenthal, Lisa, and Sheri R. Levy, "The Colorblind, Multicultural, and Polyculture Ideological Approaches to Improving Intergroup Attitudes and Relations," *Social Issues and Policy Review*, Vol. 4, No. 1, 2010, pp. 215–246. As of June 17, 2022:
https://cpb-us-e1.wpmucdn.com/you.stonybrook.edu/dist/e/2677/files/2018/04/ContentServer.asp-2929fhi.pdf

Rubin, Donald B., "Estimating Causal Effects of Treatments in Randomized and Nonrandomized Studies," *Journal of Educational Psychology*, Vol. 66, No. 5, 1974, pp. 688–701.

Ryan, Carey S., Jennifer S. Hunt, Joshua A. Weible, Charles R. Peterson, and Juan F. Casas, "Multicultural and Colorblind Ideology, Stereotypes, and Ethnocentrism Among Black and White Americans," *Group Processes and Intergroup Relations*, Vol. 10, No. 4, 2007. As of June 17, 2022:
https://journals.sagepub.com/doi/pdf/10.1177/1368430207084105

SAF/IGS—*See* Air Force Inspector General.

Schneider, Benjamin, Mark G. Ehrhart, and William H. Macey, "Perspectives on Organizational Climate and Culture," in S. Zedeck, ed., *APA Handbook of Industrial and Organizational Psychology*, Vol. 1, Building and Developing the Organization, Washington, D.C.: American Psychological Association, 2011, pp. 373–414. As of June 30, 2022:
https://doi.org/10.1037/12169-012

Schulker, David, Nelson Lim, Luke J. Matthews, Geoffrey E. Grimm, Anthony Lawrence, and Perry Shameem Firoz, *Can Artificial Intelligence Help Improve Air Force Talent Management? An Exploratory Application*, Santa Monica, Calif.: RAND Corporation, RR-A812-1, 2021. As of July 21, 2022:
https://www.rand.org/pubs/research_reports/RRA812-1.html

Setchell, Joanna M., "Editorial: Double-Blind Peer Review and the Advantages of Data Sharing," *International Journal of Primatology*, Vol. 36, 2015. As of June 15, 2022:
https://link.springer.com/content/pdf/10.1007/s10764-015-9860-2.pdf

Shadish, William R., Thomas D. Cook, and Donald T. Campbell, *Experimental and Quasi-Experimental Designs for Generalized Causal Inference*, Boston, Mass.: Houghton Mifflin, 2002.

Smith, Candis Watts, and Sara Mayorga-Gallo, "The New Principle-Policy Gap: How Diversity Ideology Subverts Diversity Initiatives," *Sociological Perspectives*, Vol. 60, No. 5, 2017, citing Eduardo Bonilla-Silva, *Racism Without Racists: Color-Blind Racism and the Persistence of Racial Inequality in the United States*, 4th ed., Lanham, Md.: Rowman & Littlefield, [2003] 2014. As of June 15, 2022:
https://journals.sagepub.com/doi/pdf/10.1177/0731121417719693

Sue, Derald Wing, Christina M. Capodilupo, Gina C. Torino, Jennifer M. Bucceri, Aisha M. B. Holder, Kevin L. Nadal, and Marta Esquilin, "Racial Microaggressions in Everyday Life: Implications for Clinical Practice," *American Psychologist*, Vol. 62, 2007, pp. 271–286. As of June 17, 2022:
https://www.cpedv.org/sites/main/files/file-attachments/how_to_be_an_effective_ally-lessons_learned_microaggressions.pdf

Sun, Mengyi, Jainabou Barry Danfa, and Misha Teplitskiy, "Does Double-Blind Peer Review Reduce Bias? Evidence From a Top Computer Science Conference," *arXiv*, 2021. As of June 15, 2022:
https://arxiv.org/pdf/2101.02701.pdf

Tomkins, Andrew, Min Zhang, and William D. Heavlin, "Reviewer Bias in Single- Versus Double-Blind Peer Review," *Proceedings of the National Academy of Sciences*, Vol. 114, No. 48, 2017. As of June 15, 2022:
https://www.pnas.org/content/pnas/114/48/12708.full.pdf

Tsiatis, Anastasios A., and Marie Davidian, "Comment: Demystifying Double Robustness: A Comparison of Alternative Strategies for Estimating a Population Mean from Incomplete Data," *Statistical Science*, Vol. 22, No. 4, 2007, pp. 540–543.

Tynes, Brandesha M., and Suzanne L. Markoe, "The Role of Color-Blind Racial Attitudes in Reactions to Racial Discrimination on Social Network Sites," *Journal of Diversity in Higher Education*, Vol. 3, 2010, pp. 1–13. As of June 17, 2022:
https://psycnet.apa.org/record/2010-05836-001

U.S. Equal Employment Opportunity Commission, "CM-604—Theories of Discrimination," guidance document, August 1, 1988. As of June 8, 2022:
https://www.eeoc.gov/laws/guidance/cm-604-theories-discrimination#

van Rooyen, Susan, Fiona Godlee, Stephen Evans, Richard Smith, and Nick Black, "Effect of Blinding and Unmasking on the Quality of Peer Review: A Randomized Trial," *JAMA: Journal of the American Medical Association*, Vol. 280, 1998. As of June 15, 2022: https://jamanetwork.com/journals/jama/fullarticle/187750

Webb, Thomas J., Bob O'Hara, and Robert P. Freckleton, "Does Double-Blind Review Benefit Female Authors?" *Trends in Ecology and Evolution*, Vol. 23, No. 7, 2008. As of June 15, 2022: https://www.sciencedirect.com/science/article/pii/S0169534708001389?via%3Dihub

Williams, Patricia J., "The Emperor's New Clothes," Chapter One in *Seeing a Color-Blind Future: The Paradox of Race*, New York: Noonday Press, 1997. As of August 28, 2022: https://archive.nytimes.com/www.nytimes.com/books/first/w/williams-future.html

Wilton, Leigh S., Jessica J. Good, Corinne A. Moss-Racusin, and Diana T. Sanchez, "Communicating More Than Diversity: The Effect of Institutional Diversity Statements on Expectations and Performance as a Function of Race and Gender," *Cultural Diversity and Ethnic Minority Psychology*, Vol. 21, No. 3, 2015, pp. 315–325.

Zisk, Nancy L., "The Future of Race-Conscious Admissions Programs and Why the Law Should Continue to Protect Them," *Northeastern University Law Review*, Vol. 12, No. 1, 2020.